A BETTER WORLD
A BETTER YOU

A BETTER WORLD
A BETTER YOU

The Proven Lou Tice
"Investment in Excellence" Program

LOUIS E. TICE
WITH ALAN STEINBERG

Prentice Hall, Englewood Cliffs, New Jersey 07632

3-3-95

Library of Congress Cataloging-in-Publication Data

TICE, LOUIS E.
   A better world, a better you : the proven Lou Tice "investment in
excellence" program / Louis E. Tice, Alan Steinberg.

   p. cm.
ISBN 0-13-073479-9
   1. Success. I. Steinberg, Alan. II. Title.
BJ1611.2.T53 1989   89-3621
   158'.1—dc19   CIP

Editorial/production supervison
and interior design: BARBARA MARTTINE
Cover design: LUNDGREN GRAPHICS, LTD.
Manufacturing buyer: ROBERT ANDERSON

©1989 by LOUIS E. TICE and
ALAN STEINBERG

The publisher offers discounts on this book when ordered
in bulk quantities. For more information, write:
   Special Sales/College Marketing
   Prentice Hall
   College Technical and Reference Division
   Englewood Ciffs, NJ 07632

Printed in the United States of America

10 9 8 7 6 5 4 3 2 1

ISBN 0-13-073479-9

PRENTICE-HALL INTERNATIONAL (UK) LIMITED, London
PRENTICE-HALL OF AUSTRALIA PTY. LIMITED, Sydney
PRENTICE-HALL CANADA INC., Toronto
PRENTICE-HALL HISPANOAMERICANA, S. A., Mexico
PRENTICE-HALL OF INDIA PRIVATE LIMITED, New Delhi
PRENTICE-HALL OF JAPAN, INC., Tokyo
SIMON & SCHUSTER ASIA PTE. LTD., Singapore
EDITORA PRENTICE-HALL DO BRASIL, LTDA.. Rio de Janerio

*To the memory of Larry Webb,
and to his parents.*

CONTENTS

Contents

Build a Better World

"Build a better world," said God.
And I answered,
"How? The world is such a vast place,
And so complicated now,
And I'm small and useless;
There's nothing I can do."
But God, in all His wisdom said,
"Just build a better you."

unknown author

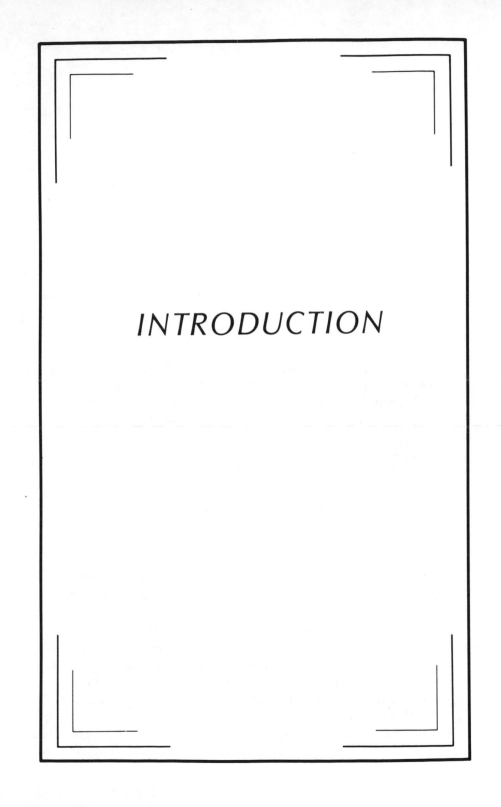

INTRODUCTION

I am about to share some very powerful information with you. In this book, I will introduce you to the same concepts that I have introduced to millions of people around the world over the past eighteen years. This information will help you make better decisions—about earning a living, raising a family, doing what you want with your future. This information is so powerful that I can make an unequivocal guarantee: If you absorb and apply these concepts properly, you will grow more in the next few years than you've grown in all the years to date. No matter who you are or what you do, you will experience the kind of phenomenal growth at every level—emotional, intellectual, spiritual, financial—that you never dreamed possible.

At some point, we all wonder, "Who's running my life?" One view is that of the determinist: "It's the circumstances outside of me that determine my life. I was born into this family, or into this tribe, or into this race, or into this ghetto, or into this town. It's fate; it's my genes; it's the weather; it's the government; it's my parents . . ." In other words, most people believe that everything that happens to them is out of their control.

I will show you that the locus of control is *inside you*. I will prove to you that you can alter the circumstances of your life by *controlling your own thoughts*. "How can I influence the way people treat me?" "How can I influence my economic situation?" "How can I influence the direction of my marriage?" "How can I influence my family?" I will show you how.

Do people react to you the way you expect them to react? How do your preconceived ideas about people and life affect what happens to you? How do your body language, tone of voice, and facial expressions elicit responses from others? What good is it to have a successful career if you're struggling internally? What good is money if you're unhappy with your life? What good are goals if you don't feel good about yourself? Ask yourself these tough questions, and then ask: *How much garbage am I willing to put up with?*

This book will talk tough to you about how much garbage you are willing to take in your life before assuming control. It will empower you to create the kind of life that you really want for yourself. It will prove that if you change the way you *think*, you can change the way you *act*. If you accomplish that, you can change your entire life.

You might say, "He's conning me. This stuff can't work for me." Good—be skeptical. Healthy skepticism is a critical ingredient of high-performance thinking. However, also allow yourself to be open-minded and option-seeking—because, if you permit me, I will prove that this information *can* work for you. This curriculum will show you that what holds you back is not external reality but internal reality; not events but your interpretation of events. In other words, you are held back by *what you believe.*

You may say, "We've seen all this before. How is your approach any different?" I am a great interpreter of this information. Other presentations make it easy for you to see *someone else* living a better life, or they imply that you might be able to make some changes *sometime in the future.* My presentation of these concepts and techniques will enable you to say, "I can see *me* using this *right now.*"

Some people believe that creation is over. Some believe that "things have never been better. Let's maintain the status quo." However, I think the world is constantly evolving, and that human beings are co-responsible with God for that evolution. We want to build a better world. We want to develop better families, better schools, better communities, better government, a better life, a better future. But who will take responsibility for these changes? Are we going to ask, "Well, why doesn't somebody else do it for me?" Or will we assume full responsibility and say, "I will do it"? That's what this book will teach you to do.

Keep in mind that these concepts aren't magic. Lou Tice doesn't have a magic wand for instant excellence, success, or happiness. What I do have is a proven blueprint for positive change and growth.

However, assimilating this blueprint is only the first step. Believing that a book can change your life is just as big a trap as believing that circumstances completely control you. It is simply another way of shifting the locus of control to something outside of you. If you're not careful, you can become a great contemplator who lays back and says, "I can see how this would work. I can see how that would work." Yet, contemplation without action is meaningless. The real adventure is *applying* these concepts to your life on a daily basis.

The concepts presented in this book are so important because they prove to you that change is possible, and enable you to notice a change in your thinking *as you read.* As you absorb these concepts, you will experience the sort of "Aha!" feeling you get when you discover, for the first time, something that was already obvious. And you will continue to feel these "Aha!" feelings throughout your life. You will constantly be telling yourself, "Look at that! How did I ever keep from seeing it?"

I believe in this curriculum for another reason: *I live it myself.* I encourage you to read the last chapter—"Longer Legs for Bigger Strides"—*first.* It will give you a good idea of how I have applied this information to make a difference in my own life, and in the life of someone I love. In fact, throughout the book I constantly relate numerous experiences in which I used the skills that I teach. That's why I consider this special presentation of my concepts a shared journey between every reader and me.

In my life, I am guided by three basic principles. The first is *authenticity.* Be yourself. Recognize that you are constantly building your uniqueness. The second principle is *progressiveness.* Make everything you do practice for the next time. Choose to be better, brighter, more productive tomorrow than you are today. The third principle is *effectiveness.* Develop ways to become a more effective human being. Always strive to translate your ideas into reality.

The information in this text has made me a more authentic, progressive, effective human being. It has made me especially effective in delivering these concepts to areas of the world where I had not previously allowed myself to venture. I started teaching these concepts in high school, and today I make a difference by teaching them to the highest-ranking members of government and the military; to strife-torn people in foreign countries; to caretakers and inmates of correctional systems; to educators and students; to factory workers, farmers, administrators, laborers, and athletes; to the health, welfare, and political systems—and to many others.

This curriculum has made a difference to me economically, socially, environmentally, personally. It allows me to be a greater influence at higher levels, and to help people create solutions to their most pressing needs. At my company, we talk about dealing in miracles: "It would be a miracle if you could find a solution to the conflict in the Middle East"; "It would be a miracle if you could come up with a cure for Alzheimer's disease or AIDS"; "It would be a miracle if you could get labor and management to work together"; "It would be a miracle if you could reduce the recidivism of criminals"; "It would be a miracle if you could develop a sensible way to get people off of welfare"; "It would be a miracle if you could improve the quality of our educational system."

And I say to myself, "*That's* what we should attack." However, with the information in this book, you can do miracles in your own families, communities, companies, teams, and organizations: "It would be a miracle if we could get our people more jobs"; "It would be a miracle if I could get my friend off drugs"; "It would be a miracle if we could get our parents to stop screaming at each other"; "It would be a miracle if the kids picked up their clothes."

There are two lines in Henrik Ibsen's *Peer Gynt* that apply to the thrust of this book. This statement about a "reckoning" at life's end addresses the use, or squandering, of our potential: "*We are thoughts; you should have formed us. Legs to run with; you should have given us.*" I interpret this to mean that all the thoughts, ideas, and dreams that we have in our life are worthless—unless we give them legs. And that's what I want to accomplish with this book. I want to help you bring form to your ideas, and give "legs" to your thoughts and dreams.

A final thought: Imagine yourself in prison for thirty years. Then someone comes along and says, "By the way, you didn't need to stay in jail. You imprisoned *yourself*." In other words: You are your own judge and jury. You sentenced yourself to unhappiness. You sentenced yourself to a life of poverty, or mediocrity, or to being an ineffective person. The key to the cell door was always in your pocket. At any time, you could have unlocked the door and walked out free.

In a very real sense, that's what this book is all about. I'm saying, "Look, the key is in your pocket. All you have to do is unlock the door and walk out free."

LOUIS E. TICE

Acknowledgments

To the Cursillo movement, and to all my teachers and mentors, and to my family.

Nothing is done by yourself. All that there is, and all that we are is a cumulation of our faith, our family, our friends, and all who touch our lives.

LOUIS E. TICE

1

SPECIAL GLASSES:

Change the Way You View Your Life

In January 1986, Jack Fitterer, the president of our company, and myself went to Fort Campbell, Ky. The Commanding General asked us to come because they had recently experienced a great tragedy. On Dec. 12, 1985, they lost 248 soldiers of the 101st Airborne division in the terrible airplane crash in Gander, Newfoundland. So we were going in to see if we could help those remaining to re-focus on the future.

At the civilian airport, we were picked up by some young people who were going to fly us to Fort Campbell in a Blackhawk helicopter. It was dark outside, yet these soldiers wanted to show us how fast the helicopter could go at 150 feet off the ground. So all of a sudden, we were flying at speeds in excess of a hundred-miles an hour, 150 feet off the ground, which was quite scary to Jack and myself. But these pilots were wearing special glasses that allowed them to see outside as though it were daylight. These glasses were like starlight scopes; they allowed the pilots to see the darkened landscape which Jack and I couldn't see. The glasses also allowed them to travel very fast, whereas most people would have wanted to go at a very timid pace.

That's like the journey you're about to embark on with me. The concepts I'll teach you in this book will be your special glasses. When you know how to use them, they will completely change the way you view your life. They have the power to illuminate not only your self-imposed barriers, but also your inner resources and unlimited potential. They will help you take the biggest strides of your life toward fulfillment of your goals. With these special glasses, you will

2

see new aspects of vision and reality, perception and belief, high-performance thinking and success. And with the power of your new sight, you will see the way to becoming much more fully yourself.

You might say, "He's talking 'pie in the sky,' he's talking 'Pollyanna.' Maybe for somebody else, but it can't be for me." Yes it can. And I'm going to show you how. But you should continue to question and doubt. As you'll see later, it's important to be skeptical and analytical, especially when other people try to tell you "the truth." At the same time, you will want to remain open-minded, aware of possibilities, alert to options. Don't lock on too quickly that "This can't be" or "That won't work."

For the moment, I want you to withhold judgment. Otherwise, you'll become too realistic, too sensible, too much of a linear thinker. Once you put on the special glasses, you'll see how to *transcend* current reality, how to *transcend* sensibility, how to *transcend* linear logic. With this special sight, you will be able to change the beliefs that are holding you back, and move to the head of the line.

I'm not a hypnotist, I'm not a preacher, I'm not a magician. I didn't invent these concepts and techniques. I'm simply an interpreter. But I'm so darned good at interpreting this, and you're so eager to change and grow, that you will not only grasp these concepts easily, but you will be able to apply them immediately to your life. That's how powerful this information is.

So I want you to consider this more than a journey; it's also a curriculum. I don't want to just inspire, I want to educate. And I promise you: If you wear my special glasses, if you finish this curriculum, if you complete this journey with me, it will be the most significant learning adventure of your whole life. Because, afterward, you will *think differently* forever.

2

THE BELIEF BUSINESS:
Leap-frogging Current Reality

The Pumpkin Jug

Years ago, a farmer brought a pumpkin to a county fair. It was in the exact size and shape of a two-gallon jug. He won blue ribbons for it. Everybody "oohed" and "ahhed" and said, "That's really spectacular." Finally, somebody asked, "How did you get a pumpkin to look like that?" And the guy said, "It was easy. As soon as it started to grow, I stuck it inside a two-gallon jug—and here it is."

Your reality is the same size and shape as the container you hold it in. What most people do, subconsciously, is confine their creativity, their imagination, their whole future, inside an *aspirin bottle*. But what would it look like if you just let it grow without a container? You're thinking, "Damn, that sounds too simple." It's not simple; it takes a firm understanding of the concepts I'm going to teach you, and a lot of dedicated effort. But it's possible. And worth the effort.

You are in the belief business. What you can accomplish is largely a matter of what you believe. Some twenty years ago, I was a teacher and football coach at Kennedy High School in Seattle. But information I learned from a brilliant visiting professor at the University of Washington changed my whole way of thinking. I wanted to make major changes in my life, so I decided to leave Kennedy High. One of the first visions, or goals, I set for myself was to use the information I'd learned to help improve the correctional system in America. That was the size of my first pumpkin jug.

"Oh, so you wanna change the correctional system?" "Yes, that's right." "Well, how long you been a warden?" "*Never.*" "You

6

got a doctorate in criminology?" "*Nope.*" "Then, where'd you do your field work?" "*Nowhere.*" "Well, what the heck are your qualifications?" "Quite frankly, *none.*"

See, ordinary people do things in ordinary, predictable, usual ways. They follow rules, they wait in line. I decided that ordinary wasn't good enough for me, so I went right after my vision. Based on my current reality at the time, and how far my vision was from that reality, I might have thought, "How can I possibly make an impact? It'll take me twenty years." But I knew differently. I didn't know *how* yet, I just knew I would invent a way to achieve my goal.

Within a year after I left Kennedy High School, I met Gordy Graham. Gordy had spent seventeen years in maximum security inside the penitentiary. One year on bread and water in solitary confinement. He was a boxer and a tough guy; ruled the prison with his fists. He referred to himself as "No. 28203—a consumer of correctional services." But Gordy changed his self-image after he went through one of my seminars at Port Ludlow. After just one day, he formed his first vision. He thought, "Every prisoner in America should have access to this information." He didn't know *how* yet, either. He just had the vision.

Two days after that seminar, Gordy and I were talking in the parking lot outside the Pacific Institute—the company my wife, Diane, and I founded to develop our business of education through seminars. I said, "Gordy, you have a doctorate that nobody would ever pay for. You could reach people who'd never listen to me. If we combine your experience with the concepts I teach, we could change the correctional system of America." We were thinking the same thing: "To anybody else, the idea of an ex-convict and a former high school football coach teaming up to improve this country's correctional system would seem absurd." But *we* believed we could do it.

We were the most unlikely candidates to instigate change in such a massive system. If we had followed the ordinary, expected, usual route—earning doctorates, doing research, gaining experience—we'd still be *preparing* to make an impact. But I knew how to leap-frog present reality, how to move to the head of the line. I taught that to Gordy, and we did it together.

Within two years, we became one of America's most respected and sought-after resource teams for implementing correctional training programs—not only for prisoners but also for the custodial, psychological, and administrative staffs. We contracted with the state of Washington to operate our own community facility, where we housed fifty people as they made the transition out of the system. We introduced videotape training programs in a great many federal and state prisons throughout the country. We developed programs for the Navy and Marines; we were consulted by wardens, associate wardens, and prison directors who became our close friends; we were invited to be guest speakers at national conventions.

Pretty soon, I was the key resource for two world conferences in the field of corrections—and corrections is *not* my business. I point that out not so you will say, "Oh, how wonderful," but to re-emphasize that I leap-frogged over present reality to achieve my vision. I became my own expert, I made an impact—and I did *not* wait in line.

Through this curriculum, I will teach you how to transcend your present circumstances to attain your goals. I will teach you how to look beyond who you are at the present moment. I don't mean that you should entirely deny present reality, because recognizing reality will be a very important step in the process of change. But don't be *fixed* by your present state. The universe is not fixed. Creation is not fixed. Human beings are not fixed. I'm going to teach you how to choose your future, how to create it, how to invent it *now*.

Shortly after starting our corrections work, I set another vision: to enhance the quality of the military leadership in America. I had no background in that, no special qualifications. Yet, recently, I was at Fort Meyer in Washington, D.C. where, for the second year in a row, I gave the closing address at the graduation dinner for the Brigadier Generals Orientation Course—a course designed to prepare newly promoted generals for their transition to positions of much greater responsibility. Then I was invited to the Pentagon to talk to staff members from offices throughout the Department of Defense. From there I went to Fort Bragg, Fort Hood, U.S. Army Europe . . . all across the United States and overseas, working with our top military leadership.

I am from Burien, a small suburb of Seattle. I'm a high school teacher and a coach by training; I am not a soldier. There were people in those audiences far more skilled at soldiering and military leadership than I—people like the Chancellor of West Point. And look how far I was, at the time, from where I set my vision. How'd I do it? "What are your qualifications?" "*None.*" "How long you been a general?" "Who, *me* from Burien? Quite frankly, *never.*" "Well then, how can you do it?" "I don't know. I just decided I *wanted* to."

A few years ago, I decided that I wanted to work to enhance the quality of political leadership in America. I was the most unlikely candidate for that job, it was so far from my current reality. I didn't even care about politics; I disdained it. I didn't know one politician personally. "How long you been a Congressman? How long you been in government? When did you get your degree in political science?" "*Never.*" I just decided I *wanted* to."

Ordinarily, you would first run for local office; then state office; then maybe Congress; work your way up through committees and run for Senator; do well and then—. I don't have that kind of time. I'm busy working over here in corrections, and over there in the military, and someplace else in—. See? "Well, it's impossible. You'll never succeed."

But I did succeed. Within a year we put on an educational program for a group of powerful national political leaders, including one who ran in the 1988 presidential primaries. That was the first political group I had worked with—and I didn't know any of them before. Then the Speaker of the House praised our work in a declaration for the Congressional Record. Then I was the opening speaker for the first Democratic Party Educational Caucus in the history of America. I shared the spotlight with some of the best speakers in the world, including Lee Iacocca.

How'd I do that? I just dropped myself right into it. And I do that all the time. So can you—when I show you how. You cannot lay back and cunningly plan yourself into those situations. When you set a goal, you immediately feel compelled to ask yourself, "How do I do it? How can I get it?" And you start planning a strategy. But there is no blueprint or strategic plan that could have dropped me into the correctional system of America—or the military system, or the political system—from where I started. It took something else.

It took a willingness to let myself get off the old track and to leap-frog my present reality. Right now—before you learn about Gestalt, self-talk, and comfort zones—this leap-frogging of present reality might seem like magic to you. Ever watch a magician do an amazing card trick? You see the end result, not the process. You don't see the magician slide the card up his or her sleeve. It looks amazing because you can't see the process, you can't see the "how." That's a key concept. Don't be too concerned with *how* you're going to be what you intend to be in the future. I'll teach you how to create and invent the process on the way. You are so creative, so intuitive, so powerful inside—you're a creative genius. But you've got to allow yourself to get off the old track.

Not long ago, the head scientist at Atari made a brilliant statement. He said, "It seems that the best way to control your future these days is to invent it." So how do high-performance people invent their future? How do they get off the old track? How do they leap-frog their current reality and drop themselves into their vision? By fixing on the goal and ignoring the "how." That will take some work but, as we move through the curriculum, I will show you how to make it easy for yourself.

Meantime, what you must know is this: If you're going to transcend current reality to achieve great things, you need to stifle the "how," you need to punch the "how" down. Otherwise, you'll shrink your vision. If you can't logically, realistically tell yourself how to get your goal based on what you think you can do at the moment, you will deny what you're capable of doing in the future because it seems unrealistic. "Oh, it's just a 'pie-in-the-sky' dream anyway." "Where will the customers come from?" "Where will I get the money?" "I'm not qualified enough. I'll need a degree first." You will invent a hundred rationalizations to keep you from doing what you really want to do. You'll tell yourself that your goal is too far out to reach, and then you'll back it up to where it seems more realistic, more attainable. Then it could take you *years* to achieve that goal—and you might never use your vast creative potential to make a better life.

Inventing your future is today's way of thinking. For young people, it is estimated that you will have at least five careers in your lifetime. It's going to be difficult for you to say what you're going to be when you grow up. You haven't invented it yet. But if you remain a logical, linear thinker, you'll buy one of those planners and you'll plan out December and January and February based only upon how inventive and creative you are at the present moment. That is yesterday's way of thinking. The old linear, cause-and-effect thinking, the old method-orientation, is already outdated. I will show you how to go on hunches and follow a direction that, at first, may seem impractical and insensible. I'm here to help you take giant leaps, not baby steps. For now, we don't *care* how. We're going to invent it on the way.

"Is-ness" Is Not Fixed

Most of you believe that your current reality is fixed. You get trapped in your own mistaken sense of "is-ness." In other words, "This is the way it is. It's always been this way and it will always be this way." But "is-ness" is not fixed; the present is not permanent. Ever hear of the Newtonian world view? Or the Whiteheadian? The Newtonian view was that God created a perfect world—with just one exception: *people*. People were considered basically sinful. They were always trying to ruin a good thing. The idea was: "If God created a perfect world, then why are you trying, with all of your imagination and creativity, to *change* it? You'll screw things up." Some of you were raised and conditioned by parents who felt that way. Some work for bosses who think this way. Some had teachers who felt that everything should stay the way it is. "We don't want any of your bright ideas, thank you. In fact, we will discourage any new ideas you have."

But there's been a shift the other way—to the Whiteheadian world view. Alfred North Whitehead, like Sir Isaac Newton two centuries earlier, was a philosopher and mathematician. But he saw a dynamic world, not a fixed one. He saw a world in which human beings were co-creative agents with God. To him, creation was ongoing, and so were the lives of human beings. They weren't stuck, they were always in motion. So, if you share that view—as I do— then what do you think about people who say, "Well, I'm going to lay back and let God, or Fate, or Destiny, or Nature, or The Powers

That Be, direct my whole life for me"? What will their lives be like? "Okay, if I'm a bum, I guess it's meant to be. If I'm lazy and I can't control this terrible temper, it isn't my fault. If I'm wallowing in debt and I never pay my bills, that's just the way it *is*." In other words, what a wonderful excuse for not being accountable or responsible for your own life. What a simple way to cement yourself into a fixed reality and never try to change.

High-performance people live in a Whiteheadian world. For them, present reality is only temporary. Instead of saying, "Well, I guess this is the way it *is*," and accepting the limits of their present reality, they build a *new* reality every day. They don't sit around cursing Fate, or wishing for change, or hoping their lottery number comes up. They create change for *themselves*. If you choose to, that's what you will be able to do in your life from now on: *create change*.

But if you're going to become a high-performance person, you must first learn to decide on the end results you want. Exactly what do you want for yourself? What kind of career? What kind of income? What kind of community? What kind of home? What kind of spiritual life? What kind of relationships? You must create a vivid mental picture of the end results you want. Once you imprint that vision in your mind, your subconscious will get very creative to find information that you can use to help achieve it. Later, I'll show you how that works when I explain about an amazing alerting device called the *reticular activating system*. But not yet. You might not be too sure about all this stuff.

For now, remember that your vision must be more than just a vague desire, like, "I want to do good for mankind." There are literally thousands of ways to do good for mankind. You must focus vividly on something specific. Ordinary people just wish for things. They never focus their desires into specific visions. I'm encouraging you to discard wishes; they're very destructive. "I wish I could win the Irish Sweepstakes." "I wish I had a better job." "I wish somebody would sweep me off my feet and marry me." Nobody's rushing to grant your wishes. I used to wait for the Fairy Godmother, too. She isn't coming today. Neither is Santa Claus. And, by the way, don't wait for the Easter Bunny either. You need to make things happen for yourself. I know what you're thinking: "That's easy for *you* to say. But how do *I* get started?"

Simple. Turn the page.

3

BLOCKS, TRAPS, AND LIDS:

Breaking Barriers That Block Your Growth

You are creative and powerful enough to become much more than you presently are. But you constantly build barriers to block your growth. Often, the barrier is not the circumstances *outside* you. It's the way that you think *inside*—the way you view yourself and the rest of the world. Your own belief system can prevent you from using your potential. Beliefs are so powerful, they can build sensory barriers to the real truth, sealing in your old beliefs and blocking out the new. That's why accomplishing more and improving the quality of your life won't be a matter of working harder. It will be a matter of *thinking differently*.

One thing we know—and it is the first basic premise in this curriculum: *Human being's think and act not in accordance with the real truth, but the truth as we believe it.* Our self-image will cause us to behave exactly as we believe ourself to be—whether it's good for us or not. So the second basic premise is: *If we change the way we think, we change the way we act.*

Nine Dots

Let's take a look at what really holds you back. We'll start with a puzzle. This will be fun, so don't be too worried about it. Your life doesn't depend on it.

Using a pencil, try to connect the nine dots with just four straight lines—without lifting your pencil from the paper or retracing any of the lines. Remember: four straight lines, no lifting your pencil from the paper, no retracing the lines.

14

Figure 3–1.   Nine dots puzzle.

I'll give you a clue as you work on it: *We limit ourselves by the way that we think. We must learn to think outside of our limitations.* The whole curriculum will have a lot to do with this premise.

Have you solved it yet? Looks simple, doesn't it? It isn't. But keep trying.

Okay—time's up. If you didn't find the solution, don't feel embarrassed. The person who gave me this puzzle many years ago gave me a few *weeks* to figure it out—and I couldn't do it. Extra time doesn't help. Neither does trying harder. Why is it so difficult? *Because of the way that we think.* What holds most of us back is that we try to solve the problem by working within the confines of the nine dots. To solve it, we have to venture *outside* the dots.

Now, you might argue, "You didn't *say* we could cross the lines." That's right. but I didn't say you *couldn't. You* did. Or you might claim, "You didn't *say* we could go outside the dots." But I didn't say you *couldn't. You* did. You gave yourself limitations that weren't really there. We all do that: "I can't quit my job, I don't know anything else," "Oh, I'm too old," "I'm too young," "I'm not the right color," "I'm not the right sex," "I'm too tall," "I'm too short," "There's no way," "It takes ten years before you can get

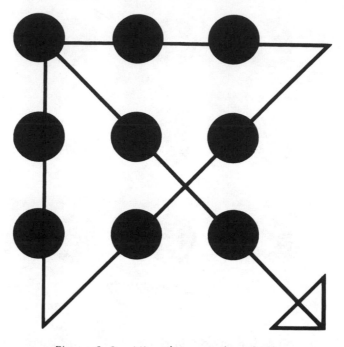

Figure 3-2. Nine dots puzzle solution

ahead in a company like this," "It's impossible to beat that team," "I can't—." See?

This kind of limited thinking blocks you the same way as when you trapped yourself inside the nine dots: "Oh, I *can't* cross the lines. I *can't* go outside the dots." You are constantly blocking yourself by the way that you think—about your business, your future career, how hard it is to make ends meet these days, how long it takes you to get ahead, how lucky other people are, how inept you are at certain skills. Your limiting thoughts recur all the time. You could be driving with your spouse, who might suggest, "Let's visit the Taylors." And you might say, "We can't. They're probably not home." That's like when a friend says, "Why don't you try for that job?" and you say, "They wouldn't hire me anyway. I don't have what they want." Or a business associate suggests, "Let's call this client" and you say, "No. They'd never buy our product." Sound familiar? Like, *"I can't cross the lines?"*

Born with It

Here's another way you hold yourself back. Many of you were raised and conditioned in the past to believe that you were either "born with it" or "born without it." You've heard people say, "She's a born leader" or "He's a born loser." In other words, you either have "what it takes," or you don't. And most of you took I.Q. or aptitude tests to find out what you were "born with" or "born without." I believe that I.Q. and aptitude tests are among the greatest injustices ever perpetrated upon human beings. After you took those tests, you were informed, "You aren't very good at this and you're only average at that." Those notions became hypnotic beliefs: "I'm no good at science; I don't have the aptitude." "I could never be a lawyer; I'm not analytical enough." "I'll never be a—."

Who said so? *You* did. The real truth is that I.Q. and aptitude tests measure only what you *have* learned, not what you *can* learn. They measure what you *have* been, not what you *can* be. But if you accept the test results as part of "the truth" about yourself, your subconscious says, "Okay, whatever you say," and then causes you to act like the person you believe yourself to be. From then on, as long as you hold that belief, you remain trapped within your own nine dots. You *will* be lousy in science; you *will* be poor in English; you *will* be awful in—. So it's not really something outside of you that prevents you from using your potential. Often, it's simply the beliefs that you hold in your mind. The question is, what if you engineered your career, or your whole future, based upon limiting, devaluative, erroneous beliefs?

Here's one more thing. You are hindered not only by what *you* think, but also by what *I* think—if I happen to be your leader, parent, teacher, manager. If *I* believe that you don't have "what it takes"—if *I* believe that women aren't meant to be police officers, blacks can't manage pro baseball teams, or the elderly are slow—then I will set up situations to prevent you from being all that you are capable of being. After all, I'm not crazy. I know "the truth," don't I? Just like the teacher who knows, "Well, I don't expect *you* to do well at math. I had your sister, and she wasn't smart either."

So it isn't just the beliefs that you have about yourself that block you. It's also the beliefs that others have about you—or about your age ("You know how teenagers are."); skin color ("That's the way white people are." "That's the way black people are."); ethnic background ("That's just like a Jew." "That's just like an Oriental."); even your vocation ("Politicians are crooked." "Doctors are cheap."). Or it could just be an attitude about the way *everybody* is: "It's human nature. There's nothing you can do about it."

Again, that's why the real key to achieving excellence in whatever you pursue won't be a matter of trying harder. It will be a matter of *thinking differently.*

Remember: *"Is-ness" is not fixed.* Your future reality needn't be the same size and shape as your present reality—unless you believe it should. You have a nearly unlimited reservoir of potential for growth; you just need to learn how to tap into it. I'm here to give you tools to help you become more than you presently are. But these tools won't do any good until you get past that one mistaken belief: You are *not* born with it.

A Day-and-a-Half Ahead

How frequently we limit our potential because of social or self-imposed beliefs. When I say this, I always think of the bumblebee. Some time ago, aeronautical engineers examined the bumblebee. They measured its wing span, computed its body weight, noted its outsized fuselage, and concluded that there was no rational reason why a bumblebee can take off and land safely. The bumblebee doesn't know this. It doesn't know that its wing span is too short, or that its fuselage is too heavy to sustain flight. So the bumblebee flies anyway. Remember that.

A few years ago, Diane and I were in Australia. The rave of Australia when we were there was a fellow by the name of Cliff Young. He was a potato farmer who had just won the 544-mile footrace from Sydney to Melbourne—one of the world's most grueling endurance tests. This guy didn't just win the race, he slaughtered the course record by finishing more than a *day-and-a-half* ahead of the pack.

What's so spectacular about that? At the time, Cliff Young was sixty-one years old. He had never run a marathon race. His opponents were world-class runners with trainers who knew that you had to train regularly, dress properly, eat correctly, and run strategically to sustain strength through a five-day race. On race day, Cliff Young showed up in long pants and old running shoes. He didn't know much about long-distance training techniques and diets. He didn't know that, to win, you obviously needed the best training and the finest equipment.

Before the race, the press interviewed Cliff like he was an amateur standing in the wrong line. When they asked him how he trained, he said, "I got a ranch with some cows. I don't have any horses, so I herd the cows on foot." Even though Cliff was in shape, it defied logic that this sixty-one-year-old potato farmer could finish *a day-and-a-half* ahead of everyone else. It just didn't make sense.

I was in Melbourne when the race ended and, by then, Cliff Young was a national hero. It turned out that the accepted strategy in a race like this was to run for eighteen hours out of every twenty-four, and sleep six. The thing is, *nobody told that to Cliff Young.* He didn't know "the truth" that everyone else knew. He had no idea he needed thirty hours of sleep over the five-plus days, so he slept only *fifteen.* He didn't know that it was impossible for anyone to finish a day-and-a-half ahead of the field. So Cliff Young unwittingly demolished another "impossible" barrier. He ran beyond conventional truth and discovered the real truth. And, by the way, since his victory, several others have broken his record.

Remember Dick Fosbury, the Olympic high jumper who introduced "The Fosbury Flop"? He was the first international competitor to go over the bar backwards. Back then, coaches told their kids, "Don't watch this guy. He's a freak." These days, *everybody* goes over backwards. Our belief system is so powerful. *If you change the way you think, you change the way you act.* And barriers in your life begin to fall.

Prior to 1954, everybody "knew" you couldn't run a mile in under four minutes. That was their current reality—their two-gallon pumpkin jug. Then Roger Bannister crashed through the barrier. Within the next four years, the four-minute barrier was shattered more than *forty* times. Why? Was it coincidence? Was it luck? Did runners train differently? No. They just *thought* differently. After Bannister did it, they knew it could be done. They added just one key ingredient to their regimen: *belief.*

A few years ago, the athletic director of the University of Texas was on the NCAA Track and Field Qualification Committee. He relayed this story to my friend, Roy Vaughn, U of T alumni director, who told me that, at the time, the minimal standard for qualification for the high jump nationals was a jump of six feet, ten inches. But since too many people qualified, they raised it to six eleven. The same number qualified. The committee said, "We have to weed some of them out"—and they raised it to seven feet. The same number qualified. They raised it to seven one and then seven two, thinking, "That'll definitely stop them"—but the same number qualified.

If we change the belief, the performance follows. If you change the belief, you can change the way you run your life; you can change the way you run your company; you can change the way you run your family. *You* build the barriers. It's often only the *belief* that makes something so. Belief puts a lid on your potential. But you will see how to remove that lid as we go along in this curriculum. It isn't a matter of inspiration or working harder; it's a matter of changing what you believe is "the truth." I'm talking about cutting a day-and-a-half off the race. Your belief system is *that* powerful.

"Sure Enough"

How does the belief make it so? Once we think we know "the truth" about something, we seal it in our subconscious as a belief and we start acting like it. We don't even know we're doing it. That's because our subconscious causes us to behave like the person we believe ourself to be. For example, if you believe you're clumsy, you'll behave like a clumsy person. You'll have a date over for dinner and, somehow, you'll find a way to spill or drop something. Or let's say you're a golfer who averages ninety for eighteen holes. One day, you're on the sixteenth hole and you realize, "Oh man, I'm shooting *seventy!*" Silently, you'll remind yourself, "That's not like me." And your subconscious will say, "Don't worry, I'll correct for the mistake." Then you'll shank it, slice it, hack it into the sand, the woods, or the water. You'll wind up with a twenty on the last two holes. That's because our physiology is tied to our self-image; we behave as we believe ourselves to be. So you'll come in at around ninety, where you believe you should be. And you'll tell yourself, "That's more like me."

This touches on *Gestalt psychology*, which comes up later in the curriculum. But it's so essential, I want to give you some of it now. We know that the job of the subconscious is to maintain order and sanity. To achieve that, it works very hard to assure that whatever you believe *inside* matches what you see *outside*. Let me give you a light example. Ever listen to Bill Cosby? In one of his early albums, he does a routine called "Chicken Heart." It's about a time when Bill is a youngster who keeps climbing out of his crib to go listen to scary radio shows on the Philco in the living room. His parents want to go out one night, but they don't believe in babysitters. So they try to scare Bill into staying in the crib. His mom comes in and says, "We've placed over a hundred poisonous snakes around your crib. If you so much as put a toe out there, they're gonna bite you, and you'll swell up and die until morning." Bill says, "I don't see no snakes!" And his mom says, "They're *invisible*."

Now remember, *we act not in accordance with the real truth, but the truth as we believe it*. So, if you're a little kid, what is "the truth"? It's what anybody bigger than you says. And certainly, it's anything your *parents* say. I wonder what "the truth" is when you're *forty*-four.

Anyway, Bill's parents leave the house, so he stands by the edge of the crib considering the snakes. He says, "Are you listening to me, snakes? I'm gonna put my toe out there. Don't you bite it! Just give it a little snakey lick. Okay, you could bite it a little bit. But don't put none of your *juice* in it!"

Now, *you've* been that way and *I've* been that way. If you think your company, or your marriage, or your career, is full of snakes, you're going to act like they're full of snakes. And, pretty soon, there *will* be snakes. Unless you change the belief. Ever read your horoscope? If you believe in horoscopes, you'll go out and find that the predictions are true.

That's the *"Sure Enough" Principle*. You expect a rotten day and, sure enough, it's a rotten day. Why? Because once you've accepted the horoscope as "the truth," your subconscious says, "Sure enough. Here it is." It works like that for more than just your horoscope. "Oh, I never win at chess." Sure enough, you'll lose. "I'll go

21

to the party, but I know I won't have a good time." Sure enough, you'll have a lousy time.

We *are* our present beliefs. And we've locked on to many partial and false beliefs, which affect the way we think and act. Have you ever seen a hypnotist work? Let's say you believe you can't sing. A hypnotist performing on stage can get you to sing. How does that happen? Well, when you were little, and you were trying to sing, somebody might have screamed at you, "Who's making that awful racket?" And you said, "It's me. I thought I was singing." Or you started singing and someone said, "That's terrible! It's hurting my ears!" And you eventually built the belief, "Gee, I can't sing." Once you lock on to a belief like that, psychologically and physiologically, you will act like your belief. If you don't believe you can sing, you will not *consciously* sing.

So hypnotists can appear to zap a strange power into someone and cause them to act differently than what they believe is "just like me." What hypnotists do, actually, is *un*-hypnotize you from your present belief, and release you to realize your true potential. Then you act like the new belief—"I can sing"—until that belief is gone. That's why, sometimes, you can put a child who stutters under hypnosis and, zap, the stutter disappears. But then, coming out of hypnosis, the child stutters again. We *are* our present beliefs.

This touches also on *psycholinguistics.* For example, we know that the human mind thinks in 3-D. We think in words, which trigger pictures, which stimulate emotion. Words, pictures, emotion—that process is called *self-talk.* It's the conversation we carry on with ourselves in our own mind. Another term for self-talk is *affirmation.* I want you to become very aware of affirmations from now on because they are the key to your future success. Affirmations are statements of fact or belief. It could be a prayer, the pledge of allegiance to the flag, an oath. Affirmations are also, "I'm scared to death" or "I'm good at this. It's easy for me." It's estimated we have about 50,000 thoughts a day, so we obviously make affirmations constantly.

Since your subconscious works to keep you from thinking you're crazy for believing what you believe, it accepts your affirmations *literally.* For example, if you say, "She makes me sick," your subconscious very cooperatively says, "Okay, if that's what you say. I'll make you sick when you're around her." And when you're around her, you will actually feel sick. Just like when you were golfing and you realized, "I'm shooting *seventy!* That's not like me. I'm a *ninety* golfer." Your subconscious then obliged by causing you to shoot a twenty on the last two holes. "Okay, if that's what you *want.*"

How would you act every day if you told yourself over and over, "Life is a bitch"? How would you behave if you said, "All good things must come to an end"? Keep in mind that *we move towards, and we become like, that which we think about.* It's hard to be depressed if you don't think depressing thoughts. It's all in the thought. So you must be very careful about what you affirm to yourself. Because if your subconscious believes something, it will work hard to make it happen.

You know about the placebo effect in medicine—the sugar pill? When a patient is allergic to a necessary medication, the doctor might provide a placebo instead. The doctor says, "Take this. It will make you well." The patient believes it's the real medication, so despite the fact that it's only sugar, the patient starts getting well. Amazing, isn't it? Well, if you can get well on a positive placebo, can you get sick on a negative placebo? What if your doctor examined you and said, "Tsk, tsk, tsk. And so young. I had a case like yours in Detroit, and they didn't make it either." I wonder if you could be *talked* into sickness.

What about a basketball team that collectively thinks, "In the big game, we can't beat the Lakers at The Forum"? Think it's likely they'll beat the Lakers in the big game at The Forum? How about a baseball team that loses twenty-one consecutive games? The press constantly reminds them, "The team needs only ten more losses to break the record," "They need only six more losses," "They need only three more losses—." If the players listen to this, I wonder if their self-talk will be, "We're *losing.* We *keep* losing. We only need three more losses to break the *record* for losing." Do you think that this team will then find ways to keep losing long enough to do what they expect themselves to do? *Sure enough,* I think they will.

Flat Worlds

Remember Columbus? Just about everyone he knew believed the world was flat. Knowing the world was flat, how would they sail? They'd sail out only so far because they "knew"—just as Bill Cosby "knew" about the snakes—that disaster was just ahead. Then they'd lose their courage, turn around, and come back. But to them, it wasn't losing courage. They thought, "If we sail any further, whoops, off the edge we go." See? Tremendous fear of overcoming limitations.

So here comes Columbus with these crazy notions of an earth without edges! People thought, "Why's this nut allowed to walk the streets like us *sane* folk?" So his problem wasn't just what *he* believed, his problem was also, "How do I get *someone else* to believe it, so I can get financing to prove it?" It's the same in your company or your family. "I know this approach will work. How can I convince the others it will work?"

So if I'm Columbus and I come into your bank for a loan and I lay the blueprints in front of you, what do you say? "Boy, those are awfully big ships. What on this flat earth will you use them for?" And I say, "I'm sorry you asked that. I've got this idea that the earth is round. I want to sail out there and prove it." You look at me like I'm crazy, and you say, "Not with *our* money."

Now keep in mind, for me to win, I can't just walk away, thinking, "That's stupid." I have to recognize that people have their own beliefs, and they aren't being deliberately obstinate. They honest-to-goodness don't see—and they think I'm nuts. So, how do I win? I've got to assume the accountability to help them see. Do you know the loser's motto? It's not, "If at first you don't succeed, try, try again." It's, "If at first you don't succeed, *fix the blame fast.* It isn't *me!* It's these stubborn people I have to work with." "*I* know the world's round. Why don't *they* know it?" Because you weren't good enough to show them.

Now, once Columbus got the money, he had another problem: getting a crew. You think you have problems leading your family or your company? Columbus had to convince a crew to sail with him off the edge of their flat earth! Same thing for us today. Everybody has potential, everyone's bright enough—if you're good enough to help them see. Moms and dads know what their kids can do, but the problem is, "How do I get my *kids* to see what they can do?" And that's what I'm going to teach you. Not only how *you* can do what you're capable of doing, but also how you can help others to do the same thing.

Everybody has flat worlds inside them. That's what you must overcome. But first, you must be willing to accept that the earth might be round. And you must be ready to sail out there to see for yourself. If you change your level of expectation and your level of belief, you *can* change your performance. The belief makes it so. Keep in mind that, before Columbus believed strongly enough that the earth was round, the earth, in effect *was* flat, wasn't it? Yet, where is that flat earth today? It's out there keeping the four-minute mile company.

So I would encourage you to reflect on the beliefs you've accumulated in your mind that are presently controlling your behavior on the job, with your family, in your relationships. Because to change the way you act, you will need to change the way you think. I want you to become an option-thinker, a creative thinker, a possibility-thinker. I want to persuade you to think of Columbus and Cliff Young, and open up your own flat-world thinking. You must ask yourself, "What attitudes, what habits, what skills, what beliefs have I locked on to that are no longer relevant?" Eventually, to grow and change, you must know these things. Because each unique person has his or her own unique "truths" and flat worlds to overcome.

So, from now on, whenever you encounter a nine dots situation in your life, instead of saying, "It can't be done," I want you to say, "What if I cross the lines? What if I go outside the dots? What if—?" Like Columbus and Cliff Young, I want you to become an explorer of all the "what ifs." That's the route to success.

4

THE WIZARD:

How Beliefs Are Built

Liver and Onions, and Meat on Friday

Do you know that you aren't even close to using your potential? You are locked into your own limited belief system—and it's holding you back. I'm talking about the way you've been conditioned by the nine dots of your past experiences, your "born with it, born without it" attitudes, your "Sure Enough" snakes on the floor, and your flat-world thinking. Limiting forces which cause you to believe and act according to how you were taught and reared. I'll show you how to overcome all that—but there's something else you must overcome first. As you'll see shortly, it has something to do with *The Wizard of Oz*.

Remember about affirmations—statements of fact or belief? When you give yourself a strong affirmation about something, it becomes part of your belief system and affects how you think and act, until you change the belief. Well, the affirmations of *others* can do the same thing. In the past, you accepted other people's versions of reality as "the truth," and you accumulated a lot of "garbaged-in" junk that might still be part of the way you view yourself and the world.

Let's say, for example, that when you were a kid, you vowed to yourself, "I hate liver and onions. It tastes awful." Keep in mind that your subconscious doesn't know you're exaggerating. It accepts your affirmations literally. In this case, it said, "Okay, whenever you eat liver and onions, it'll taste awful. You'll hate it." Sure enough, you hated it. When you grew older, you didn't need to re-

28

member the vow; you automatically acted like it. Even though you may have forgotten that particular vow, you hate liver and onions to this very day. That one-time affirmation keeps working—and you don't question why.

As kids, we make all sorts of vows: "I'm scared to death of heights," "I'm afraid of the dark," "I'm frightened of—" When we get older, we're still scared of those same things simply because we *said* we were. That's the power of words to build belief. So, if you talked yourself into believing your own vows about "the truth," who else's vows did you believe? What did your brother or sister tell you about reality that you believed? What did your parents tell you that shaped your self-image? How about your grandparents, your relatives, teachers, employers, coaches, friends? How many of *their* liver-and-onion vows have you digested without a second thought?

It's like the placebo effect—the sugar pill that has the power to make you feel well. The power isn't really in the *pill*, is it? It's in your acceptance of the doctor's affirmation that "This pill will get you well." It's the *belief* that makes you well. But belief can also make you sick, can't it? It's a matter of what you tell yourself—or what someone else tells you—that you *believe*.

Throughout your life—in your home, in your neighborhood, at your job—people will constantly give you negative placebos that will make you feel sick. A lot of people will tell you, "Ain't it awful?" and "There's no hope" and "You can't get that job" and "It's a waste of time to—." Got anyone like that in your life right now? Someone who knows "the truth" and wants you to know it, too? Beware. Because your subconscious can't distinguish between positive or negative placebos, happy or depressing thoughts, healthy or harmful beliefs. It doesn't care if you're happy or sad, healthy or sick. It simply accepts whatever you tell it, literally, like a vow. So, you can talk yourself *into* or *out of* self-limiting, denigrating beliefs. You can talk yourself *into* or *out of* excellence.

From now on, I want you to become very cognizant of the affirmations you continually tell yourself. And be especially aware of the affirmations that others give you. Because you're constantly acting and making decisions based on their false, irrelevant, "garbaged-in" information. I remember a funny example in my own life. I am a Catholic. When I was a kid, a lot of what Catholics learned was

29

taught through fear. You didn't do something because you wanted to, you did it because you were afraid *not* to. You feared the punishment. It was a sort of "or else" motivation: "Either you do it this way, *or else*." In my Catholic grade school, I was taught to believe that you couldn't eat meat on Friday, or else you'd go to hell. The nuns who taught me that painted a picture of hell that would frighten an adult. They had it down real good; they knew "the truth."

They painted it so vividly that I "knew" if I so much as nibbled meat on Friday, I'd be hurled into the fire pits of hell. But most of the kids in my neighborhood weren't Catholic. So every Friday, someone would say, "You wanna come over to my house for dinner?" I'd always ask, "What are you having?" They'd say, "Hamburgers." And I'd think, "*You* maybe, but not me. *You* can go to hell if you want to, but *I* ain't goin'." Pretty soon, along came a guy by the name of Pope John, and he had the power to make a few changes. One change he made was "It's okay. You can eat meat on Friday now. It's your choice." Boy, that was so sudden. I mean, after centuries, now we had permission to eat meat on Friday? I thought of the people who'd already gone to hell for that, and I said to myself, "Oh no." *You* eat it!' But, eventually, I gave in. And when I finally did eat meat on Friday, it tasted like the flames of hell! That sensation lasted for weeks. With every bite, I wondered, "Is he *sure*?"

See what happened? Even though I had the Pope's permission to choose for myself, my *conditioned fear* wouldn't allow me to change comfortably. It takes a lot of effort to overcome powerful, past conditioning. But that's what I'm leading you to. You're going to stop affirming things that can ruin your future happiness and success. You accomplish that by being careful who you listen to, controlling your self-talk, writing affirmations, and visualizing what you want, not what you don't want. I'll show you how later. The key for now is to remember this: Successful, high-performance people *choose* whom they listen to. They build blind spots to the junk. When they want to try something new, instead of thinking, "*Fear*," they think, "*Challenge*." But if you're not careful about letting negative, limiting junk get through, you might alter your whole life based on what someone else tells you.

"Who-Said" of the Greatest Magnitude

It's important for you to realize that even a one-time affirmation by another person can alter your behavior drastically. "You're a troublemaker," "You're just like your sister, and she wasn't bright either," "You'll never be a doctor, you don't have the aptitude," "You're too awkward to be an athlete." In the past, you affirmed these kinds of proclamations from people you regarded as authorities. I call such people *"Who-Saids."* As in "Who said?" "Well, *they* did." "Oh, then it must be so."

A "Who-Said" can be anyone you admire and respect whose words have the power to influence how you think and act. If you're a small kid, it could be a big kid: "The big kid said so." It could be your boss: "My supervisor said so." It could be your spouse: "My wife said so." It could be someone you've never met: "I read it in the paper. Dr. Expert said so." It could even be something impersonal: "The Farmer's Almanac said so," "The encyclopedia said so," "The horoscope said so." "Oh, then it must be true."

Know what a rite of passage is? It's a ritual associated with a change in status. Generally, it's a formal ceremony presided over by a *"Who-Said" of the Greatest Magnitude.* Like a wedding ceremony. Either a minister, priest, rabbi, or judge is the presiding "Who-Said." They're like the doctor who gives you the placebo; you believe they have the power. You're willing to accept what they say in the ceremony as "the truth."

Here's what happens. Two people come in knowing they're single, and acting single. Then this "Who-Said" says, "Do you take this man to be—?" And with just one statement of fact, the woman vows or affirms, "I do." Then "Who-Said" proclaims, "By the power vested in me by God—or by the Holy Church, or the State of Washington, or affirms, "I do." The "Who-Said proclaims. "By the power vested in me by God—or by the Holy Church, or the State of Washington, or the City of Las Vegas—I now pronounce you man and wife." Now the couple believes they're married. Think about that. See how simple it is? You come in acting single, a "Who-Said" proclaims you married, and you go out acting married!

Conversely, for some people, if the marriage doesn't work out, a judge puts them through another rite of passage: "By the power vested in me, I hereby dissolve this marriage." Now they go out and act single again! Isn't it amazing? All it takes is *words* in a one-time affirmation by a "Who-Said" of the Greatest Magnitude. Then the belief is changed, and so is the behavior. Because whether you believe you're single or married, you don't need to consciously remember. Your subconscious will make you act like the person you believe yourself to be.

The military knows this. Let's say you're a soldier, and you don't believe you're brave. They put you through some rugged training, at the end of which they have a ceremony with pomp and circumstance, in front of a lot of "Who-Saids" of the Greatest Magnitude, and they give you medals and proclaim you brave. Suddenly, you *feel* brave. You didn't before, but now you do. So what happens? You leave there acting brave: "They gave me medals. They say I'm brave. It must be so."

That's what graduation from school with a degree is all about. Somebody studies for seven years to become a surgeon. They're called an "intern." The day before graduation, they wouldn't consider operating on anyone because, in most states, it would be illegal—and you wouldn't think of letting them cut *you* open, right? You'd say, "No way. You don't have a diploma. You're not a doctor yet!"

But the next day, they go through a graduation ceremony, with caps and gowns and pomp and circumstance, and they march down a carpeted aisle to a stage. On the stage, there's the dean of the medical school in his robes and tassled cap—a classic "Who-Said" of the Greatest Magnitude. He proclaims, "By the power vested in me by the State of --, I grant you a doctor's degree. Go and cut 'em open." *Now* you'd let them do an operation on you, right? Because now you believe in them. As soon as they have their diploma, you say, "Oh, then it must be so."

See how that works? Yesterday, they couldn't. Today, they can. What changed? Only the *belief*. They went through a rite of passage with a one-time affirmation by a "Who-Said" of the Greatest Magnitude—and now they have the power to change your life. Just *words*! Of course, not just anything that anyone says has that power. It has to come from someone you believe in. And the circumstances and spirit of intent behind the words are essential, too. For example, two people meet in a bar for the first time and, after a few minutes of conversation, the guy says, "Oh, I love you." And the woman says, "Well, yes. I love you, too." The bartender says, "And I pronounce you man and wife." That won't work, will it? It's the same words, but the bartender isn't a "Who-Said," and the circumstance and spirit of intent are significantly different. You don't accept the bartender's affirmation, so you don't act married. Your subconscious knows it isn't so.

Do you see how powerful belief is, and how powerful the "Who-Saids" in your life can be? But the real truth is: "Who-Saids" don't possess the power. It's *you* who grant it to them. "Who-Saids" have power partly because we've been conditioned to need someone else's blessing or approval: "I wonder if they'll let me go to elementary school. Oh, thank you." "I wonder if they'll let me go to high school. Oh, thank you." "I wonder if they'll let me go to college. Oh, thank you." "I wonder if they'll hire me. Oh, thank you." "I wonder if they'll grant me a raise. Oh, thank you." "I wonder if I'm handsome." "I wonder if I'm pretty." "I wonder if I'm—"

Always waiting for other people to give you permission, or to affirm that you're capable of doing what you already know you're capable of doing: "Here's your football letter. Now you're an official member of the team." "Oh, thank you. I've played two years, but I didn't know I was an official member of the team until you gave me this letter." "Here's your pilot's license. You're officially a pilot." "Oh, thank you. I've only flown sixty hours. I didn't know I was a pilot until you gave me this license." See what I mean? I'm not saying, "Fly without a license" or "Break any laws that you don't make yourself." That would create chaos; we're striving for *order*. I'm simply saying that when you grant other people undue influence over what you think and do, you've given up accountability for your own life. Somebody tells you, "Okay, you're ready now," and you say, "I *am*? Oh, thank you. I wouldn't have known if you didn't tell me." But you *do* know. You just won't let yourself believe it.

Now reflect for a moment. Name the "Who-Saids" in your life whose opinions you've sanctioned as "the truth." How do *they* know "the truth"? What did they tell you about yourself that you didn't already know? Why do you need them?

The Wizard of Oz

Let's take another step. This is vitally important. It's a little story about how our beliefs are built.

A few years ago, on my way back from Australia, I stopped in Hawaii. One of our clients there is a native organization that asked me to talk at their graduation ceremony for people who'd gone through our highly popular "Investment in Excellence" program. I expected it to be a little luau. Anyway, I arrived late and they said, "We're so glad you came. We were afraid you wouldn't be here in time to give the commencement address." I said, *"Commencement address?"* I thought I was just going to say a few words at a party.

Well, they led me up in front of the entire student body and gave me a big introduction. I realized that this audience would consider me a "Who-Said," so I had to come up with something appropriate very quickly. I looked at them: They were people who seldom got out of the eighth grade. They believed they couldn't hold jobs. Their self-esteem was so low, they felt they were on the bottom rung of the social ladder. So I told them about one-time affirmations, rites of passage, and *The Wizard of Oz.*

I said, "You have been listening to a great many people who have told you that you aren't capable. I want you to know that's garbage. They're wrong. They don't know the real truth. It's not that you aren't capable, it's just that you *believe* you aren't capable. The reason is, you've let other people tell you that you aren't very smart, that you aren't worthwhile, that you always flunk out of school, that you can't hold jobs. And then you go and act like those beliefs. But listen, it isn't just *you* doing that. *Everybody* does it."

I explained about rites of passage, one-time affirmations, and "Who-Saids" of the Greatest Magnitude. I said, "You have given all these 'Who-Saids' the power to transform your belief so completely, it has altered your behavior." I needed a concrete example to illustrate this, so I said, "That's exactly what happened in *The Wizard of Oz.*" And I told the following story.

"Just about everybody knows about *The Wizard of Oz.* Now, in that story, when Dorothy's house lands in Oz, it kills a wicked witch. That witch's sister is after Dorothy, so Dorothy wants to go back home to Kansas. The good witch, Glenda, advises Dorothy to go to the Emerald City to see the Wizard of Oz. 'Only the Wizard', she says, 'has the power to send you home.' Wizards, of course, are 'Who-Saids' of the Greatest Magnitude. They have 'the touch,' you know. At least, everybody believes they do.

So Dorothy sets off to see the Wizard, the wonderful Wizard of Oz. She's off to see the Wizard—why? Because of the wonderful things he does. You think *you* got problems getting through life? On her way to the Emerald City, Dorothy meets a scarecrow who claims he has no brains. Then she meets a tin man who says he has no heart; Finally a lion who insists he has no courage. If that's not enough, the wicked witch dispatches flying monkeys to attack them; she causes trees to throw fruit at them; she tricks them into smelling poison poppies, so they'll fall asleep. It isn't a fun journey.

"But Dorothy, the Scarecrow, the Tin Man, and the Cowardly Lion persist—with brains and heart and courage, by the way—and they arrive safely at the Wizard's palace. But it turns out that the Wizard isn't a wizard at all. He's an ordinary person, just like Dorothy. He knows he doesn't have any special powers. But everybody believes he does, so he hides behind a curtain and *pretends* to be the omnipotent Wizard of Oz. He tries to live up to everybody's expectations. Sound familiar?

"Dorothy has to force an audience with the Wizard because he's as hard to see as the pope. Then everybody tells the Wizard what they want. The Scarecrow wants some brains. The Wizard says, 'Every smart person needs a diploma. By the power vested in me, the Great and Powerful Oz, I hereby give you this diploma. Now you've got brains. Go and act like it.' The Tin Man wants a heart. The Wizard says, 'Everyone who has a heart can hear it tick.' So he gives the Tin Man a clock and says, 'By the power vested in me, I hereby give you this clock. Now you've got a heart. Go and act like it.' The Cowardly Lion wants courage. The Wizard says, 'Every brave person needs a medal. By the power vested in me'—and he pins a medal on the Lion. 'Now you're brave. Go and act like it.'

"Just a one-time affirmation from a 'Who-Said' of the Greatest Magnitude, and it changes belief, which changes behavior. But the important lesson the Wizard teaches Dorothy, the Scarecrow, the Tin Man, and the Cowardly Lion is this: *The very things they wanted from him were attributes they already possessed—if only they would think differently.*

"What I want to convey," I said, "is that Dorothy and her pals went to see a positive wizard. Even though he was a fake, he was a good person. He gave them courage and heart. He raised their self-esteem. Whereas you may have been to see too many negative wizards who, by their negative appraisals of you, have taken away what you already had. We all run into negative wizards. They tell us we're not smart enough, or we're not the right color, or we're not the right sex, or we don't have what it takes. It could be a grandparent who says, 'Oh, she's one of my *slow* grandchildren'—and she doesn't mean foot-speed; it could be a manager who shouldn't be managing; or a husband who shouldn't be married. That's why you must stop waiting for somebody else's approval. You've got to learn to grant *yourself* the approval to use the potential God gave you.

"You must teach yourself and the people around you to be very cognizant of whom you listen to. We've been taught to respect authority, even though we're not always sure if the authority knows more than we do. Throughout your life, you'll run into negative wizards in positions of authority. They'll try to tell you who you are and what you can do; they'll try to take away your heart, your courage, your brains. But, like in *The Wizard of Oz*, that can only happen if you *believe* them.

"So the important lesson from *The Wizard of Oz* is that you must become your own positive wizard in order to control your own thoughts. Reject the negative affirmations of others. Don't allow them to steal your future and your hope. You are smart, you are bright, you are capable. *You* have 'the touch,' too. You have the power to be a very positive, constructive wizard to yourself and to the people you love.

"For example, Little Scotty Fitterer traveled back from Australia with us. His dad is president of our company. Scotty was going to dive into the swimming pool for the first time in his life. He'd chickened out all through Australia, but this time he did it. He said, 'Mama, Mama, come see!' Scotty didn't really want his mama to come see. He wanted her to come and declare him brave. Because she has 'the touch' with her own children. Just as you do with your children, and others who love and respect you.

"Let me give you a great example of how, with thoughtful use of 'the touch,' you can affirm something positive for others. One time, I was traveling to an Army base where they develop America's elite soldiers. I was met at the airport by a General, two helicopter pilots, and two bodyguards in camouflage fatigues. The General said, 'I'm here to escort you to the base.' As we walked to the helicopter, I noticed he had a star on his shoulder, which indicated he was a brigadier general. He said, 'Excuse my two bodyguards. I'm a great target for the KGB.' And I thought, 'What am I doing with *this* guy?'

"When we got in the helicopter, he said, 'We're doing some very important exercises here, and we could be watched by the Russians and the Chinese. We know I could be captured.' He explained why our enemies would be interested in him; he was really a big catch. That night, at dinner in the officer's club, this General and I were engrossed in conversation. I found out that he had a doctorate degree, he was a graduate of West Point, he'd served four terms in Vietnam, and he was multilingual. He was a very interesting character. As we were talking, a Colonel walked by. The General reached out, grabbed him by the arm, and introduced him to me this way: *'This is the bravest man I know in the world.* He spent five years in solitary confinement as a P.O.W. in North Vietnam. He escaped in his fifth year. He's here to teach us how to be brave and how to survive.' Then he let the Colonel go.

"The lesson for me was that the General used me to affirm for the Colonel how much he admired him, and how brave he thought he was. But he couldn't just throw his arms around him and tell him. So he told the Colonel by telling *me.* That's called third-person affirming. The General did that continually over my twenty-four hour stay.

"Just before we left, a young officer was saluting us off in the car, and the General stuck his own foot in the door to keep it open. He pointed at the officer and said to me, 'One day, this man will be the finest officer in America.' And he meant it. That officer saluted so smartly, so proudly. Why did he believe this guy? Because everyone knew that if *he* said something, it must be so. By continually third-person affirming in this manner, the General showed that he was a Positive Wizard of the Greatest Magnitude—a master at building positive belief in others.

"Sometimes, you do that for your children. You brag about them, in their presence, to somebody else. Physicians do that when they want someone to get well. They'll stand at the patient's bedside and tell an intern that the patient is doing well and will be leaving soon. The doctor can't tell certain patients directly because the patient won't believe it. Yet, when they overhear it being said to a third party, they believe it.

"So you must learn to use the tremendous power you've got to help people become what they are truly capable of becoming. But beware. You can also become a very negative wizard. If you devalue, belittle, or criticize someone negatively, watch out. Once they believe you—just like with the placebo or the marriage vow—they will act like what you've affirmed. What do you think happens when a father tells his son in Little League, 'Don't strike out?' When the kid comes up to bat, he strikes out. The father says, 'Geez, why can't you hit? I taught you everything I know, but you can't do it.' I wonder why. When the kid goes up to hit, I wonder if his subconscious says, 'You can't hit. Your *dad* said so. It must be true.' Is that kid gonna hit? He might when he realizes his dad is a Negative Wizard of the Greatest Magnitude, and then takes back the power.

"So my questions for you today are: Do you do this in your family? In your marriage? In your social relationships? In your business relationships? Who are the negative wizards you listen to? Have you been a positive wizard to anyone else? My challenge to you is: Stop letting other people feed you negative junk. Be in charge of your own life by taking back accountability. Become your own positive wizard.

"In conclusion," I said, "are you familiar with the words in that beautiful *Wizard of Oz* song: 'We're off to see the Wizard, the wonderful Wizard of Oz?' Well, that will be relevant to you if you change two words. Change, 'We're off to *see* the Wizard,' to '*I'm* off the *be* the Wizard.' That's how I want you to think from now on.

"And to any of you doubters, I say, 'By the power vested in me today, I declare you Associate Wizards. So go and act like it.'"

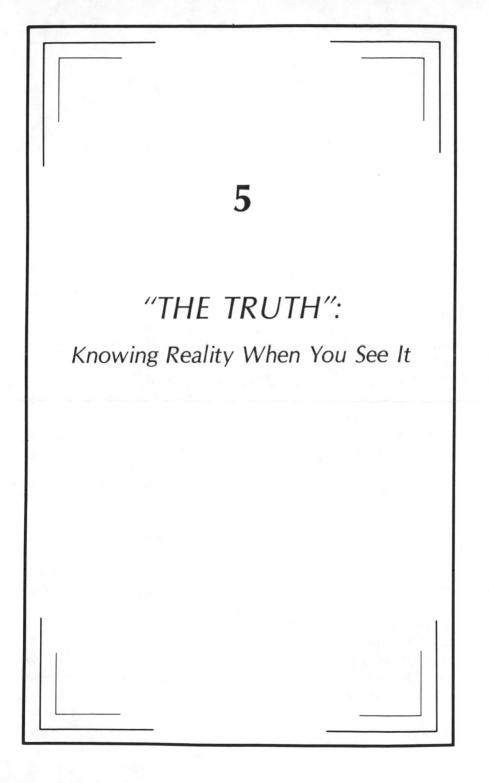

5

"THE TRUTH":

Knowing Reality When You See It

Where is "the truth"? What do you know to be true *for sure*? Are you hearing all the answers—or just the ones you want to hear? Are you seeing all the possibilities—or just the ones you've been conditioned to see? You and I must ask ourselves these questions because we're constantly blinding ourselves to aspects of the real truth that don't match what we believe.

Our image of present reality is only a partial picture. Our physical senses are limited absolutely. For example, we can only see between red and violet. So, if there's light out there beyond the red-violet spectrum, without augmenting our vision with special glasses or scopes, we might deny it existed. If we want to see details of the planets, we need a telescope; if we want to see inside the human body, we need an X-ray; if we want to look into a living cell, we need a microscope. So, what else are we missing about reality?

Human beings hear low-pitch sound at about 50 vibrations per second and high-pitch at about 19,500. Did you ever blow a dog whistle? No sound comes out, yet the dog responds. It makes no sense. It does make sense to *dogs* because they hear at about 24,000 vibrations per second—well beyond our range. Bats hear at 80,000, and some porpoises at an even higher rate. There's sound out there we don't even know about.

Our sense of smell is also very limited compared to animals who rely on it for protection and to find food. One of the world record holders for the sense of smell is the male silkworm moth who can detect the odor of the female moth more than a mile away. And that female moth emits only .001 of a milligram of the odor-producing chemical. Now that's *really* being aware of one's environment.

I'm saying our senses are limited in detecting the outside reality in which we live our lives. We still haven't discovered all there is to be discovered, and we can't perceive all there is to perceive. So don't go by what is *apparent*. What is apparent may be only what you're able to see—or what you've allowed yourself to see.

"Lo—Lo"

We all tend to think, "I'm not wrong. I know the truth when I see it, don't I?" The answer is no. In fact, we can look right at something and not see it. I'll prove it to you.

Here are pictures of two ladies. First, study the picture on the left.

Figure 5–1

That picture shows an old lady with no teeth, a big chin and a big hook nose. She's facing to your left, with her pointy chin in the center of her black coat. She's wearing a black hat with a feather sticking out. See the old lady's face now? She looks like the kind of "old hag" we see in cartoons.

Now take a moment and study the picture on the right. This picture shows a young lady who's looking back over her right shoulder. She's wearing a black choker on her neck. She has the same hair as the old lady, same black coat, same feathered hat. Can you see the young lady's face?

Study both pictures a moment before reading further.

Okay, you can stop now. Obviously, the two pictures are identical. So how can one be an old lady and the other a young lady? The answer is that each picture shows both ladies. I'll show you how to see them. *The old lady's mouth is the young lady's choker.* Concentrate on that until you see the two ladies. They should jump right out at you, once you know how to find them.

What you've just experienced is called the *"Lo-Lo Principle"* or the *"Lock on-Lock Out Principle."* Remember the nine dots puzzle? Remember: *"We limit ourselves by the way that we think?"* Well, if you locked on to the old lady first, you locked out the young. If you locked on to the young lady first, you locked out the old. Why couldn't you see both? Because human beings have difficulty holding two conflicting thoughts, or "pictures," at the same time. If you see the old lady first, you think, "Got it. It's the old lady." And that becomes your belief; it becomes "the truth." If somebody said, "No, it's a *young* lady," you'd say, "You're crazy. I know what I see."

But it's likely you're not seeing the whole truth. We tend to lock on to conventional and conditioned ways of thinking, which lock out options that would be open to us through possibility-thinking. You might wonder, "What the heck *is* 'possibility-thinking?'" Very simply, it's being able to see beyond convention, beyond conditioning. It's being able to stop looking at what you *don't* want in life, and start focusing on what you *do* want. That's the way high-performance people think, and it's one reason why they succeed. They constantly search for options and new ways to get things done. If one way doesn't work, they try others—until they win. So you must ask yourself, "Do I lock on more to the problem than the solution? Would I *see* the solution if it was right in front of me? Or have I built a blind spot in my mind that says, 'It can't be done?'"

Scotoma

In talking about blind spots, I use the word "*scotoma*," which is Greek for blindness. When someone complains, "I don't get it" or "It doesn't make sense to me," they have a scotoma. Scotoma is when your senses lock out the environment. It's not just visual, it can affect *all* the senses. You can be in a conversation and not hear what the other person says; you can be having fun at a party and not smell the smoke from a fire outside; you might not taste something you normally hate in your food; you could be boxing, and not feel the punch that breaks your nose.

Scotomas cause us to see what we expect to see, hear what we expect to hear, think what we expect to think. "They can't win—they never do." "She won't go out with me—she never does." "We can't sell to that company—we never have." This blocking out of the optional truths around us is a common human trait. When you lock on to an opinion, belief, or attitude, you build scotomas to anything else that doesn't verify what you believe. You become a prisoner to your preconceived ways of seeing things and your habitual ways of doing things.

Scotomas block change, flexibility, and creativity because they make us selective information-gatherers. Keep in mind, when you saw the old lady, you literally blinded yourself to the young. You didn't see her, even though she was right in front of you. Ever look for something, and tell yourself you lost it? As soon as you say, "I lost it," your subconscious builds a scotoma to the object—click, just like that.

Remember the *self-talk concept* I mentioned earlier? I explained that your mind takes everything you say literally, and then causes you to act automatically like your belief. Your subconscious is more concerned with proving that you aren't crazy for believing what you believe than with discovering the real truth. So, if you tell yourself you've lost your keys, what would make you look crazy? *Finding them!* That being the case, your subconscious says, "Oh, you lost your keys?" and, click, it builds a blind spot to your keys. Just like it did to the old lady, or the young. The keys can be six inches away, but you won't see them. Then somebody will come along and say, "Here they are. You're looking right at them!" You know what you'll say? "Who *moved* them?" They weren't there a minute ago." You ever do that?

Make no mistake, scotomas do exist. They cause friendships to dissolve, marriages to fail, nations to go to war. Each side thinks, "What's the matter with you? Are you blind?" Quite frankly, the answer is yes. *Everybody* has blind spots. This is a key concept because once you understand scotomas, you will be able to see many more options and opportunities in your career, your social life, and your emotional life. I want you to apply this to your whole growth. Apply it to the way you live, the way you look at your business; the way you look at your children, and, particularly, the way you look at yourself.

Remember: *When we lock on, we lock out.* What have you locked on to about your life? What have you locked on to about your business? What have you locked on to about your spouse, your children, your clients, your friends? Have you locked on that, "I can't win," "This won't sell," "She's no good," "He's all right," "That won't work," "This will work"? Be aware that you manipulate your very senses by these conclusions. You blind yourself to other options, even when you're immersed in them.

How quickly do you lock on? "Oh, I've *had* one of those positive motivational courses. They don't work." Click. You won't hear another word I say. Ever been around people who lock on forever and ever, Amen? They honest-to-God don't see. "This is how I live. There *is* no other way." "I've been in this relationship forever. There *is* no other relationship." "It's tradition in this company. My grandfather did it this way, my father did it this way, and I do it this way. There *is* no other way." For them, there really isn't. Why? Because when they lock on that this is the *only* way, they build a scotoma to the old lady, or to the young. No matter what you say, you can't show them. They sincerely believe, "I know the truth when I see it."

"I'll Be Darned! Look at That!"

Let me just relate something funny and dumb that happened to me years ago when I was a teacher and football coach at Kennedy High School. I had my players for four years, so I thought I knew them better than most people know anybody. See my locked-on opinion? Watch how you use this in your life and you don't even know it. By the end of the third year, I had locked on that my quarterback—a kid named David—couldn't pass the ball ten yards. To me, that's how weak his arm was; that was "the truth." How did I know? Well, I'd seen him play for three years, hadn't I? I was his coach; I ought to know.

See the detrimental attitude? But that was all right because I had also locked on that my ends couldn't catch. I knew "the truth" about them, too. I mean, they'd been dropping them all along, hadn't they? Keep in mind that once I "knew" they couldn't catch the ball, I built a scotoma to every catch they made. That whole year, I never saw my ends make a catch.

I'd also locked on that we had no speed. Being the great coach that I was, I figured the only possible way we would move the ball was if I took this big, 225-pound kid by the name of Don out of the line and made him a fullback. So we slammed that kid into the line over here for three yards, and then we slammed him over there for three yards. And to fool you, we'd come back over here with him because you thought we'd go over there. We would win 7–6, or lose 6–7. Imagine watching games like that. They were so boring, even the kids' mothers fell asleep in the stands.

I remember this one game so vividly—it must've been twenty years ago. We were ahead of Stadium High School out of Tacoma 7–0 in the second quarter. Third down, eight yards to go on Stadium's twenty-yard line. That was a long-yardage situation for us because we averaged three yards a carry with our "Belly" plays—fullback into the line. So David called time out and came over to me and said, "Coach, what're we gonna call?" That made me madder than the dickens. We only had two plays, and he'd wasted a time out like that? "Hell," I thought. "Now I'm gonna have to give these kids some inspiration."

Ever get people around you who try to inspire you because they can't tell you what to do? That was me. I said, "Run 'Belly at Six' and tell those darned kids to block harder." And David said, "But Coach, couldn't we pass the ball to Marty?" Now, Marty was an end that we split way out there for a decoy. Everybody knew we wouldn't throw to him. When David said, "Couldn't we pass the ball to Marty?" that was insubordination! A bad-mouther! A kid telling you how to run your company! I said, "Don't you bad-mouth me. I got another guy that can play." I didn't, but you always say that. And they see right through it.

In exasperation, this sixteen-year-old quarterback got up enough courage to look me in the eye and say, "Well, Marty's not only been open the whole game, he's been open the whole *year!*" Oooh, that made me mad. So we ran my play again, naturally, where we crunched into the line for three more yards. But David sent Marty downfield anyway—and here went this kid right down the middle of our opponent's field without anybody near him. But that wasn't so bad. Every step of the way, he was making faces at me! And then he stood wide open right under the goal post. I looked at him and thought, *"I'll be darned! Look at that!"* Just like when you saw the old lady and then, click, you saw the young. You couldn't see it, then you could. *"I'll be darned! Look at that!"*

On the very next play, we sent Marty downfield again, and David faked a handoff to the fullback and threw a wobbly ol' touchdown pass to Marty. "Wobbly," of course, was my perception because, after all, I *knew* the kid couldn't throw. Well, we scored three touchdowns in that game on the same play. I got to thinking, "Not all *year*. It *couldn't* have been that easy. Not as hard as *we've* been working."

You're going to have the same feeling about your life from now on. Because it isn't just me being dumb and blind, and locked on and locked out. You'll see that you and many of the people around you are the same way. And when you see a new option for the first time, you'll be very embarrassed. You'll say to yourself, "Why didn't I see that before?"

Hold on. There's more to the story. The next day, Sunday, I went down in my basement and looked at our game films. I found out it wasn't just Marty in the clear; we had *other* kids in the clear all over the place. But we never called their plays. I sat there watching the film, thinking, "I'll be darned. Look at that. Look at that. Look at that." I could *see* now.

On Monday, I went to my office in the locker room and called in this cocky, egotistical, know-it-all junior by the name of Tommy —a halfback who was always trying to tell me how to run my team. You got any of those in your company? I said, "Tell me, Tommy. How can we score?" He said, "You know that play where you got me knocking the end down, and everybody else goes the other way? Well, once I knock him down, everybody leaves me. Even *he* gets up and leaves. If you wanna score, just throw me the ball." That sounded too easy. Why didn't *I* see that?

In the next game, so help me, that "know-it-all" kid scored six touchdowns. Not points—*touchdowns*. The game after that, he scored six more. That's twelve touchdowns in two games—and, before that, we had trouble scoring just one a game. Why hadn't I *seen*? I knew why: because I was so opinionated.

The next week I asked another kid, a halfback by the name of Joe, "Hey Joe, what's *your* favorite play?" And I'll be darned, I became a good coach. How come? Wasn't I working at it before? Wasn't I trying hard? Wasn't I studying? Of course, I was. But I was too locked on to my own vision of the way things is, was, and always will be, forever and ever, Amen. I was so locked on to what I thought was "the truth" about everybody else, that I couldn't see the old lady, or I couldn't see the young.

You could be blocking yourself the same way—to your children, to the client, to earning a living, to getting ahead in a new career. Open-mindedness, flexibility, option thinking—that's what I want to encourage. "What can I be? What can I do? What don't I see? How can I see it?" Right now, you may not know, but by the time you finish this curriculum, you will have the tools. Whether you apply them or not is your own business. Having an intellectual understanding of this stuff is worth nothing. It is the application of these principles that counts. I could have an intellectual understanding of "Lock On-Lock Out" and never see Marty in the clear.

By the way, Marty went on to become a high school All-American. Tommy became the state's leading scorer. And we got to the point where we talked about winning games by forty points. Not "Could we win?" but "Could we win by forty points?" And I started treating the kids with dignity. I locked on that they knew as much as I did, that they could see options. And I accepted my own limitations, which allowed me to grow. I found out that my self-esteem was so low that it had blocked me from listening to the kids on my team. "What would people think if I asked the *players* what to do? Aren't *I* supposed to know it all?" I knew I didn't know it all, but my low self-esteem made me too embarrassed to ask for help. *Now* if I don't know something—or if I think I have a scotoma to it—I say, *"Please show me."*

The Answers Are There

There's bad news and good news about scotomas. The bad news is that we don't know we've got them. We continue our daily routines—raising a family, running a business, doing our jobs—in a state of semi-myopia. We don't see all the optional truths around us. Scotomas not only prevent us from finding the solution, they also block us from seeing the problem. "It's right in front of your nose!" "No, it isn't. Where?" "Over *there!*" "Well, it wasn't there before. Who *moved* it?"

Did you ever get in an argument with your children or your spouse, and say, "It's so obvious! How can you deny it? You're just being stubborn and belligerent!" And they say, "No, *you're* being stubborn and belligerent!" In other words, you're gonna show them the young lady, and they only see the old. They think you're crazy, and you think they're nuts! Amazing, right? So, the important thing to recognize about scotomas is that we don't know we have them, but everybody does have them.

The good news is, when you know you've got them, scotomas can be highly constructive. The locking-on process—building your own scotomas to outside distractions—helps you focus intently on the challenge at hand. High-performance people use locking on to help them tenaciously accomplish a goal: to make more money, create a successful marriage, beat racial prejudice, make a speech, throw a football under pressure. But be careful. This very strength—the ability to concentrate singlemindedly on an objective—can become your weakness. Because you *are* so strong and opinionated, and because you need that very strength to win, you may be blind to the other options. Along with distractions, you may also be locking out a better way.

So the trick is to *lock on and open up.* Don't *know* all there is to know about your business; don't *know* all there is to know about your relationships; don't *know* all there is to know about the way it *is*. We look at successful people and, often, we say, "They're lucky. Things break well for them." *Are* they lucky? Or do they just see more than you see? Do they see *differently*? Funny how a different point of view can suddenly open up so much more. Click, there's the old lady. Click, there's the young. Click, there's Marty in the clear. Click, there's Tommy. Click, click, click, click.

What sets high-performance people apart is that they seem to have fewer scotomas than other people. They are intensely focused on their goals, yet they remain skeptical and analytical. They recognize that they don't see the whole truth, so they take creative risks in search of *more* truth. As the quantity of truth that they see increases, so do the lucky "breaks" in their lives. That has little to do with coincidence. It has little to do with intelligence. It has little to do with luck. It has nothing to do with being born with it. It has to do with the way that they think. And if you can learn to use these skills, your life will "break" better for you all along the line. Every time you look around, you'll see an option you never saw before: "I'll be darned. Look at that. There's another one."

So we really must keep an open mind. Through this curriculum—and forever forward—we must hold this belief: *The answers are there. I just don't see them yet. But I will see them soon.* That's the way to attack life. Think in terms of what you want—the family, the career, the resources. Don't delay it by asking yourself, "How?" But keep in mind, if you're my subordinate or employee, and I lock on that you don't have what it takes, it'll be difficult for you to succeed. I will build a scotoma to anything you do that would make me look crazy for believing what I believe. You could struggle and struggle to improve, but if I believe that you were born without it, I won't see you make the catch. So you may have to become a *Scotoma Buster* for someone else. More on that later.

What I'm trying to do now is show you how to be your *own* Scotoma Buster; how to see what you may not presently see; how to make life easier for yourself and your children. You've got to learn to resist negative conditioning. You've got to keep reminding yourself: *"The answers are there. I just don't see them yet. But I will see them soon."* You've got to *uncondition* yourself in areas where you're working too hard to make things happen. With that approach, you'll be off on a great treasure hunt: "I gotta find out how. I gotta see differently. I'll find solutions along the way."

Right now, the big questions are: "What have I locked on to about me? What attitudes, what beliefs, what 'truths?' How do I even describe myself?" But beware. By your very description, you put yourself inside of nine dots. "I'm a teacher." "I'm, a nurse." "I'm an accountant." "I'm a—." Once you label yourself, you build scotomas to other things you can be. There are options, there are alternatives. I want you to be flexible, open-minded. I want you to experience that "I'll be darned" feeling. Not just now, but next week, next month, next year. Remember: The only difference between average and high-performance people—those who constantly seem to have excellence "break" for them—is that *they see more* because *they think differently*.

"GIGO"

The whole truth is elusive. So we often act on the basis of partial truths, half-truths, or untruths. We accept all kinds of information as "the truth," even though we don't know it's true for sure. In computerese, this is called *"GIGO"* or *"Garbage In-Garbage Out."* If you feed misinformation into a computer, you can't expect the right answer to come out. The same with the quality of your decisions. They won't be any more accurate than the information on which you base them. Would you finance the construction of ships to sail around a flat earth?

It was written a long time ago: "A man thinketh in his heart, so is he." In those days, they believed the brain was in the heart. The saying meant that you would behave according to whatever you felt in your "heart" to be true. What we surmise now is that thinking takes place in the neuron structure of the cells of the brain, and you can think the way you choose to. In other words, *"Is-ness" is not fixed.* If you change the way you *thinketh*, you change the way you *is-eth*.

It starts in the mind where *thoughts accumulate to build beliefs.* If you accumulate false or partially true beliefs about your capabilities or your potential, then that's how you'll behave. How would you behave if you believed "It is easier for a camel to slip through the eye of a needle than it is for a rich man to get to Heaven?" If you had the opportunity to be rich—but you also wanted to go to heaven someday—your subconscious would cause you to push away riches with both hands. It's not just money. If you believe, for example, that because of a mistake you made in the past, you don't deserve happiness, then every time happiness approaches you'll unconsciously shove it away with both hands. And you'll wonder why your life isn't going so well. *Garbage In-Garbage Out.*

Years ago, I worked with some ex-convicts. There was this one guy who'd just gotten out of prison after being in for a long time. His name was Emmett. He was about sixty, and he'd been a drunk and a burglar—but not a very good burglar or he wouldn't have been in prison. I taught Emmett this information, and he decided, "I'll try to go legitimate." He chose the upholstery business—reupholstering furniture. He'd never been in business before, but he'd learned that skill in prison.

He had a problem, though. He needed a sewing machine. Now, those machines cost hundreds of dollars, but all Emmett had was fifty-six bucks. Right away, he figured: "I can't do it." You know, "*Impossibility*-thinking." I said, "How do you know that?" He said, "Well, Don told me." Don was a prisoner inside Walla Walla who'd been locked up for thirteen years. He was the tough guy who ran the prison, and he knew it all. So the "garbaged-in" information that Emmett got from Don was that ex-convicts can't get credit. To Emmett, that was "the truth."

I said, "Why don't you just try it"—and, finally, he did. He went down to Lacey, a community near Washington's capital, and somehow he got a sewing machine on credit. He came back to one of our follow-up sessions and told me his success story. He said, "I went in and put my fifty-six dollars down, and the guy *gave* me a sewing machine on credit!" That wasn't so bad. It was Emmett's next statement that screamed "Garbage In." He said, "And the guy didn't even ask me if I was a convict!"

Well, how many times have they asked *anybody?* See, they *don't* ask. But let's suppose that, in your mind, you know you're an ex-convict, and you drink a lot, and you just got out of prison, and you know you'll probably be going back. How would you apply for credit? You'd go in and sit down, and your facial expressions, your body language, and your tone of voice would say, "You wouldn't give credit to a guy that drinks a lot and just got out of prison and might be going back, would you?" Almost like wearing a sign: *"I'm a crook. Just got out. Probably go back."* What's the guy in the store going to say? "No!" And then, what would you tell yourself? "See. Don was right. Ex-cons *can't* get credit."

Now, that didn't happen to Emmett. He got his sewing machine because he understood enough of this information to keep his old attitudes from sabotaging his goal. The point is, we constantly make flawed decisions and judgments based on "garbaged-in" information. So this curriculum will help make things much easier for you in the future. You're going to be able to make better decisions, and accomplish goals quicker and more effectively. I'm going to teach you how to be "luckier." It isn't magic; it isn't working harder—it's simply a matter of *seeing differently*.

Which, by the way, you already *do*.

How to See a Fly

But you need to take another step. Study this difficult puzzle by concentrating on the objects in black.

Figure 5-2

The easiest one to identify is an arrow. Everybody gets that one. The next easiest seems to be a comb with some teeth broken away from the top and bottom. Got the comb? Can you also see the silhouette of an Indian-brave's head with a feather on top? How about a log cabin with a chimney? One of the hardest to see is a top view of an architectural blueprint of a living room with a fireplace in it. Most people don't get that one. The toughest is the letter "F." Can you see that? How about the letter "L"? The letter "Y"? Can you see the word "FLY" in there?

Remember: This curriculum is also about *psycholinguistics*. The power of language on your perception, your beliefs, your behavior. You've got to become very analytical about what people tell

52

you. Because if they say, "It'll take you five years to get that job" or "There are snakes on the floor" or "The word 'FLY' is the toughest to see"—and you *believe* them—your subconscious will say, "Sure enough" and you'll act like your belief.

So—can you see the word "FLY"? Not yet? Does this help?

Figure 5-3

It should jump right out at you—like the old lady and the young. You were looking right at it, you just didn't see it. One reason is because *the letters in the first illustration (Figure 5-2) are in white with black spacing*—and most of us have built a scotoma to that. That's because blind spots are the result of how we've been *conditioned* to see the world. For years, you were conditioned to read black lettering with white spacing. When you look at white lettering with black spacing, you literally can't see the letters.

Another reason you had trouble seeing "FLY" was that I focused you on the objects in black, not the letters in white. I said, "There's a comb, there's an arrow, there's a brave's head." Then you saw what you *expected* to see—a comb, an arrow, a brave's head—even though they aren't there! And you missed the only thing that really *is* there: the word "FLY."

A third reason you had a problem was that I said it would be very difficult to see the word "FLY." If you accepted that, your subconscious said, "Fine. I'll *make* it difficult." You told yourself, "This will be hard," and then that's what you expected. So, sure enough, it *was* hard.

Who really blocked you from seeing "FLY"? *You* did. But be careful what you're telling yourself right now. You might be saying, "Something's wrong with me. I didn't get it. I must be stupid." No. It's just that your conditioning wouldn't let you see. This sort of thing happens all the time. If you're not careful, you will constantly imprint a false opinion of yourself into your subconscious: "I'm not good enough. I can't do it. I don't have what it takes." But it has nothing to do with intelligence, and it has nothing to do with aptitude. It has to do with years of conditioning to see things one way.

When I first found the word "FLY," I was on a Western Airlines flight from Los Angeles to Seattle, and I read it in a magazine. On the *children's* page. I had to look up the solution in the back. I was so disgusted with myself, I tore the page out. When I got home, Diane was in the living room. I hurried in and held it up and said, "Diane, tell me what you see here." I couldn't wait to surprise her like I had been surprised.

You know what she said? *"FLY."* Darn, that made me mad. I didn't tell her I had to look it up. I said, "How come you saw that so quickly?" She said, "It was simple. It's just a reverse print." You see, Diane has two degrees from Seattle University in art education. She said, "We were always taught to look at spacing first, and then lettering." So her conditioning made the word "FLY" practically jump right out at her, while all *I* saw were arrows and combs with missing teeth.

That's going to be true of your future associates, employers, supervisors, coaches, and teachers. They're going to know it says, "FLY." They won't be brighter than you; their conditioning will just match the situation. When Diane found the word "FLY" so quickly, I could have felt stupid. I could have said, "I don't have it!" and quit. But I know better. Now you do, too.

Let me explain something else about the way our brain works. The main reason we left out the word "FLY" is because *we don't see only with our eyes. We see with our minds as well.* Remember that; it will have a lot to do with you finding new business, resources, opportunities. We only perceive light with our eyes—off a flower, a car, a person. Then our brain interprets the light based upon how we've been conditioned to interpret the light. If what we're *looking at* doesn't match what we've been *conditioned* to see, we won't see it at all.

So your senses leave out the word "FLY" for the same reason they leave out information that could help you accomplish your future goals. You could be looking right at a new job, new customers, finances. But if your past conditioning, education, and way of perceiving things doesn't match what you're looking at, you'll conclude, "There's no way. It's not there." It's like, "I looked all over and there's no new business." "I looked everywhere and there's no money." "I looked a hundred times and there is no 'FLY.'"

Throughout your life, you'll meet many people who will tell you why you aren't ready yet, and what you have to do to get ready. They'll say, "It's a jungle out there." If you believe them, you'll be out there seeing combs with broken teeth when you should be seeing—what? *"FLY."* If you're not careful, scotomas can sabotage your success without your knowing it. I know what you're thinking: "How will we ever see what we're conditioned *not* to see?"

Here's the fun part. You may not know it, but you possess a remarkable device that can help you see whatever you want to see. It's so "user-friendly," you can program it an unlimited number of times to help you find whatever you want. The trick is in knowing how to use it properly. But once you learn that, it'll be like money in the bank.

Want more? Stay tuned.

6

RETICULAR ACTIVATING SYSTEM:

Inventing Your Future

A Good Executive Secretary

We know that the way you've been conditioned, trained, and educated can blind you to options and opportunities in your life, just as you were blinded to the word "FLY." We also know that, even if you're open-minded, your senses can't provide all the information that's available. Some of it simply isn't accessible at present. And if you were made aware of everything bombarding you within your perceptual capability, you'd go stark raving mad. You ever get a haircut and have the hair fall down your back? You get itchy and scratchy. That's exactly how you'd feel, because the movement of every hair on your body sends a message to the central cortex of your brain for a response. If you needed to be aware of all the light and all the smells and all the tastes and all the sounds, it would drive you nuts. So you have a filtering device in your brain which screens the information for you, and lets only some of it get through to your consciousness.

In an earlier chapter, I emphasized the importance of fixing, in your mind, a vivid picture of your goals. I said that once a specific goal is imprinted in your subconscious, an "alerting device" in your brain can then help you find information you need to accomplish it. That unique device is the filtering device I just described: *the reticular activating system*. It's the most essential tool you have to lead you to success.

Reticular means "net-like." So it's a net-like system of circuits running from the middle of the brainstem to the cerebrum—the seat of all our conscious mental processes. This system controls arousal, attention, awareness. Its job is to determine which of the thousands of messages bombarding your nervous system simultaneously are the most urgent, and it lets through only those messages. It screens out the junk mail. If you were an executive, and you had everyone knocking on your door vying for your attention, you couldn't concentrate. If you needed to answer every phone call yourself, and every piece of mail, you couldn't get anything done. Like a good executive secretary, your reticular activating system knows who to let in to see the boss.

While it's letting urgent information through, it is also filtering out and building scotomas to irrelevant information. That prevents an overload. The reticular activating system only sends you information that you've decided is of value to you *right now*. It locks out everything else. Once you achieve a goal, the information of value about that goal no longer gets through. So the reticular activating system keeps *current* with your needs. When you understand this, you can set bigger goals with broader vision because, once you set a specific goal, you know that the information you need will start rushing through.

Here's how it works. Let's say you have a mother, a father, and a four-month old baby who's ill. The mother takes a leave from her career to devote herself full-time to the baby's care. The father works long hours, so he can't contribute much right now. At night, the parents are sound asleep in their bedroom, while the baby is asleep in another room. The parents sleep through airplanes roaring overhead, trucks gunning by, radios blasting—you name it. They don't hear that noise. But if the baby emits the slightest cry or cough in the middle of the night—click—out of an altered state of consciousness, the mother awakens to attend to her child.

Why does she hear a barely audible cough or cry, but not all these other noises that are a hundred times louder? Because it's not the decibel level that gets through to the subconscious, it's the *value of the information*. And *you* determine the value. If you don't clearly define the essential information for yourself, you can be immersed in it and never know it. For example, why does the father continue sleeping soundly through the baby's cry? Because it's not essential for him to hear it. He knows his wife will. In the present situation, *she's* the one who needs the information. Of course, that can change as their circumstances change. When he's ready to share more fully in the care-giving, he, too, will start awakening to the baby's cry.

You ever get ready to buy a stove or refrigerator or television set? As soon as you make the commitment and decide exactly what you're looking for, you start thumbing through the paper and say, "Look at that. They're having a *sale* on it at 'The Bon.' And there's another one at 'Frederick & Nelson. And another one at—. Boy, are we *lucky!*" That afternoon, you go to lunch and you overhear a stranger talking about the very item. On your drive home, you notice somebody delivering one to a neighbor. Later, you're watching television and there it is on sale again. You think, "What a coincidence!"

The fact is, they're *always* having sales on those things. They're advertised in newspapers and on TV in every large city every day of the year. But you build a scotoma to it because it isn't important to you at the time. Until you decide you want one, you read through the paper and never see it. Once you want it, though, it screams through like the baby's cry. That's the reticular activating system screening out the hairs falling down your back, and filtering through only what is vital to you *now*. That's why, when you have an appendicitis attack, no matter what else you're doing, the pain gets through. Pain is a vital message *now*. It says, "Hey, pay attention!"

Another example: You're strolling through the airport unaware of the continual announcements coming over the P.A.—until *your name* comes through. That's another one: "Alert!" Or you're walking downtown, oblivious to the traffic. The moment you start to cross the street, traffic gets through, doesn't it? Because now you need to know about the threat. It's the *now* that matters. This concept will be essential to inventing your future. Because what you're going to learn is: *The goal comes first and then you see. You do not see first.* In other words, you open up your awareness to the information you need—to the "how"—simply by deciding what's important. *Then* the "how" screams through like the baby's cry.

Know anybody who can always find a parking spot downtown? Here's how you do it. You program your reticular activating system by telling yourself, "I want a parking spot on Fifth Avenue close to the theater." While you're approaching Fifth Avenue, engaged in conversation, thinking about other things, watching traffic and people crossing the street, your subconscious is scanning for cues—any bits of information that will lead you to a parking spot. It alerts you to flashing tail lights three blocks ahead, people approaching their cars near the theater, exhaust from cars backing out, heads moving in cars on both sides of the street—all the information you need to find a spot. Suddenly, "There's one! And there's one! And there's one!" They're all over the place. Because: *The goal comes first, and then you see. You do not see first.*

Knowing how the reticular activating system works, I don't wait in line. I set goals based upon what I *want*, and I find out how to accomplish them along the way. In our company, I never say, "How can we do business overseas?" I say, "Where would we *like* to do business? How about Australia?" Somebody says, "But you don't know any potential clients in Australia," and I say, "That's right. Let's go find some." Years ago, I set a goal to get our company into the video business. I knew nothing about making videos. I didn't need to know, I just decided I wanted to do it. I opened up my reticular activating system and, immediately, information screamed through from Seattle, San Diego, Los Angeles, San Francisco, Chicago. And now, 95% of our business world-wide is video business. I found the information all over the place. So can you—when you know how.

Keep in mind: Threats get through, too. One time I was flying from Seattle to Twisp, where we have a ranch. And all of a sudden, click, I woke up. You know why? The engine shut off. It's amazing; silence can wake you up if it's a threat. A friend of mine, a policeman in Detroit, told me about some tough bars he used to have trouble in all the time. There'd be arguments and brawls and people busting things up. My friend and his partner used to go in with shotguns, and they'd yell, "Police! Knock it off! Sit down and shut up!" Nobody paid attention. They just kept slugging each other and breaking things.

This one time, my friend and his partner went into this bar during a fight, and my friend loaded a shell into his shotgun. All of a sudden, total silence. The place froze. My friend couldn't figure it out. But from then on, he kept doing the same thing—and it worked every time. Finally, he learned about the reticular activating system and figured it out. The *threat* got through. In the past, when he went in there and yelled, "Police! Knock it off!" no one heard. But the

61

much less noticeable sound of a single shell being pumped into his shotgun, *everybody* heard. Threats get through.

Athletes can really use this information to their advantage. Some inexperienced players can't tell what is important, so they don't filter out the junk. It's called having "rabbit ears." Their reticular activating system lets *everything* through, so there are too many messages bombarding their brain simultaneously. That's one reason why, for example, a rookie quarterback will often be blind to receivers standing wide open in the end zone. He hasn't filtered out the distractions, so he sees *everything* instead of focusing on only what he *needs* to see.

A veteran quarterback knows exactly what to let through. Even though he's immersed in feedback from eighty thousand people yelling all around him, when he drops back to pass, click, he focuses instantly. Like one of those automatic zoom lenses, his consciousness zooms in on his primary receiver in the end zone. Then, click, he spots his secondary receiver open on a curl. Click, out of the corner of his eye, there's his halfback open in the flat. And while he's busy with his main goal—seeing his open receivers—click, he starts sensing the threats. Five yards to his left, he "feels" a six eight, 300-pound monster from the other team charging in, ready to rip his head off. He also sees two other Goliaths breaking free of their blocks.

He sees value and he sees threats; he builds scotomas to everything else. He doesn't see the crowd, the vendors, the cheerleaders, the officials, the players on the bench. There could be other players frothing at the mouth to kill him, but as long as they're being *blocked*, he doesn't need to see them. You could offer this guy a hundred thousand dollars to describe the umpire standing three feet away, and he wouldn't win his money. He might be looking right at the umpire, but he won't see him. *No value.*

How many times have you gone shopping for Christmas gifts, spent the whole day at it, and come home with nothing? Why didn't you find anything? Because you didn't decide beforehand that it was a twenty-dollar portable radio you wanted for your brother. If you're looking for real estate, you don't just go looking for listings, you go looking for *specific* listings, like: $250,000 homes in the Queen Anne District. Click, now you can't keep them out: "There's one! There's another one! There's another one!"

Do you see what I'm encouraging you to do? See why it's important to be vision-oriented, goal-oriented, end result-oriented—even though you presently don't know where the information, resources, and people you need are coming from? I'm talking about having *belief without evidence*. Mediocrity demands the evidence before building belief: "Show me. Where's it coming from? How will we get it done?" High-performance operates in the reverse. Once you set a specific goal, you have the belief—the faith that you'll find what you need—and *then* the evidence starts shooting through. If you don't have faith in how you work, you don't see the evidence: "It's right in front of your nose." "No it isn't. *Where?*" The old lady won't get through, the young lady won't get through, "FLY" won't get through.

So the key to your future is realizing that your goals should always *transcend* your current reality. If you visualize the goal as if it's already been achieved, you will then find what you need to achieve it. Remember: Most people base their future only on what they know presently. If they can't figure out how they'll accomplish a goal based on their present resources and skills, they'll say, "Well, we can't do it yet," and they'll back the goal up closer to their present reality: "We have to wait a few months before we go ahead." If you know about the reticular activating system, you don't wait. You define your goal without the slightest idea, *beforehand*, about how to accomplish it—and, click, the "how" comes through like it was invented for you. Business opportunities, knowledge, resources, finances—whatever you need.

I tell you this to give you great hope. This is information that most people don't have and won't use. But those of us who use it have tremendous fun getting things done in our lives. We find people, money, resources, adventure—everything. That's the way I learned. And that's what I'll teach you. Once you switch on your reticular activating system—click—you become a Selective Information-Finder of the Greatest Magnitude!

My Boxing Show

Years ago, when I was teaching at Kennedy High, I came up with an idea to make some extra money for some of the kids at school. I got these ten kids who wanted to fight these ten other kids, and I said, "We'll put on a boxing show and we'll sell tickets to the public." The kids thought it was a great idea because they were going to fight anyway, and now they could beat each other up in front of the whole school.

In the first month after announcing the show, I sold about two thousand tickets. The only problem was, I'd searched all over King County and I couldn't come up with a few necessary ingredients. I couldn't find a boxing ring, regulation boxing gloves, or a referee. Everybody said, "You better give up the idea. What's gonna happen when people show up and you can't put on the show?"

I kept selling tickets. Finally, here I was on Thursday, with the fight scheduled for the coming Wednesday, and I had printed ads and programs, and I'd sold about three thousand tickets—but I still didn't have a ring, gloves, or a referee. "Man, you're up the creek," people told me. "You'll never pull it together in time." But knowing about end-result thinking and the reticular activating system, I just kept selling tickets. I could visualize the fights underway in my mind, so I believed the information would eventually get through.

I remember teaching a new night class for adults that week. We were sitting around afterwards, talking about my boxing show, and I said to one student, "Why don't you come to the fights? We're still selling tickets." He said, "Okay, I will." And I said to another one "Why don't you come, too?" He said he would. I was on a roll, so I asked a third student, "How about you? Wednesday night—ten bouts." I'll never forget what he said: "I think I will. You know, I was a fighter when I was in the Army over in the Pacific." At first, I thought, "That's nice, but so what?" It seemed trivial to me. But then he said, "I got a friend who runs a boxing club in Auburn." That's a little town near Seattle. *Click!* When you needed a boxing ring as bad as I did, that information was like the baby's cry screaming through to its mother!

I said, "That guy wouldn't let us use his ring, would he?" He said, "Probably." So I called the guy up at 9:30 that night, and he said, "I don't have that ring anymore. But I got a friend who runs a boxing club in Kent, and he rents it out." So I called the guy in Kent, which is next to Auburn, and I said, "I understand you have a boxing ring for rent." He said, "What night do you want it?" I told him, and he said, "It's yours for fifty bucks." I said, "Man, I'll take it!

But I can't use the ring unless you know where I can get a referee." The guy said, "All right, I'll ref. Same price." I said, "Great. But there's no sense in your coming to ref if I don't have any boxing gloves." He said, "Well, what in the heck *do* you have?" I said, "Just the tickets sold and the kids to fight." He chuckled, and I said, "By the way, if you have any protective helmets, bring them, too. And stools, and water buckets, and a bell to ring. But don't worry," I assured him. "I got everything else."

Now, would *you* have sold the tickets before you had the boxing ring and the referee—or at least the gloves? Most people wouldn't. I didn't know where to find that stuff; normally, it would just be trivia to me. But remember: Once you set the goal, you don't need to know where the information, the finances, the resources, are coming from. If you don't set the goal, you won't find them anyway. So you need to set the goal, become accountable for accomplishing it, and have the faith and guts to ride it through.

The point is this: You don't need the Sears catalogue under this arm, and the Montgomery Ward catalogue under this arm, and the Yellow Pages over here. All you need are the goal, the belief that you'll find what you need to succeed, and the reticular activating system. Then, click, there's the boxing ring. Click, there's the referee. Click, there are the gloves, the helmets, the bell. It's like magic; it works every time. Whereas most people set a goal and the first thing they say is, "How do I do it? How do I get it?" They ask their associates, "Do you know where it's coming from?" "No." They ask their friends, "Do you know?" "No." They ask their spouse, "Do you know?" "No." "Well, unreasonable! Unrealistic! Pollyanna! Pie-in-the-sky! There no way! We can't do it right now!"

I'm saying you don't *need* to know where it's coming from. High-performance people don't know. Because, for them, as it's going to be for you after you finish this curriculum: *The goal comes first, then you see. You do not see first.*

Hang on. Much more to see.

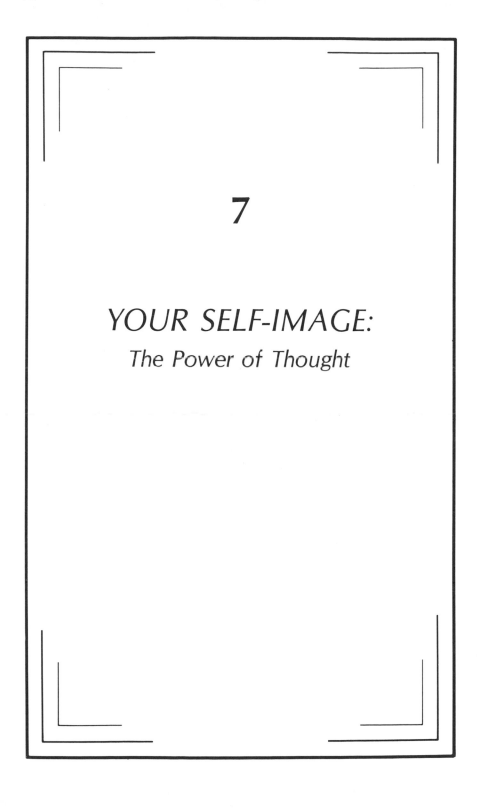

7

YOUR SELF-IMAGE:

The Power of Thought

The Power Inside

I am going to teach you some fascinating things about what we presently know of how our minds work. This will help you to understand why growth and change is possible. It will allow you to direct your own future and give you the confidence to bring out the best in yourself.

Let's start with what I call the processes of thought. If we break the thinking process down, we can identify three parts: *the conscious, the subconscious,* and *the creative subconscious.*

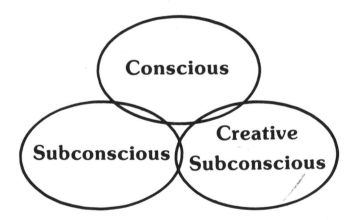

Figure 7–1   Thought Process

They aren't really separate compartments in our mind; they

comprise an integrated whole. But they do represent the mind's different functions. If you understand those functions, you can learn more about why you think and act as you do. In the conscious process, there are four basic functions: *perception, association, evaluation, decision.* I want to dwell on perception because that has so much to do with the development of your self-image.

Through your senses, you perceive your feelings, thoughts, and emotions, as well as the external world. Your senses have been telling you, "This is the way the world is" from the time you were in the womb. That's when you first perceived movement, balance, and sound. Then, as you grew up in the world, you recorded and stored all the information gathered through your senses in a sort of "data bank" in your subconscious: your first words as a baby, the books you read, every fight you had, every time you cried, people you met, places you went, secrets that people have told you, the joy of every triumph, the pain of every loss.

That information is part of a subconscious encyclopedia about you that you're continually updating with new memories. We don't know quite how memory works yet. We do know that there is a chemical change in the neuron structure of the cells of the brain that helps us store information we perceive. Since we have billions of neuron cells—each one capable of storing millions of bits of information—we have a virtually unlimited storage capacity.

You and I refer to this stored information as "reality" or "the truth." But it isn't the absolute truth, is it? Remember: *We don't see only with our eyes. We see with our minds as well.* We don't even actually see objects, we just see light reflecting off objects. Often, we see only what we want to see, expect to see, or are conditioned to see. In other words, our own version of "the truth." And because we have scotomas to other people's versions, ours sometimes leaves out the old lady or the young, arrows and combs, and the word "FLY." You and I could view the same event and someone would ask me, "How was it?" and I'd say, "Wonderful!" They'd ask you and you'd say, "Boring!" You recorded your view, I recorded mine. If we expressed them to each other, we'd both think, "We weren't at the same event."

It's like when those critics do a movie review on TV. One says, "It's an original film with real people full of real passion. I give it four stars." The other says, "'Original?' Oh, c'mon! It was one long cliché. 'Real people full of real passion?' More like stick figures full of *baloney*! I give it half a star. Save your money." They saw the same film, yet they recorded completely different versions of "the truth."

Now, the subjective version of "the truth" that you perceive about *yourself* is called your *self-image*. Your self-image is just your subconscious opinion of you—based upon the countless beliefs and attitudes you've recorded about you in your "data bank." It's your inner "picture" of who you are and what you expect of yourself. "I'm outgoing," "I'm shy," "I'm a fast learner," "I don't like books," "I have rhythm," "I can't dance," "I'm popular," "I'm a loner." Your "picture" is a composite of everything you've learned since you were little, when your family, neighbors, mentors, and teachers—all the positive and negative wizards you respected—told you "the truth."

You have beliefs and expectations about every aspect of your life—how efficient or lazy you are on the job, how tough or easy-going at home, what kind of person you are morally, socially, spiritually, intellectually, how brave or timid, attractive or repulsive, tall or short, fat or thin you are. So you don't just have one overall self-image, you have thousands. And within any given one of them, you have multiple opinions. For example, you can have a belief about what kind of leader you are—and within that one belief, you may have many related opinions. You may think, "I'm a leader on my softball team and as a teacher at school"—but also, "I am *not* a leader in my community or in my church." You can have an opinion about what kind of athlete you are, "I'm great at tennis, golf, and bowling"—but also, "I can't sky-dive and I'm a lousy swimmer." You might think, "I'm an effective driver in traffic, rain, and snow"—but also, "I'd never race on the Indianapolis Speedway. I don't drive that fast."

You've recorded a self-image for every skill or experience, real or imagined. Each one is built with a belief, and these beliefs control your life. I want to remind you here about the major premise of this curriculum: *We think and act not in accordance with the real truth, but the truth as we believe it.* That's important because if you've built your self-image on negative beliefs—"I'm awkward," "I'm slow"—those beliefs will be recorded in your mind as "Just like me," and that's how you will behave. If you don't change your beliefs, you can't change your self-image—and you will continue to act as awkward or slow as you believe yourself to be. That's your *creative subconscious* at work—which I'll explain later in this chapter. It can make change very difficult, or very easy.

At some point, you may wonder, "How in the world did I get these beliefs?" The answer is: through your own self-talk. In an earlier chapter, I explained self-talk as the conversations you have with yourself in your own mind. Well, thoughts make up those silent conversations. And we know that *thoughts accumulate to build beliefs.* That happens, remember, because we think in *words* that trigger *pictures*, which bring about *emotions.* All your thoughts and emotions are recorded in the neuron structure of the cells of your brain, as "the truth." Then you start reinforcing "the truth" with your "Just like me" behavior. So your self-talk is the foundation of your self-image.

Your self-image is so powerful, it controls not only what you presently are—what sort of person, how accomplished, how happy—but also what you will be in the future. It controls how much of your potential you will use. We don't really know how much potential we have. Not so long ago, few people imagined we could fly human beings to the moon and bring them back. When President Kennedy announced that we would do it within "this decade," we began to think differently. We really don't know, for sure, what we can achieve, until we remove our self-imposed limitations.

We do know that self-image is not fixed. If you aren't satisfied with the way your life is going right now, if you aren't happy with how you presently think or feel or behave, you have an option. You can change your self-image. In fact, if you're going to become the happy, successful, high-performance person you're capable of becoming, you'll be revamping your self-image *regularly*. You'll be constantly revising it to help you achieve new goals. Because we know that to change circumstances outside, we have to change inside first.

We live our lives immersed in two essential realities—internal and external. If you change one, you can change the other. Everyone would like to change their external circumstances, but few know how to do it. Some may think that making more money will bring about the change they want, or driving a particular car, or wearing certain clothes, or marrying the right person. They're wrong. The power doesn't reside in money, material goods, or other people. The power is inside. So keep in mind: *All meaningful and lasting change starts on the inside first and works its way out.*

You're wondering, "What exactly is this 'power' we have inside us?" The answer is: the power to change the way that we think. To accomplish that, you will need to know a little more about the process of thought. So now let's explore in greater detail the interrelationships between the conscious, subconscious, and creative subconscious.

Conscious Mind: The Unzipped Fly

Through our senses, the conscious mind perceives and maintains contact with external reality. Its job is to rationally investigate and interpret that reality. It does so in at least four stages:

1. *PERCEPTION:* I've just explained this. To briefly review: We perceive information about internal and external reality through our senses. The information is stored in our subconscious "data bank," and we refer to it as "the truth." Based on this "truth," we fashion our self-image.

2. *ASSOCIATION:* Once you perceive something, you associate it with anything similar stored in your "data bank" by asking yourself, *"Have I experienced anything like this before?"* Say you're a passenger on an airplane that's flying through a storm and the plane suddenly dips, but then recovers. You immediately ask yourself, *"Have I experienced anything like this before?"* If you've had a similar experience, this event will make sense to you: "Oh, it's probably just the wind. Nothing to worry about." If you haven't had a similar experience, the information is meaningless: "What was *that*?"

3. *EVALUATION:* After associating what you perceive, you evaluate it against previous information in your "data bank" by asking yourself, *"What is this probably leading me toward?"* And you assess the probabilities. "Is it leading me toward happiness, pleasure, fun?" Or "Is it leading me toward stress, discomfort, pain?" In other words, "Will this be good or bad for me?"

4. *DECISION:* Lastly, you decide on a course of action based on your immediate needs and goals. You may react by taking action; you may let someone else make the decision; you may choose to

72

ignore or repress the matter entirely. Now here's an insight that will help you achieve greater levels of excellence in the future: Many of the conscious decisions you make are based not on what is happening to you *presently*, but rather on what has happened to you in the *past*.

Here's a simple example of how this works. A ten-year old boy gets up in front of the classroom for his first "Show and Tell." As he starts telling his story, he is very intent and serious—yet everybody cracks up laughing. So he gets flustered, forgets what he wants to say, and hurries back to his seat. His friend leans over and says to him, "Dummy! Your *fly* is unzipped!" The youngster's emotional response to this event—his feeling of humiliation—is recorded in his "data bank" as a strongly negative experience. His life goes on; twenty-five years pass. At age thirty-five, he has an opportunity to speak to a local Boys Club. He thinks, *"Have I experienced anything like this before?* Darn right!" He evaluates, *"What is this leading me toward?* Nothing good!" So he makes the decision: "I'm too busy to give the talk." He makes this decision, at thirty-five, very likely because his pants were unzipped when he was ten.

Remember *"Garbage In-Garbage Out:" Our decisions aren't any more accurate than the information on which they're based?* Ever known anyone who went through a traumatic break-up in a relationship? A few years later, they have a chance to get involved with someone else, but they associate, *"Have I experienced anything like this before?* Darn right!" They evaluate, *"What is this leading me toward?* Nothing good!" Then they decide, "No thanks. Don't want any part of it." The decision is not based on feelings for the *new* person, but rather on the trauma caused by the *old*.

Again, the point is: Many of your decisions about your future are not based on what you *can* do in the future, but rather on what happened in the past. So, to improve the quantity and quality of your future success, you will need to modify and update "the truth" recorded in your subconscious "data bank." In other words, you must learn how to change your picture. Those techniques—internal goal-setting, affirmations, visualization, imprinting—are coming up in later chapters. But first, we need to consider the functions of the subconscious and the creative subconscious. Once you understand how they function, you can start making decisions at home, on your job, and at leisure, that are much more accurate and appropriate to the person you are today.

Subconscious Mind: The "Real" You

Think of your subconscious mind as a high-fidelity sensory tape recorder, whose task it is to record and store your version of "reality." It stores all of your experiences—what you think, say, sense, feel, and imagine about yourself, along with your emotional attitudes and reactions to your experiences. Or think of it as a blank canvas at conception. With every life experience, you dab a little paint on the canvas. Eventually, you paint your own picture of "the truth" about yourself—in other words, the "real" you. Every artist paints their own version. Like fingerprints, no two are alike. Once you dab on attitudes and opinions about yourself and the world— no matter how detrimental they are—you're stuck with them. Until you decide *consciously* to repaint the picture.

The subconscious has a second job: to handle the automatic, or unconscious, functions of living—like heartbeat, circulation, breathing, digestion. It also handles learned functions, like tying your shoelaces, walking, driving, playing sports, adding, and subtracting. These activities originate on the conscious level. But through repeated brush strokes, a picture emerges on your subconscious canvas, incorporating them as habits. You perform them with a free-flowing ease because you no longer have to consciously think about them.

Tying your shoelaces, walking, and knowing how to add and subtract are positive habits. They allow you to function efficiently. But some subconscious habits can become barriers to growth. They can become obsolete—like an old, ribbon typewriter in the computer age. They still do the job, but they lock out change. Because they're so "comfortable," they can keep people from venturing into new personal situations—accepting a new job, adjusting to a new living environment, risking a new relationship.

Creative Subconscious: The Enforcer

Now we come to the most important subconscious process: the *creative subconscious*. It isn't a separate area of the subconscious, but it's easier to explain if I isolate it. The creative subconscious enforces your behavior. It maintains your present version of reality by causing you to act like the person you believe yourself to be. Its main job—as I said in earlier chapters—is to *maintain order and sanity*. It maintains the inner picture of "the truth" that you've come to accept as "Just like me." It does this by making sure your beliefs and opinions *happen*—without your needing to think about them consciously.

So once you get an idea about what kind of person you are, you don't need to get up every morning and remember how you are. As long as that self-image is imprinted into your belief system, you will automatically behave like you. Now, that's not so bad because it keeps you from being different every day in every situation. There's something inside you that allows you to consistently be you. Suppose you've convinced yourself that you always get lost when you drive to unfamiliar places. You don't have to wake up every morning and remind yourself," Don't forget to get lost if you drive someplace new." Your creative subconscious will take care of it automatically. Maybe you feel you have a mental block when it comes to remembering people's names. You won't need to remind yourself to forget; your creative subconscious will take care of that for you.

This is a critically important principle: *Your creative subconscious always maintains your presently dominant self-image*. It maintains your present idea of how good you are, how successful, how athletic, how smart, how loving, how much money you earn. It isn't concerned with what you *used* to be, what you *want* to be, or what you have the *potential* to be. It simply maintains whatever you've decided is good enough for you right now.

Your creative subconscious is so powerful in maintaining your present self-image, it can influence how other people act toward you. We know, for example, that body language and tone of voice are tied to self-image. In communicating to others what you really believe, words carry only about 7% validity; tone of voice about 37%; body language about 58%. So you can negate what you say with your body language and tone of voice. Let's say you think of yourself as shy, and you're invited to a cocktail party where you don't know anyone. Your creative subconscious will invent ways to keep people away. You might stand in a corner, arms folded, feet crossed, eyes averted. Your body language will scream, "I'm shy. Leave me alone." If people get too close, you'll escape into the bathroom fifteen times in an hour. Or you'll invite yourself into the kitchen— away from the crowd—and start doing the dishes so you can stay. Afterwards, when you're home alone, you'll re-affirm for yourself, "See? I *am* shy."

Or suppose you've always wanted to be a leader, but you believe you're a follower. When a crisis occurs, you will automatically act like you believe yourself to be. Say there's a fire in a theater. As people rush for the exits, you might try to be a leader and, in a trembling voice, say, "Uh, listen. Why not, uh, follow me? I'll, uh, get us, you know, out of here." But you're still standing in the middle of the row, clutching a seat so hard that your knuckles are white. Well sorry, I'm sure not following *you*. Why not? Because your body language and tone of voice are screaming, "I'm scared to death! We're all gonna *die!*" No thank you.

If you feel out of place, one thing that happens is tension constricts your vocal chords so your voice changes. That's why, when someone gets up in front of a group of people to talk, and says in a squeaky, timid voice, "I'm really looking forward to this," you sense they're lying. By the way, the Internal Revenue Service knows this information. You know what their investigator's handbook says? Something like, "Do not listen to the *words* people use, listen to their *tone of voice*." So, if you're being questioned by an IRS agent, and your voice changes, watch out. That agent will probably pursue the questioning: "Are you sure you've reported *everything* you were supposed to report?" Oh, yes. You don't uh, think I'd, uh, want to go to jail—uh, do you?" That agent will say, "*Follow me.*"

Now, remember: To your creative subconscious, maintaining your present idea of "reality,"your idea of how things are supposed to be, is more important than gregariousness, leadership, staying out of jail, wealth, happiness, success, even health. Its job is to maintain your sanity by making things on the outside match what you believe inside. Then you won't seem crazy to yourself for believing what you believe.

Let's say you're thirty pounds overweight, but you suddenly decide to look better and feel healthier by losing some weight. So you skip breakfast and lunch. But your creative subconscious knows you don't really see yourself as thin. So it goes to work, subliminally, not to make you look thinner and feel healthier, but rather to maintain your presently dominant self-image. So, when you consciously override the mechanism by skipping breakfast and lunch, it *corrects for the mistake*. How? By getting you to eat *two helpings of dinner*! You say, "What's the matter?" Your creative subconscious says, "Well, you didn't eat enough." You say, "Enough for what? I want to *lose* weight!" It says, "You don't believe that. It's not like you. You believe you're thirty pounds overweight. If you get thin, you'll feel *crazy*." In other words, if you lose weight, your external picture (your body) will no longer match your internal picture ("It's like me to be thirty pounds overweight"). So your creative subconscious sets off its sanity alarm: "Hey! Don't try to be thin! That's not *you*! Get back to being you." And, suddenly, you've eaten two helpings of dinner.

The creative subconscious won't quit pressuring you until the two pictures match again. So, after dinner, it works even harder to correct for the mistake: "Hey! Get hungry again! Get hungry again!" Finally, at about 10 P.M., you feel starved. You say, "Geez, I gotta have a piece of cake—but no frosting." That's your conscious mind talking. Your creative subconscious says, "Oh no. We need all the frosting we can get. And some ice cream!" So you go back in, and you not only eat that one piece—with all the frosting—but you end up eating *the whole cake*! And some ice cream for the road. You wake up the next morning and say, "Why'd I eat the whole cake? That's dumb. It doesn't make much sense!"

It really doesn't—*consciously*. Because you told yourself that you wanted to look better and feel healthier. But your creative subconscious knew you couldn't stay thirty pounds overweight if you didn't eat the whole cake. It did its job of automatically maintaining your present picture of you. And it goes on doing its job until you change that picture.

What would happen if you knew you didn't deserve a good marriage, but your spouse was always gracious, warm, loving, and kind, and the marriage was going well? Your creative subconscious would correct for the mistake by causing you to do dumb things to mess up your marriage. In other words, it would make you eat the whole cake. And your spouse would say, "What did you do that for?" And you'd say, "I don't know. Doesn't make much sense, does it?" It made sense to your creative subconscious, because it made you act like the person you believed yourself to be. Not what you *want* to be, not what you *can* be, but what you *"is."* See? Maintaining sanity is more important than a happy marriage.

I wonder if that's why the rich keep getting richer, and the poor keep getting poorer. You ever hear about the bum who won about three hundred grand in Reno, and in a few short weeks was broke again? He got rid of the money so fast, he didn't have enough to cover the *tax*! It was like the money literally burned a hole in his pocket. He gave it away, threw it away, gambled it away, drank it away. Could his self-image have been, "I'm poor. I don't deserve all this money. It's a mistake for me to be rich"? Do you suppose his creative subconscious corrected for the mistake?

On the other hand, have you ever observed rich people who "know" they should be rich, and then they suddenly go broke? They will correct for the mistake and come right back to being rich again. Here's a term you should know: "Poverty Consciousness." It applies to more than simply money. It applies to an attitude about life in general. People know, subconsciously, whether they're supposed to be rich or poor with regard to life's bounty—relationships, friendships, family, spirit, career, love. If you know you're supposed to be rich in life, and things start to go wrong, you correct for the mistake: "Hey, it's a mistake that things aren't going right." But if you believe you're supposed to be poor in life, and you have an opportunity to get a raise, go into business for yourself, or have a better house in a nicer neighborhood, your creative subconscious will sabotage your chances for success to get you back where you belong.

Remember: We behave not according to the real truth, but "the truth" as we believe it. In other words, "Why'd you eat the whole cake?" "I don't know." "Why'd you blow all that money?" "I don't know." "Why'd you do that dumb thing to break your marriage up?" "I don't know. It doesn't make much sense." Maybe not *consciously*. But, subconsciously, it makes perfect sense. Because your creative subconscious keeps you from coming unglued. It keeps you from being one thing today and something else tomorrow. It maintains consistency in your behavior—whether it's to your benefit or not. That stability is good; it's necessary. But it also makes it tough for you to change—unless you know how to alter your inner picture of what you deserve.

My wife, Diane, and I have a number of foster and adopted children. Three young boys we adopted at the same time were very badly abused. They were shot at, they were beaten, they were run over—a lot of horrible, traumatic things happened to them when they were very young. So they "knew," subconsciously, that the world was a rotten, miserable place. They believed, "I'm not a good person. People always hurt me." That "truth," became their "reality." They believed: "I'm worthless. I don't deserve to be treated well."

At the time, Diane and I didn't know much about self-image psychology. We just wanted to be the best parents anyone could possibly be. We were going to give them all the care and love they missed. So whenever these little kids—at five, six, and seven—did something right, we told them how wonderful they were: "Geez, we're so proud of you." See, we didn't know. We thought positive reinforcement would be helpful. But every time we put our arms around them and praised them for doing something good, they corrected for the mistake. They stole mail, trampled the neighbors' flowers, got in trouble at school.

One time, I told one of them, "I'm so proud of you." Do you know what that kid did? A half-hour later, he started a fire behind the couch! So I hollered, "Why'd you start that fire?" He said, "I don't know." That made me so mad. I said, "What do you mean, you don't know? It was only a half-hour ago. Your memory's not *that* bad." He said, "I don't know." I said, "Well, get into your room until you can figure it out." Know what he said then? *"Good."*

The kid was setting me up to punish him. His subconscious picture was, "The world punishes me, but you don't punish me. You're treating me too good." Even though his world was improving by living with people who loved him, it didn't make a difference. His picture hadn't changed. So his creative subconscious kept correcting for the mistake—even if it meant getting me mad at him. Because, subconsciously, the important thing wasn't love and support from mom and dad. The important thing was making sure that what happened *outside* matched what he knew, *inside*, was supposed to happen. And inside, "the truth" still was, "I'm worthless and bad. I deserve to be punished."

Now, another of these boys had been badly abused when we got him at age seven. His parents tried to toilet-train him by flushing his head in the toilet. They beat him, too. He never knew he had birthdays; he didn't even know his own name when we got him. What he *did* know was: "I'm a bad person. People do mean things to me." When we put him in school, the other kids started picking on him. I wonder if his self-image might've been, "The world picks on me. They always have."

Years later, we sent him to a junior high school where nobody knew him. But you know what? The kids picked on him again. Then he went to high school, where people took advantage of him. Then he went into the Army and got stationed in Germany—and guess what. The same thing happened. The Sergeant took advantage of him; his fellow soldiers took advantage; he couldn't seem to catch a break. Wasn't it an amazing coincidence that, even in a foreign country, everybody still picked on him?

When he got out of the Army and came home, we bought him a couple of tow trucks so he could start a little business. We hired a guy named Bill to manage it for him, so all he had to do was drive the truck and do the towing. Do you know what he said one day? "I quit! Bill's always picking on me." Hell, *he* owned the company, not Bill. Yet he blamed it on Bill. Shortly after that, when he was sitting around one day, he said, "You and mom always treat the girls better than us." He started giving us the "Poor me. Everybody always picks on me" routine. So I told him, "You have to change your inside point of view about yourself or you'll end up the kind of person, when you're forty, who'll come back here one day and tell us your *wife* is beating you up. Because, if you stay with what you believe about yourself right now, you'll *find* a wife who'll beat you up! You have the idea that the world is against you, so you go out and unconsciously do things to get the world to be against you. It isn't genes, it isn't coincidence, it isn't the world, and it sure isn't luck. You can't *have* that much bad luck. It's *you!* Change you, and the world will change around you." And today, he is doing just that.

What you must have to discover—and that's what I'm leading you to—is how to change your picture, your belief, your self-image, and bring it closer to your real potential, so you will then automatically behave like that until you change the picture again. Examine the beliefs that you hold. Ask yourself, "What is the 'truth' I believe about me—intellectually, socially, spiritually, financially?" "Who have I allowed to see 'the truth' for me?" "What negative wizards have I listened to?" "Do I tell myself, 'Oh, it's impossible to change. You can't teach an old dog new tricks?'" "Do I believe, 'I was born this way. It's just my nature?'" "What do I expect of me—as a parent, a spouse, a friend, a professional?" "What's good enough for me?"

Keep in mind: *If you change the way you think, you change the way you act.* If you change the way you think about yourself, your children will respond differently to you, your friends will respond differently, your spouse will respond differently, your business associates will respond differently. You aren't born "lucky." You make your own breaks based on "the truth" that you believe about yourself. You make your own "reality." But I guarantee you, if you don't change your negative self-image, people will keep behaving toward you the way you see yourself—and you'll go on believing you were born that way.

8

YOUR SELF-TALK:

Changing the Way that You Think

Right into the Rock

Remember when I said that human beings think in three dimensions? We think in words, which trigger pictures, which create emotions. These words, pictures, and emotions are recorded in your subconscious, which then fashions them into beliefs. As I explained earlier, in the world of *psycholinguistics*, this three-dimensional form of thought is called *self-talk*. It is the continual dialogue you have with yourself. It is also the raw material from which you manufacture your own self-image: "Oh, I'm clumsy," "I'm graceful," "It's easy for me," "It's hard for me," "I'm—." Keep in mind that your subconscious believes what you tell yourself, and then makes sure you act like your belief. I'm talking about the power language has on behavior. I'm talking about controlling your self-talk so you can use your subconscious to help you become more successful.

It's important to remember that when you observe an event in the external world—in your community, your family, your marriage, your career—you're not recording the actual event. You're *interpreting* it with your own self-talk; you're telling yourself what you think is happening: "She was angry, but she didn't mean what she said. I know what she *really* meant." That's technical, but essential. Because if you're aware that the world you perceive through your senses is only your *version* of the world, then you realize you can change it anytime you choose. You can't change the event, but you can change your interpretation of the event. How? By controlling your self-talk.

84

To set the stage for how self-talk works, consider these two major premises: (1) *You move toward, and become like, that which you think about;* (2) *Your present thoughts determine your future.* Whatever you repeatedly tell yourself with your own self-talk determines your beliefs and self-image, which affect your behavior. So unless you change your stored beliefs by changing your self-talk, you won't alter your future behavior. It will stay pretty much the same as it is now. This is why, for the most part, people don't seem to change much. It's like hypnosis. If I hypnotize you and hold a pen to your hand and say, "This is a lighted cigarette," a blister will form where the pen touches your hand. Hypnosis bypasses your conscious mind and goes directly to your subconscious. And your subconscious, remember, is like a sensory tape recorder which records whatever it's told. So when the pen touches your hand, your subconscious says, "A cigarette burn!" and it immediately triggers a "fire alarm" to the brain: "Hurry! Send water!" And you get a blister. That blister is really your belief, your self-talk that "A cigarette burned my hand." And your mind will continue forming blisters for as long as you believe it. That's how powerful a single thought can be. And repeated thoughts—your self-talk—can be that powerful.

Suppose your boss fires you, and you tell yourself, "I'm worthless without this job. I don't want to live." You may choose to kill yourself, directly or indirectly. Who's responsible for your behavior—your boss because he or she fired you, or you? Now change the scenario. After being fired, instead of telling yourself, "I'm worthless. I don't want to live," you think, "I wasn't growing there anyway. Now I can find a much better job." And you go looking for another job. Who's responsible for that behavior—your boss or you? In both cases, you are responsible. Because it isn't the event—the firing—which causes your behavior. It's the way you choose to *interpret* the event. "I'm worthless" is your self-talk version of what happened to you. "I don't want to live" is your self-talk "truth." Instantly, that most obedient slave, your creative subconscious, says, "Okay, whatever you want"—even if it means self-destruction.

You know the saying, "That which I feared most has come upon me"? *Why* does it happen? Because when your self-talk makes a "take" in your subconscious—when you give it sanction—it controls your body as well as your mind. If you dwell on something you *don't* want to happen, your fine motor muscles will work to bring about what you're picturing. Remember when you were a kid riding your bicycle, and you weren't very good at it yet? You were pedaling along and you spotted this big old rock in the middle of the road, and you didn't want to hit it. But being inexperienced, you kept staring at the rock—until you steered your bike right into it! Then you got mad at the *rock*. The problem wasn't the rock; the problem was that you told yourself, with your own self-talk, to focus your attention on the rock.

Do you know any accident-prone people? What do you suppose they think about? *Having accidents!* The insurance industry found out that most accidents are caused by accident-prone people out looking for each other. When you "know" you're accident-prone, you create an accident. And if you temporarily forget, people close to you might keep reminding you: "Be careful, dear. You know how you are." "Oh, thank you. I almost forgot." "Well, I only tell you that, dear, because I love you." "I know. I came *that* close to having an accident yesterday. Good thing you reminded me, before I left, to watch out."

To the degree that you focus on what you don't want, you will be drawn in that direction. You ever know anybody like that? How about yourself? It will take discipline to control your focus because you'll have people in your family, your company, and your social groups who will want to sit around and talk about what's wrong in life. They'll say, "Business is no good" and "This equipment isn't worth a darn" and "That food was terrible." That's negative, destructive talk. The way to think is, "What will it look like when we *don't* have the problem? What will things look like when they're *fixed*?" Otherwise, you know where you're headed? *Right into the rock.*

Do you drive a car? Once you learn the skills, driving becomes an unconscious habit. You simply picture where you *want* the car to go, and you automatically turn the steering wheel in that direction. You don't have to consciously think, "Turn left, turn right, foot on the brake, foot on the gas." You automatically adjust according to the image you hold in your mind of where you want to go. So how do accidents occur? They occur when you start picturing what you don't want to happen.

Imagine yourself teaching a teenager to drive. The kid's driving down the road, crowding the center line, and you can visualize a head-on collision any minute. So you say, "Watch out for the oncoming cars." Where's the kid gonna look? At the oncoming cars! Automatically, his subconscious tells his fine motor muscles, "Aim for those cars!" When the kid drifts over the center line, you really get upset and you say, "Get over on the curb!" Those words trigger another picture, and the kid drives—where? Onto the curb! You get mad as heck and say, "Watch out for that parked car!" Smacko! Right into the parked car. Remember the loser's motto: *"If at first you don't succeed, fix the blame fast"*? Well, you think, "It's this problem *kid*! Why won't he *listen* to me?" Well, that's just it; he *did* listen.

What you visualize most vividly and most often is what you get, whether it's good for you or not. Those of you who golf—do you have any hooks or slices that always put you in the sand or the water? What do you think about when you're playing? I wonder if you're affirming that you've got this terrible slice. And that produces—what? The most perfect slice you could ever picture! Just like steering your bike or driving your car. Once you self-talk that "skill" in there— "I always slice the ball"—your body will automatically re-create your inner picture on the outside so the two pictures match. Not what you *want*, but what you *think about*.

You say, "No, not me." But when you're approaching the tee on that most treacherous hole, if you really see your ball landing on the green, why are you taking out your bad ball? See, the difficulty is in controlling your self-talk. If you know there's a water hazard, and you tell yourself, "I don't want to slice it into the water," even though you may think you're doing the opposite, your subconscious draws you toward your most dominant picture. The "don't want to" doesn't create a picture. "Water" is the picture, so water is where you're drawn. In other words, *right into the rock*.

But then, as you're walking down the fairway, what are you saying to yourself? "There I go again. That's just like me." So you not only slice it once when you hit it, but you do it again every time you think about it: "I must've sliced a hundred times if I've sliced once. In fact, I've always had this slice." By the time the game is over, you've mentally "hit" about five hundred slices! You're better than you give yourself credit for; you've been slicing so often, you're an *expert* at it!

So, with your self-talk, you're setting yourself up for failure. Some people continually set themselves up by anticipating what will go wrong in their marriage, what will go wrong in their company, what will go wrong with their health. Worrying is negative goal-setting. It focuses you on what you *don't* want—so that's exactly what you get. Now, you leaders, managers, supervisors—forget the bike, the car, and the golf, and substitute the way you lead your people. Parents—think about how you guide your children. Coaches—how do you run your teams? Spiritual leaders—how are you counseling your people? Are you giving them images of what you *don't* want them to do? Are you leading them into the parked car?

Here's another interesting phenomenon: *Thoughts accumulate to build beliefs.* You must become very cognizant of what a powerful wizard you are to yourself. Have you ever made a mistake, and asked yourself, "What's the matter with me, anyway?" It would be all right if you'd stop there, but you go on to answer the question. You automatically visualize yourself screwing up when you were five or fifteen or fifty—as if it were happening again. Each time you and I allow ourselves to dwell on negative self-talk, we add weight to the belief. Some of us dwell on it for a few minutes; some a day; some for weeks; some have been doing it for a lifetime.

Be honest—if you had a friend who talked to you the way you talk to yourself sometimes, would you hang around with that friend very long? No—neither would I.

Your Attitudinal Balance Scale

I want to give you an image to keep in mind about how self-talk builds your attitudes about yourself.

A good definition of an attitude is "a leaning," as in the attitude of an airplane's wings. When we lean toward something, we say we have a positive attiitude about it. When we lean away from something, we say we have a negative attitude about it. Let's assume that this kid's water buckets (Figure 8–1) represent your attitudinal balance scale. You start life with nothing in either bucket. But what

ATTITUDES

Direction in which we lean

Figure 8-1. Attitudinal Balance Scale

happens if you put most of the weight in the right bucket? Pretty soon, it gets so heavy, you lean in that direction and, eventually, topple over. Same thing will happen if you put most of the weight in the left bucket. You will lean, and then topple, to the left.

Every time you make a positive affirmation—a positive statement of belief or fact—about yourself, I want you to imagine that it adds weight to the right bucket. Conversely, every negative, devaluative, destructive affirmation adds weight to the left bucket. If you accumulate more weight in the left bucket, you'll lean in the negative direction. If you accumulate more weight in the right bucket, you'll lean in the positive direction. See what I'm saying? When you build beliefs and attitudes through self-talk, you will either lean toward the positive or the negative, so you must always monitor the way you're leaning. Because, if you learn the techniques I'm teaching you, you can choose to redistribute the weight.

Why do I tell you this? Because I want you to be very careful, very selective about what you tell yourself. You can talk yourself into or out of, toward or away from, anything. Attitudes are neither right nor wrong, good nor bad—except in relation to something you *value*. Yesterday's old pictures, accumulated through repetitive self-talk, may make you lean away from something that is actually a great value and benefit to you today—or toward something of great harm. The good news is that attitudes are changed the same way they're formed: by your self-talk and affirmations of "what's so" for you from now on.

I × V = R

Let's take another step. Events don't need to keep occurring for you to build a belief. You can relive one occurrence thousands of times in your mind. All you have to do is replay the image. Every time you remind yourself about an event with your self-talk, you visualize it as though it's happening again. Usually, one thought doesn't make a solid "take" on the subconscious level. There *are* exceptions, like one-time affirmations from "Who-Saids" of the Greatest Magnitude—marriage vows, graduation ceremonies, prayers, oaths. But, for the most part, it takes repetition, repetition, repetition. The event itself does not have to recur, because your subconscious doesn't know the difference. As far as it's concerned, when you *think* about something vividly, it's actually happening.

Here's a formula for how you build your belief with self-talk: $I \times V = R$. Remember this formula because you're going to use it later for both internal and external goal-setting. The "I" stands for *Imagination*, the "V" for *Vividness*, the "R" for *Reality* (in the subconscious). Any time you imagine something vividly in your mind, and you feel the related emotions, it makes a solid "take" and becomes "reality" in the subconscious. Suppose you have a seven-year-old son who won't eat spinach. He believes, "I'll get sick if I eat it. I'll throw up." You tell him, "But you've never tried it." He says, "I have so. I eat it all the time." But you know for a fact that he's never eaten spinach. What's the problem?

The problem is that he's heard the big kids say, "Spinach is awful. I throw up when I eat it." In their own imaginations, they've seen themselves eating spinach and throwing up. It's like déjà vu; they believe it's happened before. In fact, it has "happened" so many times in their mind that, when the event actually occurs for the first

90

time, they *do* throw up. And your son's heard all about it. So, sometimes, the event doesn't even need to occur at all. You can just *imagine* it and get a "take" in the subconscious as if it has really happened. $I \times V = R$. Every time you think a negative thought about yourself—even though it might only be a fantasy, or a memory of something that happened when you were a kid—it's as if it's happening *now*. And it controls your behavior all through life—unless you change the belief.

Thoughts accumulate to build beliefs. Let's suppose you're a four-year-old kid learning how to draw. At four, you don't have an opinion yet about whether or not you're a good artist. Attitude-wise, you're starting off with empty buckets. Now you color your first picture, and you think it looks pretty good. So you go find a family wizard—your eight-year-old sister, Janet. She's been around twice as long as you; she's obviously a "Who-Said" of the Greatest Magnitude. And, by the way, she's also an expert on art. You know how you can tell? All of her art work is prominently displayed on the refrigerator door. Excitedly, you ask Janet, "Do you like this?" She takes one look and says, "What is it? Is it upside-down? You didn't even color inside the lines!" That would make a "take" in your subconscious, wouldn't it? Because you look up to your older sister, and you think she knows "the truth." So you translate to yourself your own version of what Janet told you: *"I can't draw."*

Her sarcastic, belittling statements—which you've interpreted with your own self-talk—go into your negative attitudinal bucket, and you start leaning to the negative side. She doesn't need to keep repeating her critique. All you have to do is replay it in your mind. Remember: $I \times V = R$. Every time you remember it, you reinforce the image, *"I can't draw."*

Now you're five, and you've drawn something else. This time, you avoid Janet and you go to your twelve-year-old brother, Bruce. He's a man of the world; he's got his new bike and he's ready to ride it around the world with his friends. He says, "Look at what *I'm* gonna do." And you say, "See my drawing, Bruce?" But he can't be bothered with a five-year-old hanging around. "Go away," he says. "Can't you see I'm busy?" And you say, "Look at my drawing!" Bruce glances at it and says, "Who ever heard of a blue man? That's dumb!"

This makes a "take" as soon as you give it sanction with your own self-talk: "He's right. Janet told me that, too." Plunk! More weight in your negative bucket. So you lean even more in that direction, further reinforcing the belief, *I can't draw. Everybody says so.*" Now you're six—you've colored away all morning. You bypass Janet and Bruce, and go straight to Mom. "Come see, come see!" You await her opinion with positive anticipation. She walks into the room and says, "My goodness! What have you done? That's awful! That's sinful!" "She cracks you on the seat of your pants and says, "Get that off the wall right now!"

All you did was spend the whole morning drawing an elaborate sketch of your mom, in color crayons, on a freshly painted wall—with a few "extras" because you recently found out that moms look different than dads. And it turned into, "Awful! Sinful! My kid better not think like that, let alone draw on the wall!" Of course, that won't affect your self-image unless—what? Unless you sanction it with your own self-talk: "Man, I sure can't draw, can I?" In fact, you're probably thinking: "It's downright *dangerous* to draw sometimes!" So at the age of six, you've got "the truth" about yourself as an artist firmly imprinted in your self-image. The weight's so heavy, you're toppling to the negative.

On September 8, you hit kindergarten—your first day at school. A few days later, your teacher says, "Class, I've got something really exciting for you to do today. I know you've all been looking forward to it. Today, I'm going to pass out crayons and we're all going to draw!" And you think: "Like heck we are. I can't draw. In fact, it's *dangerous* to draw!" By the time you get to sixth grade, are you going to volunteer to make the posters for the class show? "Not *me*. Never could stand that junk. Besides, I got too many other things to do." You'll creatively avoid it. In high school, when you have the chance to take art as an elective, will you take it? "No thanks. Can't do it, can't stand it, don't have the time." When you're an adult, and you have the opportunity to go to an art show, will you go? "No thanks. It's a waste of time, and I hate that junk anyway." *You move toward, and become like, that which you think about. Your present thoughts determine your future.*

Every image, every belief that you presently hold, was built the same way. It doesn't have anything to do with not being artistically inclined or not having the aptitude or whether you use a pencil or a

92

computer or if you're a slow or fast learner. You build your own reality—*"I can't draw"*—with your own self-talk.

A Victim of You

I want to remind you about *sanctioning your own beliefs*. I've been talking about building belief through self-talk, and how the garbage about yourself that you record in your subconscious becomes reality. But keep in mind that no one else can build a belief within you. It cannot be done unless you, the receiver, give sanction to the belief. "Uh-huh, I agree." I could tell you that you're the most delightful, wonderful person I've met in a long time. But you might think, "What's he up to? What's he want?" See? You can deny or reject my statement, "No. I don't believe him."

If I told you, "That's the most incompetent thing I've ever seen anybody do," would you automatically record, "I am competent" into your self-image? Not necessarily. You might choose to think, "Well, you're not so smart yourself. I don't buy what you're saying." Or you could accept it: "Well yes, I agree with you. You have always been very perceptive and wise. That is true." Only *then* would it become part of your reality. Nobody can build a belief in you until you *sanction* it first: "Oh yes, I've been thinking along the same lines myself."

So you must be careful whom you listen to. You could ask a friend, "How do I look?" and your friend might say, "You look awful." If you have low-esteem, you might think, "Well, I'm glad I asked. I almost went out looking like this." Or a little kid goes out for football, and his nose starts to bleed, so he comes to the sidelines to rest. But he's got a coach who thinks he's Mr. Macho, and he says, "You little wimp! Get your rear end outta here! We don't want any cowards here."

Now, that won't make a "take" until the kid starts thinking, "*I don't have what it takes.*" Then all the other kids say, "You know what the coach said. We don't want him here." The kid gets home and his father says, "How did practice go?" and the kid relives it again for his dad. That further reinforces—what? *"I don't have what it takes."* That night, the kid can't sleep for thinking about what happened at practice; he reviews it a hundred times in his mind. Next morning, he wakes up thinking about it, still feeling the same way. So, within the short space of twenty-four hours, that one event could've happened two hundred times in his mind. I wonder if that's enough to make a "take" in his subconscious self-image.

But remember: Language alone is an empty vehicle. It has to carry the spirit of intent. Even then, you must sanction it before it records, subconsciously, as "the truth." The power is in the *receiver*, not the words or the sender of the words. The power is in you. So the real truth is that you're not the victim of your second grade teacher, your Drivers-Ed instructor, your football coach, your spouse, your brother, sister, mom, or dad. When you sanction somebody else as a "Who-Said," ironically, you become a victim of *you*.

9

CONTROLLING YOUR SELF-TALK:

"Float Like A Butterfly, Sting Like A Bee"

Automatic Pilot

Whenever you think of changing your self-image, I want you to picture yourself fishing off the stern of a boat that's heading north. You're not catching any fish, so you decide to change the boat's direction. You walk forward, grab the steering wheel and turn the boat to the east. Then you let go of the wheel and head back to the stern. As you do, the boat starts swinging back to the north on its own. Why? Because you forgot to adjust the automatic pilot system. You only tried to override it.

You can *temporarily* act brave if you're scared; you can *temporarily* act outgoing if you're shy; you can *temporarily* act calm if you're mad. You can override your automatic pilot system at any time. But if you haven't changed your picture, the moment you let go of the steering wheel, the automatic pilot will kick in and draw you back again. If you see yourself as a smoker, you can hang on temporarily and act like a nonsmoker. But the moment the stress hits, you'll let go of the steering wheel—and back you'll go. If you see yourself as overweight, you can temporarily stick to a diet. But you're consciously hanging onto the steering wheel, and you feel the strain. The moment you let go—. See?

If that is so, then change will be rather difficult, right? Perhaps. But did you know that you can turn the boat to the east without ever touching the steering wheel? Just change the automatic pilot system, and the boat will automatically go east. The automatic pilot, of course, is your self-image. It determines the direction toward which you'll lean—east or north, positive or negative. So how do you change your self-image? *By controlling and changing your self-talk.* That's what built it in the first place.

"Float Like a Butterfly, Sting Like a Bee"

One key will be your conscious use of these two phrases: *"That's like me"* and *"That's not like me."* Remember: You affirm beliefs with your own self-talk. Once you get the belief imprinted in your subconscious, you act like it. And you reinforce the belief by reviewing it vividly in your imagination: "I'm good at this," "I'm terrible at that." You even manipulate your senses and lock things out to reinforce "the truth." So you need to consciously build your *"That's like me"* and *"That's not like me"* beliefs. For example, if you believe you're the best teacher among your peers, and you win an "Excellence in Teaching Award," you're self-talk should be, "Well, that's like me. I deserve it." On the other hand, if you believe you're an excellent stage performer, and you forget your lines one night, your self-talk should be, "That's not like me. I remember my lines." By using these two statements, you constantly affirm the future positively, and not the past negatively. So, whether you've done well at something or not, you're adding positive weights to your attitudinal balance scale. And as you add to, and update, the positive "truth," about yourself, you will change the direction in which you lean, and start using your full potential.

Now, many of you might have the tendency to sit and wait for people to affirm for you how good you are. You wait for your boss, your teacher, your coach, your friends, your spouse to come around and say, "I've been meaning to tell you how much I appreciate what you do." But if you wait only for that, you won't live long enough to use your potential. You must build your self-image on your own. You can start by denying all the negatives that people throw your way. I don't mean you should ignore it when you find yourself getting out of line. I'm talking about denying the "truths" you get from negative wizards who want to take away your courage, your heart, and your brains. All those "Who-Saids" whose opinions you sanction, but who have no authority except what you've granted them. It isn't, "By the power vested in me by the state of California."

What you need to examine is: It's really, "By the power vested in me by *you*!"

If you're going to grow, you must consciously reject the negative, sarcastic, devaluative, belittling criticism from yourself and others, because that kind of talk is conducive to a negative, small-minded, self-image. Deflect that garbage with your *"That's not like me"* self-talk. Don't let it through. You must also learn to discard excessive or false humility, and to accept more of your own *"That's like me"* self-praise. In fact, be a little more like Muhammad Ali. In his heyday as a professional boxer, he rejected anything negative that anyone said about him. He was famous for rejecting appraisals from that notorious sportscaster, Howard Cosell. Ali constantly proclaimed to the world, and to himself, *"I am the greatest! I am the greatest!"* That was his self-talk. Even his childish rhymes became part of his automatic pilot: *"I float like a butterfly, sting like a bee. His hands can't hit what his eyes can't see."* And that's exactly how he boxed. He visualized and constantly affirmed the "floating," the "stinging," the winning. He built his own self-image by becoming his own expert.

What made Muhammad Ali unique? His self-image was so masterfully built on *"That's like me"/"That's not like me"* self-talk that his opponents would affirm their own defeat! Before a match, Ali would publicly predict, *"So-and-so is not like me! So-and-so will fall in three!"* This would incense his opponent, who would then announce, "No way. He's crazy. I'll last at least *four!*" See? Affirming a loss to Ali without knowing it!

If you think more like Muhammad Ali, you will no longer dwell on "What's the matter with me anyway?" You'll start thinking better of yourself, and triggering images in your mind of only what you choose to be, as opposed to what you don't choose to be. Instead of putting yourself down, you'll start putting yourself up. Remember: Your subconscious is recording what you tell it, and it doesn't care if you denigrate or elevate yourself. It just makes sure that you act like what you believe. So start telling yourself that you believe the best about you, not the worst. Pretty soon, you'll adjust your automatic pilot to go in the direction you choose—and that's the way you'll go.

I want you to become consciously aware of how you talk to you. That's how you record positive habits and attitudes. You bring them to the conscious level and, as you repeat them with emotion and a genuine spirit of intent, you automatically start thinking constructively. That may be a whole new discipline because many of us have been taught that it's wrong, or even sinful, to think good things about ourselves. But it's essential that you judge yourself as good, loving, powerful, creative, warm, trusting, sensitive, dynamic, and deserving. You won't grow until you learn to take credit when you deserve it. If you are a genuinely accountable person, you'll take the blame when you make a mistake. So why not also accept the praise when you do something right? Give credit where credit is due, and accept it when it's due you.

How? Well, consider how you talk to yourself in areas where you are successful. Notice how you keep reinforcing the strengths with positive affirmations: "I *am* a good speaker," "I *am* a great hitter," "I *always* get the sale," "Kids *do* respond well to me." That's the positive way to accept your strengths. And when other people pay you a compliment, don't put it off. Your subconscious doesn't know you're kidding. Allow yourself to say, "Thank you very much," and *mean* it. Your self-talk should be, "Yes, *that's like me. That's how I am.*" Like Muhammad Ali, you can start affirming what is *right* with you. He was big enough to affirm out loud, but it can be done silently, too. Either way, you can imprint competence, excellence, and high performance through a simple *"That's just like me."* But you must keep affirming this until you believe it inside.

So where do you want to grow? In your golf game? Your dancing? Your stress management? Your personal relationships? Your ability to be more persuasive? Your career? Your management style? Your ability to socialize? Your leadership? Once you decide, you can start building your belief with your own self-talk. But you must do something else at the same time. You must also defend against the doom and gloom chatter and negative evaluations of others. Groups have self-talk. Organizations affirm. Nations affirm. Teams affirm. Companies affirm. Families affirm. To the degree that any group's self-talk is fault-finding and negative, the work of its members will follow suit.

You will be immersed in your social and professional groups, and you will hear the negative talk constantly going on around you: "Ain't it terrible?" "Things can't get much worse, can they?" When people start ripping and complaining, you must learn to say, "Stop it. I don't buy that." Otherwise their self-talk could overwhelm your own. When people hand you a negative weight for your attitudinal balance scale, they're saying, "Here, you deserve this." You must say, "No. That is *not* me." Don't let it in.

If you have a low self-image, you don't value your own opinion enough. You'll always think other people know more than you: "Well, she's smarter at this than me." "He's been around more than I have." "They're the experts." In effect, you're telling yourself, "My opinions aren't worth much." And you communicate to others, "Please see for me." "Please tell me, should I do this?" "Do you think I'm smart?" "Do I have a chance?" Whereas if you have a high self-image, you consider your opinion as valid as anybody else's. And that's the way it should be.

"From Now On, No More"

How do high self-image, high-performance people handle their mistakes? By telling themselves, "That's not like me," and affirming what they'll do the next time the situation occurs: "The next time, I'll be more tactful with potential clients." "The next time, I'll be more cooperative with the union." "The next time, I won't be so judgmental with my daughter." "The next time, I'll be patient with my employees." And they visualize themselves feeling and being that way the next time. They don't dwell on the rock in the road; they visualize the way around it.

Let's say something goes wrong that you haven't anticipated. You must immediately tell yourself, *"That's not like me."* If you say that often enough in these situations, your subconscious will believe you and record the mistake as the exception, not the rule. If you add, *"Next time, I intend to—,"* and finish the affirmation with whatever you plan to do next time, your subconscious imprints the way you *want* things to be in the future, not the way they were in the past. That way, the problem, or the mistake, doesn't make a subconscious "take." If it doesn't make a "take," it's as if it never happened. What you're really doing is shutting off negative input about what you *would've* done, *should've* done, *could've* done about something in the past. Instead of re-affirming the past problem, you re-affirm the future solution—and *that* becomes "the truth."

So when you make a mistake, simply tell yourself, "That's no longer like me. The next time, I intend to handle it with much more class." "It's no longer like me to forget an appointment. The next time, I intend to remember." "It's no longer like me to lose my guts. The next time, I intend to be tough and courageous." "It's no longer like me to blow up like that. The next time, I intend to stay patient, cool, and calm." In affirming what you intend to do next time, you're adjusting your automatic pilot to steer your bike around the rock. You aren't ignoring the rock, you're simply choosing to dwell on the solution. That's how high-performance people handle their mistakes.

You might wonder, "What if my subconscious won't accept my new self-image right away?" I didn't say this stuff was instant. You must be persistent in maintaining your positive self-talk. Keep driving it home every chance you get. Bear in mind that your subconscious is your slave; when you *believe* what you're saying, your slave will dutifully obey. One time, after a seminar, somebody said to me, "How come when I start affirming good things about myself, my self-talk always says, 'No, you're not!' " The reason is because the subconscious is acting on what you *believe* now. Until you decide to control and change and believe it, you're just grabbing the steering wheel and holding on against the stress until the old you regains control. So, if you allow it, your subconscious will continually deny the "new" you because its main assignment is to maintain your *present* reality. See what I'm saying? You're going to get a lot of old negative self-talk that's contrary to the new talk you're putting in. It will be important for you to control your old self-talk to allow your new self-talk to become automatic, free-flowing, habitual. You won't be perfect at it, but you'll keep getting better and better.

Let's say that you know you're clumsy. You've been telling yourself for years that you have "two left feet." One day, you trip and fall. In the past, you might have said, "That's just like me. I'm clumsy and awkward. I always trip and fall." That's the old way. The new way is to immediately correct and say, "That's no longer like me." Yet, you may get an unexpected response. Your self-talk might say, "Bull! It is so!" You need to correct yourself; you must come back with, "Up till now, I've been clumsy. From now on, no more." Just keep using these two phrases whenever you need them: *"Up till now—"* and *"From now on, no more."* That's how you go about finishing off the "old" reality. What you're after, remember, is affirming what is *right* about you, not what is wrong. This will become increasingly easy and, soon, the new self-talk will free-flow and the old will disappear.

Superstar Self-Talk

I work with a lot of college and professional athletes, and I teach them the power of their self-talk to direct their performance. For example, when I work with football players, I tell them that after they drop the ball, the worst thing they can do is return to the huddle affirming what they just did wrong: "I've got this problem. I'm dropping the ball." If that's the vivid picture they paint with their self-talk, the next time the situation arises, they'll do something physiologically to re-create the problem. They'll keep dropping the ball until—what? Until they change the automatic pilot.

That's how slumps occur in sports and in life. As you keep affirming the reality that you observe, you keep perpetuating it. Remember the "Sure Enough" principle and the placebo effect? Remember the twenty-one game losing streak? What you tell yourself is what you picture, and what you picture is what you get: "I always strike out when it counts." "She makes me sick." "I never make the sale." "We always lose." "I can't get the job." "I've always been poor." It's a self-fulfilling prophecy; you predict an outcome with your self-talk, and then you make it happen.

So you don't want to keep affirming past mistakes, or you'll perpetuate them in the future. Instead, affirm what you *want* to achieve, what you *intend* to create. Replay in your mind only past *successes*, and tell yourself, "That's like me. Next time, I intend to do it again." This kind of thinking breeds greatness.

You may be familiar with a former professional baseball star whose nickname was "Mr. October." Whether he played for Oakland, Baltimore, California, or New York, he always saw himself as the guy who performed under pressure—especially in October, during the World Series, when everything was on the line. He was a lot like Muhammad Ali; he had that positive, superstar expectancy of greatness. If you haven't already guessed, I'm talking about Reggie Jackson.

When Reggie played for the New York Yankees, he saw himself as "the straw that stirs the drink." He believed he was the heart and guts of the team—the one player you could rely on to win the game for you in the clutch. Was it coincidence, I wonder, that Reggie Jackson finished his career seventh on the all-time home run list? Was it luck that he played for five World Champions?

One year, when the Yankees played the Dodgers in the World Series, Reggie came up in the ninth inning with two men out, two men on, the Yankees two runs down. He faced a young rookie by the name of Bob Welch in a tense, dramatic confrontation. The count went to three-and-two, and Reggie kept fouling off pitches. The tension came right through the TV screen; millions watched and waited in anxious anticipation. All Reggie needed to do to be himself was hit a home run. But right in front of the whole world, he struck out.

What most people remember about that strike out was what happened immediately afterward. Reggie threw a tantrum. He pounded the bat on the ground; he punched the air angrily; he ranted and raved, cursed and yelled; and then he stomped back to the dugout, absolutely beside himself. Keep in mind, he didn't *drag* back, he *stomped* back. He couldn't accept that he'd just struck out.

That reaction was characteristic, not only of Reggie Jackson's self-image as a superstar athlete, but of *any* superstar in any career. Because superstar self-talk is performance talk, excellence talk, "I am the greatest!" talk. A superstar self-image can't accept anything less. A lot of people who saw Reggie's tantrum that night might've thought, "What a big baby." But you see, he didn't just *want* to hit a home run; he *knew* he would. Inside himself, he absolutely *believed* he would. No doubt, no pretense, no grabbing the steering wheel and holding on. It was his automatic belief that it's just like Reggie Jackson to hit a home run in a pressure situation.

If we could've gotten inside his head after he struck out, I bet we'd've heard him telling himself, *"Damn! I don't believe it! That's not me! I refuse to accept that I did that!"* Because that's what his body language was screaming from the moment he struck out. I'd also bet that once he calmed down, he told himself, "The next time I get the opportunity against Bob Welch, he better beware. The ball's *gone*, baby!" And do you know what happened the next time Reggie Jackson faced Bob Welch? The ball *was* gone. Home run. But that wasn't enough. He hit another one off the next pitcher just to make sure. And another one off the next pitcher—for pride. His three home runs in that one game tied an all-time World Series record set by only one other man—another superstar named *Babe Ruth*. By the way, Reggie hit a total of *five* home runs in that World Series—an incredible all-time record he holds all by himself.

See, you can't keep a superstar self-image down—whether it's in your business, your recreation, or your private life. But it doesn't just come to you; it isn't luck and you aren't born with it. You control it by controlling your own self-talk, or else your self-talk will control you. Control your self-talk and you can change your self-image. Change your self-image and you can change your life.

The Way Tomorrow Looks

There's another level of controlling your self-talk that affects the way you run your life. I'm talking about the way you react to and affect the self-talk of others. In your social and professional interaction with other people, you exchange ideas, attitudes, suggestions, complaints. All this talk creates a sort of feedback loop, which could be positive or negative. If you imprint what someone else is saying about you or about things in general, then you will lean toward what they've said. So, if you get negative feedback, you will lean toward the negative. Let me give you an example.

Some coaches have been notorious for using negative feedback loops in their coaching. They do it both one-on-one and with the entire team. Kirk Gibson, the Los Angeles Dodger superstar outfielder, has been through our program. Previously, when he was a rookie player with the Detroit Tigers several years ago, his manager, Sparky Anderson, wouldn't let him bat against left-handed pitchers. That was Sparky's picture of Kirk: "He can't hit lefties." Kirk hits left-handed, so when a lefty pitched for the other team, Kirk had to sit out the game. He absolutely hated not playing because that wasn't his self-image. His picture was: "I hit *everybody.*" But he couldn't get past his manager's "flat-world" thinking.

At the time, Kirk was young, impressionable, and struggling to realize his potential—which he knew was considerable. Yet he started telling himself, "Sparky says I can't hit lefties. It must be so." And, subconsciously, that made a "take." On rare occasions, Sparky would send Kirk up to bat against a lefty—and guess what happened. Kirk invariably struck out. And the fans would boo because they, too, had higher expectations of him. Every time that happened, he would skulk back to the dugout thinking, "You stink, Kirk. Sparky's right. You *can't* hit lefties." At night, Kirk would sometimes tell himself, "It's a bitch being Kirk Gibson." His negative self-talk—based, in part, on what his manager was telling him—was changing his self-image for the worse. Negative feedback loop.

Eventually, after learning some of the information in this book, Kirk convinced himself and his coaches that he could hit lefties if given the chance. To their credit, they recognized his self-confidence and started sending him up to bat against lefties. You know what happened? In 1984, the year the Tigers won the World Series, Kirk Gibson batted almost as well against lefties as against righties. I wonder if his self-talk changed back to, "It's like me to hit lefties well. I hit *everybody* well."

Another example is the way some football coaches use game films to point out their players' past mistakes. Keep in mind: You get what you picture; you move toward, and become like, that which you think about; if you dwell on the rock—. What do some coaches do? Before every Tuesday practice, they gather the team together to watch the film of last week's game. And they slow down the film to focus on—what? *Everything the players did wrong.* "See where you screwed up, Eddie? You blocked too high. Remember that play?" "I remember, coach." "Well, you said that a month ago when I showed you the same mistake. You *got* it now?" "Yes coach. Got it good." "Maybe. But I'm gonna run it back one more time just to make sure."

So Eddie starts replaying the mistake in his mind, telling himself, "I block too high." That's like the little kid saying, "I can't sing" or "I can't draw." Is that kid ever going to sing or draw for anyone? Finally, the team goes out to practice, and Eddie makes the same mistake. The coach says, "You don't listen! Don't you care? I'd be a good coach if it wasn't for these stubborn kids I got."

What happens? The team cuts the player and keeps the coach. Even though it's the coach who's telling them, "Look out for the oncoming car. Get over on the curb. Be careful, don't hit the rock. You always *do*. You know how you are." So ask yourself how you are treating the people you're leading. Are you leading them toward success or failure? Are you leading them toward excellence or mediocrity? How do you describe to them what you want them to do? Are you telling them what you *don't* want or what you *do* want? It's essential, both to directing yourself and leading others, that you visualize what you want—and *then* communicate it to your people. The opposite brings on the opposite.

I remember one time when I was coaching high school football—before I was aware of this information—and I had this very talented punter who kept booting the ball off the side of his foot. In a crucial game, his first punt went only ten yards before slicing out of bounds. Not at all the way I wanted it. So when the kid came to the sideline, I grabbed him and said, "Hey, stupid! You're kicking the ball off the side of your foot! Go sit down and think about it."

So the kid sat down and visualized—what? Kicking the ball off the side of his foot, over and over, as if it were happening again right now. And, no doubt, he felt that awful, sinking sensation in his stomach, too. See? Getting that whole 3-D picture of failure to "take" in his mind. Later in the game, the same kid had another opportunity to get us out of a hole with a good long kick. But he shanked another one about eight yards off the side of his foot. Made me madder than the dickens. Didn't I just tell that kid what he was doing wrong?

I grabbed him when he came out of the game and said, "Hey, you did it again! You didn't pay a bit of attention to me, did you? Go sit down again and think about it." Same kid kicked three more off the side of his foot in that game—all of them less than ten yards. When he came off the field the last time, he tried to hide. But I found him, grabbed his shirt, and said, "You did the same dumb thing five straight times! You're not playing for the rest of the game! You may not play for the rest of your *life!*" I was serious. I added, "Besides that, you don't even get good *grades!*" You always throw that in if you get the chance; you know, *fix the blame fast.*

Now, who do you think should've been benched? Pretty obvious, isn't it? The kid was doing what he was being coached to do. He did exactly what I described. You might say, "Well, you can't just let the kid do anything he wants to do." Right. But there's a better way to correct the problem. The first thing is to get the kid to stop making the mistake. Now I know I should have told him calmly, "Stop it. You're too good for that. It's not like you. The next time, drop the ball with the nose up." Just tell him what I *want* him to do, and how to do it *right*. That's a positive feedback loop—a positive way to manage people. You're recognizing that everybody has scotomas to their faults, and that they will see the right thing to do when someone tells them to start dropping the ball with the nose up.

Remember: If you think about what you don't want today, that's the way tomorrow looks. You will bring it about again and again. If you were a sculptor, you'd envision the finished statue in your mind before you began to sculpt. What would happen if you visualized a blemish on the statue's face? You'd end up unconsciously sculpting the blemish. That's how powerful your own feedback can be to you—and it can be just as powerful to someone else who respects your opinion.

Suppose you have an obnoxious thirteen-year-old who's driving you nuts. The kid is absolutely somebody you'd like to avoid at all cost. Bad-mouthing, uncooperative, irresponsible, can't get along with anybody. What happens if you affirm that reality? "I can't get along with this kid. Nobody can." You will unconsciously sculpt the blemish; you'll perpetuate tomorrow the reality you see today. If your verbal and nonverbal feedback to the kid is negative—"You can't get along with anybody! You're irresponsible!"—the kid will visualize and perpetuate those same problems tomorrow.

So parents, here's the discipline. While you may have an obnoxious thirteen-year-old, you must visualize not what the kid *is*, but what you want the kid to *become:* a happy, successful, responsible, cooperative, mature, twenty-five-year-old. Then, when the kid acts like an obnoxious thirteen-year-old again, you say, "Stop it! I won't tolerate that. You're much better than that. You're a much nicer person. I see you as—" and then you describe the way you expect him to behave.

See the difference? You've established a positive feedback loop; you feed back not what the kid really *is*, but what you envision him capable of being in the future. You already see him as a nicer, more mature, twenty-five-year-old. The kid will observe that, reflect back on the spirit and the power of your statement, visualize it, and, hopefully, move toward it. So, in effect, you must deny the kid's present reality and shut it off—even if it's true—and tell the kid you will not tolerate it. In other words, "You *are* cooperative. You *are* responsible. You *are* a nice person. You *are* pleasant to have around. You *are* mature—and I will not accept less from you anymore." You can do the same with employees or anyone else you manage and lead.

Here's an interesting question: Why do we sometimes treat the people we love the worst? How do you treat your siblings? How do you treat your spouse? How do you treat your parents? How do you treat your closest friends, your closest business associates—the people you absolutely rely on the most? Do you communicate to them: "What's the matter with you anyway? How can you be so dense?" Almost like you expect them to raise their hand and say, "I was hoping you'd ask me that. I never thought you'd give me the chance to tell you." See how dumb that is? But we do it anyway: "I've been meaning to tell you what an irresponsible person I am. I'm sure glad you brought it up again."

See what we do? Those closest to us are most vulnerable because they love us. We have their attention, and we know their flaws. "Geez, you're the messiest kid I've ever seen!" What's that picture look like when you're seven? What will the kid affirm with their own self-talk? Cleanliness? Order? No: "I'm the messiest kid he's ever seen. My dad says so. It must be so." And what's the kid going to continue to affirm? "It's like me. I *am* messy. Everybody says so."

Once that "takes," they act like the person they believe themself to be. So now they've *got* to throw their clothes on the floor, or else they'll feel crazy. Then you come in and you see the clothes scattered all over the place, and you think, "There they are again!" You get the kid and say, "Look at those clothes! This proves it; this is the biggest mess I've ever seen!" And the kid thinks, "I know. I'm *good* at it. You been telling me I'm the greatest at it for *years*!"

You are a very powerful person. You have tremendous power, for others and for yourself. So you must become very cognizant of the power of words and the spirit of intent behind them. *Words* trigger *pictures* that bring about *emotions*. What kind of pictures are we painting when we bring up how incompetent we think somebody is, or how messy? Does it trigger the constructive change we want? Absolutely not. It triggers the exact image for tomorrow that we want to move away from today. So if all those years I'd been describing to my children, my siblings, my spouse, my parents, my close friends and associates, what I *didn't* want in them, without knowing it I would've been helping them perpetuate those very things. Especially if they considered me the great wizard I must have thought I was.

You must eliminate from your own self-talk, and in the way that you talk to others, all the sarcasm, which is totally destructive; all the devaluation, which diminishes; all the belittling and teasing which demeans; and all the fault-finding. You must start thinking better of yourself and others, and triggering the images you want, not the images you don't want. I'm only touching on the fundamentals right now, but they are essential.

What I want to encourage you to do for the next twenty-four hours is this: I'd like you to deliberately control your self-talk for one full day by eliminating all the put-downs, hostility, cynicism, and devaluation of yourself and others. No negative affirmations. Don't allow teasing, "cuts," or sarcasm—even in jest. Remember: The subconscious has no sense of humor. It doesn't know a joke from a literal put-down. If you put yourself or somebody else down, you must immediately correct by silently affirming, "That's not like me." Then state what you'll do the next time the situation occurs. If you want to see how it really works, you might keep a chart—like the one in Figure 9-1—and score each positive put-up and negative put-down about yourself or someone else.

After twenty-four hours, check the chart, and you'll be more aware of your self-talk cycle. I know what you're thinking: "This will be the quietest, dullest twenty-four hours I've spent in years. What'll I say? What'll I do?" Everybody thinks that. Try it anyway—and see how it works.

MYSELF		OTHERS	
+	−	+	−

Figure 9-1.   Myself and Others Chart

So What?

If you stop and reflect back upon the principles I've been discussing here, the question might arise, "*So what?* What advantage is it to me, personally, to know some of these things?" Let me put it simply. Before I understood and applied these principles to Lou Tice's life, I didn't realize that *I* was responsible for my own mental health. I always fixed the blame for my difficulties on circumstances outside myself, thinking I had no control. Once I realized the power that self-talk had in controlling my life, I became a great deal more confident in my ability to direct my future. For the first time, I felt, "Now I can see the way tomorrow looks. In fact, I can make tomorrow look the way I *want!*"

You have that power, too. All I'm asking you to do now is control it.

10

HABITS AND ATTITUDES:
Resisting Change

Holding the Nose Down

As I mentioned earlier, one of the jobs of the subconscious is to regulate automatic behavior, like respiration, digestion, circulation. These are reflex actions handled on the subconscious level where they become habits. What are habits? They're automatic, free-flowing actions that we don't have to consciously think about. Habits are necessary because they allow us to comfortably do several tasks at the same time. We can talk while we drive. We can breathe while we eat. If we had to stop to consciously think about how we breathe, or how we digest food, or how we drive a car, we'd have difficulty *doing* it. If a football player consciously thought about how to run downfield between his opponents, reach up, and snare a pass, he'd probably never get off the line of scrimmage. He'd stand there thinking, "How do I *do* it? Let's see: First the right foot, then the left." He'd go nuts!

Tying our shoelaces became a habit when we were kids. It took a lot of effort at first, right? You ever watch little kids try it? Seems like their tongue has to be out or they can't do it. They give it a tremendous effort. But once they've done it twenty or thirty times, it becomes a nice, free-flowing habit. Then they can try something else that requires their tongue to be hanging out.

Tying our shoelaces is a helpful habit. But other habits can hinder our growth. You know the saying, "Practice makes perfect"? Is it true? If you're striving for excellence, practice does not make perfect. For example, when we were very young, we learned to do mul-

112

tiplication without thinking. If I asked you today, "What is two times two?" you would automatically say, "Four." If I asked, "Three times three?" you would say, "Nine." "Four times four?" "Sixteen." All very easy for you. But what if every time you practiced two times two, you came up with five? If you did it thirty times, you'd have that habit down perfectly—except that every time you did it, you'd be doing it *wrong*. So only practice of perfection makes perfection.

Suppose that instead of "What is two times two?" I asked you, "What is sixty-seven times eighty-six? You would pass on that, "Well, I uh, don't know." But you could have just as easily habituated that one. There are Las Vegas croupiers who can automatically compute all the odds—click, click, click—as easy as two times two. You must practice excellence and make it a habit. You aren't born with it.

Habits are fine, as long as everything stays the same. A habit that might have served us nicely three years ago might hinder us today. It is estimated, for example, that all of mankind's accumulated knowledge can be doubled within the next five years. Not long ago, I met some very astute computer people in England who suggested that, in a few years, anyone who can't operate a computer will be considered illiterate. That's how fast technology is changing. So we need to be aware that some of our habits will require updating if we expect to change and grow. We must change our habits as our marriage changes, as our children change, as our business changes, as our own needs change. We must keep making habits "current."

Changing habits and developing new ones is a challenge. Remember "Lock On-Lock Out"? It's no trouble for our subconscious to lock out a new routine, even if it would help us achieve ten times more than what we do now. We feel more comfortable with old habits because we don't have to think about them consciously. In fact, once you have a habit down real good, if you bring it back to the conscious level, you mess up the automatic flow. Have you ever been asked to spell a familiar word? You might say, "Give me a pen. I have to write it out." You *know* the word perfectly, but the stress of having to *think* about it causes you to be unsure. Ever try to teach somebody how to dance? You can suddenly be awkward, uncertain. You wonder, "Do I really *know* this dance?" You do know it, but you know it best *subconsciously*. Bring it to the conscious level, and you need to think it out.

Here's something to try in a crucial situation when you really need it. Let's say you're golfing competitively with a friend. At about the tenth tee, when your friend is really grooved and ready to swing, ask this all-important question: "I was wondering: Do you inhale or exhale on your backstroke?" Then watch what happens. If they stop to think about it, they'll probably mess it up. They'll shank it, put it off a tree, maybe miss it altogether. I've seen it happen. Heck, I've *made* it happen! How? By bringing their habit to the conscious level, and letting them mess it up.

Why do you need to know this? Because you're going to get a great deal of resistance to change in your organizations, your companies, your teams, your families, even from your friends. Not because they can't change, but because you're suddenly asking them whether they inhale or exhale on their backstroke. You're asking them for extra conscious effort, and they won't like the uncomfortable feeling: "You're irritating me. Stop it! I don't want to think about it." "Well, it would be nice if I could stop it, but the competition won't wait for us." "It would be nice if I could stop it, but the technology keeps changing." "It would be nice if I could stop it, but my needs are different now, and you're still treating me the same old way." See what I'm saying?

So how do you get your company to go automated for the first time? How do you get your spouse to change old habits that are hindering growth? How do you get yourself to change? I'll show you how to change with ease by using visualization and internal goal-setting. It won't be a matter of jamming in more information. It will be a matter of using visualization techniques to program in the anticipated new responses. That way, when the time comes for the actual change, you can do it *automatically*.

Several years ago, I was seated in a fully loaded DC-10 on a Honolulu airstrip. As we gunned down the runway to lift off, all of a sudden, pow, we blew out tires on the left side. The captain held the nose down, and we gouged about a thousand-foot rut in the runway. Just before we dumped in the ocean, the captain veered the plane to the left and brought it to a halt. Everybody breathed again.

The captain got on the P.A. system and calmly said, "Looks like we got a flat tire." *Flat tire*? We almost *died*!

How could that guy be so calm and cool under that kind of stress—and still get the job done right? Was it luck? Was he born with it? No, of course not. It was *habit*. He'd programed in the anticipated recovery from that kind of emergency so often and so thoroughly that he didn't need to think about it. He just reacted like he'd trained himself to react. You know how pilots train? In simulators. They sit in full-scale replica cockpits with authentic instruments, and they "fly" the simulators without ever leaving the ground. They get the skills down *safely* first; they anticipate and get a "feel" for emergencies; they repeat the proper reactions hundreds of times. When a real emergency situation occurs, they perceive the danger signals— like the tires blowing out—and then, click, their simulator habits kick right in. They automatically hold the nose down and keep the plane on the runway.

Deliberate preparation for a predetermined outcome—that's what high performance is all about. You accomplish a goal hundreds of times in your mind (your simulator) *before* you try to accomplish it. It's a matter of programming habits into your subconscious with visualization—an art which native American Indians use, which the martial arts employ, which many of us haven't used. You anticipate the changes in your business, you anticipate what the new job will be like, you anticipate what the new house will be like, you anticipate expected crises. Then, when the tires suddenly *do* blow out, click, you've got control.

The difference between the amateur and the professional is that the amateur is constantly coping with the new. The professional always anticipates ahead, knows what to expect, and has the reactions down. When the situation occurs, *"Got it!"* That's how we train our astronauts; that's how we train our elite commandos; and that's how I'll teach you to train yourself. I'll show you how to build your own simulators so you can program in the key new habits that you need. If you don't learn how to use these techniques in the future, you'll be very uptight and out of place. You'll be wondering, "Why is the world passing me by so fast? Can't we slow it down?" Quite frankly, no. In fact, look out. It's getting faster.

"Ex-Friend" and Purse

We've talked a lot about how our subconscious mind habituates us to our own version of "reality." One way it does that is by causing us to stick to our attitudes. We've developed attitudes about every aspect of our existence—how we dress, the type of car we drive, our politics, our friends, our careers, our ethics—all the "norms" of our daily life. We've kept some attitudes so long, they're part of the automatic pilot system steering our boat. If we want to change direction, we'll have to examine and change some attitudes first.

An attitude is an emotional predisposition to a given situation or stimulus. Aeronautically, the "attitude" of an airplane is judged by the angle of the wings in relation to a fixed point on the horizon. In other words, the direction in which the plane is leaning. So remember: An attitude is the direction in which you lean. If you lean toward something, you've got a positive attitude toward it. If you lean away, you've got a negative attitude.

Attitudes aren't positive or negative until you set a goal. Once you set a goal, you must ask yourself, "Does my present attitude lead me *toward* accomplishment of the goal, or *away* from it?" Toward is positive; away is negative. Negative attitudes are tricky. You might not be aware of them but, subconsciously, you may be saying, "I can't bring myself to do it." So what happens? Instead of changing the attitude, too many people give up on the goal: "Oh well. I guess I'm not cut out for this kind of job." "I guess I don't deserve that kind of car." "I guess I'm not tall enough to play on this team. That's just the way it is." No—that's the way *you* "is." All you need to do is change your attitude.

Take a moment now and visualize your residence. You have an attitude about how you run your home. If you're an orderly person, your attitude might be, "I like my house neat and clean." Suppose your brother is staying with you for a week, and his attitude is, "I like my house messy." How would you feel if you came home one night and found your brother's belongings scattered everywhere? You'd probably feel uptight, irritated. Your self-talk might be, "This isn't the way I live." You would have a problem.

Let's go one more step. Suppose you have the attitude: "I can't stand left-handed people"—and, upon reporting to the Navy for submarine duty, you discover, to your horror, that your bunkmate is

116

left-handed. You got a problem. Especially if *he* can't stand *right-handed* people. It's the same basic process through which attitudes solidify over centuries of conflict between Arabs and Jews; black and white South Africans; Irish Catholics and Irish Protestants; Sandinistas and Contras. See what I mean? Each side has an attitude about the other that limits interaction and prohibits positive change. So we must always be aware of the critical influence of attitudes on how we live.

Some of our attitudes are outmoded or inappropriate. They prevent us, and others whom we influence, from making positive changes. In the 1950s, the majority of Americans seemingly shared the attitude that "A woman's place is in the home." In the 1980s, that attitude is outmoded, right? Most women today—single and married—are in the workforce. Up until 1947, blacks were not accepted in major league baseball. Then Jackie Robinson broke the "color barrier" and integrated the game. Today, that old, restrictive, racial policy is unacceptable. Times change and values change. So attitudes must change along with them.

Years ago, after Diane and I quit teaching school and had decided to go into this business for ourselves, we were getting ready to fly to Denver to work with some people at the University of Colorado. When I walked into our house, Diane was scrubbing the kitchen floor. I said, "Aren't you going? We've got a plane to catch in a half-hour." She said, "I'll be ready as soon as I finish this." I said, "Diane, why are you scrubbing the kitchen floor?" She said, "Well, I don't feel like a mother unless I scrub the floor."

How do you argue with that? You don't. But you may not get to Denver, either. At the time, we had changed our lives dramatically—but scrubbing the kitchen floor could have prevented us from *enjoying* our new lifestyle. So sometimes you've got to give up an old attitude about what it means to be a mother. "Well," she said, "If I don't get this done, I won't feel right about going." I said, "Why not hire somebody this one time to do it for you?" She said, "No, I wouldn't feel comfortable with that." To Diane, at that time, scrubbing the floor was a mother's obligation. But that attitude was holding up our lives.

So how do you apply this to *your* life? Well, if you have this knowledge, you'll recognize that you may be lugging around a lot of outmoded attitudes that keep you from reaching your goals. And once you learn the techniques for changing old attitudes, you will see that you don't have to give up your goals. You can pursue them aggressively, with great anticipation, like a kid looking forward to Christmas. With this knowledge, you will more readily identify your own negative attitudes, and you will know how to change them.

You might say, "Well, how will I know if I have a negative attitude?" Just observe yourself in action. If you have a positive attitude about something, you seek it out and try to possess it—whether it's music, career, love, money, art, food, adventure. If you have a negative attitude, you unconsciously lean away; you try to duck it. How do you know if your child has a negative attitude about school? If they do, they'll break out, psychosomatically, in spots and a fever to creatively avoid getting out of bed. When we perceive or anticipate an uncomfortable situation, we get creative to avoid it. We're very good at that.

Most of us don't even know how we acquired our attitudes. How did you get your attitude about success; about money; about travel; about the death penalty; about red people, white people, black people, yellow people; about selling; about war; about love? I've asked myself that, and the answer often is, "Gee, I don't know." I don't even know when my attitudes jump right out at me. Let me give you an amusing example.

I have a good friend who runs a hair salon. Years ago, when this incident happened, I had the attitude that running a hair salon was a strange business for a man. At that particular time, my friend was helping me put on some seminars for convicts as they were released into our custody. While I worked on their *inside* image, he worked on their *outside* image—acquainting them with the latest clothing and hair styles.

So here I was teaching this seminar to some people who were being paroled ,and it was lunchtime, and I hadn't talked to my friend in a while. So I suggested that we go across the street to the campus cafeteria and have lunch together. He said great. So after I finished teaching, we walked outside. It was winter, and he was wearing a stylish coat, which was fine because he was interested in fashion. But the darned guy also had a *purse*! One of those "mail bags" that you sling over your shoulder.

Well, I do not walk with men who carry purses. That was my attitude. But I didn't realize it until we started across the street. What went through my mind *then* was, "I'm crossing the street with my *ex*-friend and his purse." See what I did? Subconsciously, I'd already created my avoidance. When we entered the cafeteria, I stopped to talk to the first person I met—a guy I didn't even *know*. I turned back to my friend and said, "Go ahead and get in line. I'll be right with you." I was acting as if I was busy with another old friend. That was my creative subconscious taking over; I wasn't *consciously* aware that I was avoiding my friend—and his purse.

Reflecting later, if I didn't know better, I might have fixed the blame on my friend, and quit the friendship. But he didn't have the problem; I did. It was *my attitude*, not *his purse*. And it might have cost me a valuable friendship. The solution was to simply realize that fashions change, ideas change, and so do people. All I needed to do was change my attitude, and the problem was solved. And you must do the same thing. Because your subconscious works the same way. It could be causing you to creatively avoid a friend with a purse—new jobs, new restaurants, new neighborhoods, new experiences. Often, unless we closely monitor ourselves, we don't recognize a negative attitude until the damage is done.

Here's one more personal example. When Diane and I had raised our kids, we decided to leave our old house—which the kids had pretty much destroyed—and buy a new one. So we sold the house and found a wonderful new place on three scenic acres. It was a beautiful setting, and Diane immediately loved it. I hated it: "Oh no. This is not for me." Why? Because the house had a major flaw that, in my mind, made it absolutely uninhabitable. The flaw was the three acres. It was all *grass*.

See, I had an attitude about grass. I hated *mowing* it. The old house had a patch of lawn about as big as a conference table. *That* was just right for me. But here we were moving into a new house that had *three acres* of the stuff! "No way. I can't cut all that." So I resisted—not because I didn't like the house, but really because I didn't want to cut the grass. I knew my choices: Either change my attitude or lose the house.

So I considered hiring a gardener. But I had a negative attitude about *that*, too: "What'll my friends think? I mean, what kind of person has household help?" To me, at the time, having household help was like carrying a purse. I wasn't comfortable with the idea. But I thought, "What's the alternative? *Mow the doggone grass!*" I couldn't do that, so I changed another attitude. I accepted the idea of having a gardener: "I'll still be me. I'll just be me with a *gardener*. Besides, it will give me more time to devote to other things." A gardener started making sense—and I started leaning toward the positive. Amazing, isn't it? Because, today, I can't imagine how I ever got along without one.

The point is: We must sometimes change our attitudes to allow ourselves to achieve what we're capable of achieving. It isn't just a Pollyanna matter of thinking better of yourself, dwelling on positive thoughts, and visualizing end results. You will hear a lot of that elsewhere. *I'm* saying that we will also have to work at changing old, inappropriate habits and attitudes that prevent us from attacking our full potential. If you learn how to do that, you'll experience more personal growth in the next five years than perhaps you've had in the first twenty, thirty, or forty years of your life.

I will show you how.

11

THE COMFORT ZONE:

What's Good Enough For You?

"The Ways Things Are Supposed to Be"

You and I have developed, in our minds, an idea of *"the way things are supposed to be"* in our home life, our career, our recreation, our environment. This idea regulates us like a thermostat regulates the temperature in a room. The thermostat operates largely on electrical feedback. Say you want the room to be seventy degrees. If the temperature rises above seventy, this very sensitive mechanism says, "Whoops, too high!" and sends an electrical current to turn on the cooling unit to lower the temperature. If the temperature drops below seventy, it says, "Whoops, too low!" and sends an impulse to the heating unit.

To maintain efficient climate control, the thermostat has a "dead space" of two degrees on either side of the desired temperature. If the desired temperature is seventy, it needs to rise to seventy-two before the electrical impulse is sent to the cooling unit. Once it cools down, the temperature needs to drop to sixty-eight before it sends the impulse to the heating unit again. So the "dead space" is the "comfort zone" that allows the thermostat to maintain a steady temperature without energy.

Human beings have comfort zones, too. They regulate our emotions like a thermostat regulates the temperature. Whenever we venture too far from our comfort zone in any area of our life, we get subliminal feedback that says, "Whoops, too high!" or "Whoops, too low!" This drives us back to where we belong—back to our comfort zone. For example, we've all been out in public—at a museum, a theater, a ballpark—when we had to use the restroom. Living in

America, we know we have separate restrooms for women and men and we know where we belong. But have you ever been in a hurry and inadvertantly walked into the wrong one? In your mind, you know "the way things are supposed to be"—and this isn't it! So how do you feel when you're in there? *Out of place.* What do you tell yourself? *"Whoops, wrong place! How do I get back to where I belong?"*

That's your subconscious letting you know you're out of your comfort zone. That's why you can feel out of place with the unfamiliar—a promotion to a new job, meeting new friends, trying new sports, making new investments, moving to a new neighborhood, buying a new house. You feel as though you're in the wrong restroom. Even though that particular restroom might be cleaner and nicer than the one you're used to, even though the promotion might be a boost to your career, even though the new house might be more roomy and secure for your family—it doesn't matter. It's the *difference* that makes the difference. Your subconscious isn't concerned with benefits or drawbacks. It is concerned with keeping you in line with "the way things are supposed to be" for you. It is concerned with keeping you sane.

Just being away from the familiar will trigger powerful feelings of discomfort and stress to get you back where you belong. You have the urge, you have the desire, you certainly have the potential—but it doesn't matter. When you're in the wrong restroom, it's tough to use your potential. If you don't believe comfort zones are real, just walk into the wrong restroom sometime and try to use your potential. It would be the same thing if you were sitting comfortably at home, talking to a few friends, and being very astute. But when you try to address the same subject in front of a conference of *five thousand* people, you get up there and your mind goes blank. You have the knowledge, you have the desire, you have the potential to speak about it astutely—yet nothing comes out. You become ineffective. Ever had that feeling?

Now, suppose I place a beam about as wide as a table on your living room rug, and I say, "I'll give you a *hundred* bucks if you walk the length of that beam without falling off." Could you do it? Sure, easy; no big deal. You could do it ten times in a row; you could do it backwards; you could stop halfway across and dangle a foot over the edge; you could probably do it blindfolded. But what

123

if I say, "I'll give you a *hundred thousand* bucks if you walk across that same beam"—and I stick the beam out a window on the top floor of a fifty-story building? You have the skill, you have the balance, you have the potential, and you've already done it in your living room. Would you try it?

You'd have to think about it, wouldn't you? Meantime, I say, "If you do it backwards, I'll throw in another ten grand. If you dangle one foot over the edge, I'll give you twenty more. Oh, and if you do it blindfolded, that'll get you another twenty." Doesn't matter; you won't win a dime. You'll feel like you'd kill yourself as soon as you stepped on that beam. Why? Because you can't use your potential if you're suddenly fifty stories high. It's the same beam, and the same skill you had in your living room—but the *difference* makes the difference. Fifty stories high is too far out of your comfort zone, even for a hundred grand: "*Whoops, too high! How do I get back to where I belong?*"

What causes that? Well, instead of an electrical impulse, human beings operate on tension feedback. You'll often hear people say, "I've been under a lot of pressure lately." "I've felt tense all week." "The stress has been wearing me down." Our regulating mechanism—our self-image—uses tension feedback to keep us from wandering too far from our presently dominant self-image. It makes us stick closely to our present attitudes, habits, and opinions, so we feel crazy when we don't act like ourself. To the degree that we detect ourself as being better or worse than our subconscious "picture" of us, pressure, tension, and stress drive us back to where the pictures match. This applies to *any* of our comfort zones—attitude comfort zone, habit comfort zone, success comfort zone, health comfort zone, and so on.

Let's say you see yourself as a smoker, but you know it's unhealthy and you want to stop. You quit for a week, but you're just barely hanging on. Finally, the stress hits hard and you let go of the wheel. What happens? You get very creative to maintain sanity. You reason, "You know, every time I stop smoking, I overeat. It's healthier for me to smoke than to get fat." Or, "Whenever I stop smoking, I'm unpleasant to my family and the people I work with. It's just not fair to *them*. I better start smoking again to be fair."

We not only get anxious when our golf game is *worse* than we expect, we get anxious when it's *better* than we expect. We not only get worried when we don't have *enough* money, we get worried when we have *too much* money. Too much for what? Too much for "the way things are supposed to be" for you. Who says so? *You* do: "Whoops, too high! Whoops, too low!" Whether something is better for you or not, your self-image corrects for the mistake to get you back where you belong.

This happened to me in my own family. One time, my teenage son said to me, "Dad, you never show you love us." I said, "What do you mean? Why do you think I adopted you?" He said, "I didn't say you don't love us. I said you never show it." Now, I had all the potential to be very loving and warm to my wife and daughters, but not so much to my sons. It wasn't part of my picture. My father died when I was twelve, so I pretty much raised myself. Since there were no loving hugs from dad when I grew up, I thought, "I don't need that stuff. Besides, it isn't manly, anyway." Eventually I became a high school football coach so, at the time, my idea of showing love to a boy was *yelling* at him. Putting an arm around him would've felt like carrying a purse! "What do you mean, I don't love you? I *hollered* at you yesterday! Don't you remember?" "Oh, was that love, dad?" "Well, certainly! What'd you think it was?" See?

After my son told me this, I tried harder to be loving and warm toward all my boys. I'd come into the room, give them a quick hug, and say unconvincingly, "There, I love you. Now get out of here." And guess how often I would do that. Maybe once. So the kid would have to remember it forever. Of course, it wouldn't "take." I felt pressured and uptight. I was out of my comfort zone, and that's what came across. I couldn't be free-flowing with my love—even though I *felt* it, even though I *wanted* to show it, even though I had the *potential* to show it. Every time I tried hard to show love to my sons, I felt as though I was in the wrong restroom. Nothing came out.

You and I can accomplish all sorts of things, if we can just learn to beat the stress. We can grow, we can change, we can excel. But first, we need to learn how to visualize and imprint the new situation in advance. We must make it part of our picture, part of "the way things are supposed to be" for us. Keep in mind: *All meaningful and lasting change starts first on the inside, and works its way out.* If we haven't changed our picture inside, then when we *do* get into the actual situation, we'll feel out of place, pressured, uptight—and nothing will come out. It's like taking a new job when you don't believe you belong there. You put yourself into it and hang on, but you know you're out of your comfort zone. So, subconsciously, you get very creative to get back where you belong. You miss work, you lose memos, forget appointments—whatever it takes to relieve the stress. Even if you lose the job, your subconscious is happy to inform you, "Hey, cheer up. This is the way things are supposed to be!"

Feeling Like Death

There are always signals to let you know when you are out of your comfort zone. Your memory gets blocked. If you feel out of place at an interview or taking an exam, you might know the right answers but you suddenly can't remember them. Once you get outside, click, the answers flow right through. Socially, you might go to a party where you don't know anyone. You meet someone new but, thirty seconds later, you can't remember their name. It's like when you're outside, watering the grass, and somebody bends the hose. The water suddenly stops. One second it's flowing fine, the next, nothing. That's how your memory works when you're out of your comfort zone.

If you go out on a first date with someone new, you may suddenly become awkward, clumsy, accident-prone. You spill something, you catch their coat in the door, you trip and fall on the way to the dance floor. Instead of being comfortable, easy-going, and relaxed, the way you are with close friends, you're awkward, nervous, uptight. That's your subconscious saying, "Wrong place! Get back to where you belong." Later, you tell yourself, "Stick with your old friends. Don't make a fool of yourself with somebody new. *Stay with the familiar*." So you stop going to parties and you invent excuses to justify staying home: "I'm too old for parties now." "My children need me." "I hate parties anyway. They're boring." You do whatever it takes to stay in your comfort zone.

When a boy goes from ninth grade in junior high to tenth grade in high school, that's a comfort zone leap. He comes to his new school the first day, and the coach assigns him a locker for gym. But the kid immediately forgets the combination because he feels so tense. So he keeps asking for the combination until the coach says,

"Next time you ask, it'll cost you a dollar." The kid doesn't want to keep losing money, so he scribbles the combination on a piece of tape and puts it—where? On the inside of his locker door, which he closes and locks again! The coach says, "How did you ever get out of junior high?" But the same thing happens to high school kids when they first arrive at college; to a nurse who changes professions and reports for her first day at the law office; when you stay overnight at the relatives' house; when companies merge; even when countries elect new presidents.

When you feel out of place, you can feel the muscles in your upper body pressing against your rib cage. That's what you mean when you say, "I've been under pressure lately." You're so tense, you literally feel squeezed: "I can hardly breathe." In athletics, that's called "choking." A rookie basketball player steps to the free throw line with the game in the balance, but he's so tense, he can't catch his breath. He feels so out of place, he can barely get his arm to unfold. So he shoots either an "air-ball" or a "brick." In other words, the ball either falls five feet short of the basket, or bashes off the backboard. He's in the wrong restroom, so nothing comes out.

Another symptom is your head starts pounding. That's because the muscles in your upper back, shoulders, and neck contract, impeding the flow of blood to your brain. Also, your hands get sweaty. That's one of the ways the lie detector works. They attach electrodes to the surface of your skin, and when you don't say what you believe to be the truth, one reaction is that moisture gathers instantly. Still another signal is feeling "sick to your stomach." When you're under pressure, your stomach secretes more digestive acid than it needs. As coaches, we used to think that when a kid threw up before a ballgame, it meant he really wanted to win. We'd see a kid sitting calm and relaxed before a game, and we'd get madder than the dickens at him. We "knew" he didn't care. We'd see some other kid throwing up his guts, and we'd say, "Everybody look at him! Take a lesson! This kid wants to win!" In fact, the poor kid was feeling so out of place, he couldn't contain his tension. What he was really thinking was, "Get me out of here! I don't wanna play!" But we didn't know that.

Other symptoms are: your blood pressure rises, your pulse rate goes up, your knees get shaky, you lose your balance, your vocal chords tighten to make your voice sound funny. Now, if every time you tried something new, you suddenly felt uptight, and your head pounded, and your heart thumped, and you started sweating like a pig, and you threw up, and your voice souded like Donald Duck—what would you tell yourself? You'd probably say, "Are you *nuts?* Why are you *doing* this? *Stick to the familiar!*" After enough of those experiences, if somebody said, "Would you like to try something new today?" you'd say, "No thank you. I've had my share of feeling like death."

That's why we often don't let ourselves try new things. That's why we don't seek out new friends, new careers, new recreation, new culture, new neighborhoods, new adventures. We're more comfortable staying in the same job, doing the same routine, having the same friends, bowling the same night, eating the same foods in the same restaurants. Our regulating mechanism keeps saying, "Stay with the familiar, or else you'll feel like death."

So from here forward, I want you to become very aware of the negative feedback in your own system, as well as in your spouse, your friends, your family, and the people with whom you work. You know the signs, and you know what they mean. Be more cognizant of when *you* are out of your comfort zone, and when someone else is out of theirs. Without this information, you might think, "Why do they refuse to change? Why are they so stubborn? Why are they so awkward? Are they really that incompetent? Why do they resist my leadership? Don't they want to grow?"

"Good Enough for Me"

Where and when do you feel out of place? With what people? In which business situations? During social activities? Remember: It's the beliefs you've built with your own self-talk that regulate your comfort zones. "My dad was poor. I'll always be poor. That's the way I was raised." Then you'll probably stay poor, unless you learn how to visualize yourself on the next plateau. You might say, "No, I won't stay poor. I'll just gut it out." Go ahead—but you'll be walking a beam fifty stories high. "So what? I can make it." Maybe. But you can also trip and get killed, or die of the stress.

On the other hand, what could you do, what could your company do, what could your team do if you could turn on a dime and get to the next plateau *without* the stress? What could you accomplish if you were able to attack change like a kid looking forward to opening birthday gifts? That's the way you want it; you don't want to get thrown into the situation and have to gut it out, waiting for the tension to strike. You want to have a picture in your mind of what the new situation will look like before you get there. You can accomplish that through imagery, written affirmations, and visualization.

But first, you need to know exactly what you expect of yourself. You must ask this question: *"What is good enough for me?"* That applies to all aspects of your life—emotional, physical, moral, educational, financial. Let's say you're in sales and you "know" you earn $2000 a month. That's your picture of you. If you come in one month with $1900, and someone says, "How'd your month go?" you'll say, "Oh, about like me." But suppose you have an exceptional month and you make $3500. You feel good about making the extra money, but you also feel uneasy. Why? Because, your subconscious is saying, "This isn't like me. Making $3500 is too good for me." Just as when you golf too well, it's out of your comfort zone.

So, what happens? Your system corrects for the mistake. And what better way than to have you take that well-earned vacation: "Now I can take the next three weeks off and rest." See? That's your self-image keeping your average monthly earnings closer to your comfort zone. Because the first month back from vacation, you'll only make about $500. And you'll rationalize, "Well, I have ups and downs, peaks and valleys." It can work the other way, too. If you're a $2000-a-month person and you only make $500 the first three weeks, you'll come in at about $1500 the last week. You'll do it every time. The question is: Why don't you make $1500 *every* week? "Oh, that's not like me. It's too good for me. I'm only a $2000-a-month person."

It isn't that you *can't* make $1500 every week. It's just that, in your mind, it would be stretching what's "good enough for me." A friend might say, "Why not put in a little extra time and earn $3500 every month? It would help you pay bills and provide a little extra for a rainy day." You resist: "Who needs that kind of stress? Besides, I want to spend more time with my family." You think other people don't? "I want to have more free time for recreation." You think other people don't? "I'm concerned about my health." You think other people aren't? Watch how creative you get to stay inside your comfort zone.

You see, stress comes when you know you're a $2000-a-month person and you try hard to earn $3500. On the other hand, if you believe you belong at the $3500-a-month plateau, your system will create the motivation for you to make that every month—automatically, effortlessly, free-flowingly, without stress. Remember: We only get the stress when we try to be what we "know" we're not—in other words, when we try hard to exceed our self-image. So you can expand your comfort zone, and eliminate the stress, simply by altering, in your mind, what you believe is "good enough for me."

You ever work in a company that forced change on its employees without preparing them for the stress? In effect, the company says, "Stay there in the new situation until you get used to it. It'll be good for you." This could be in relation to a new work quota, a new administrative policy, a new merger, using new equipment. The company doesn't realize that people will correct for the mistake to get back to their comfort zones. If you want to see this in action, try moving the desk of an executive who's been there for a few years. Move the desk two feet to the left or right. It might make their job easier somehow or reduce the possibility of an accident. Doesn't matter. They're out of their comfort zone; they can't get their work done until they're back where they belong. See, two feet the other way was good enough for them.

Years ago, Diane and I escorted three Catholic nuns to a seminar in Portland. One was a philosophy professor at Seattle University, one the principal of a school in Alaska, one a second grade teacher in nearby Bellevue. I remember that the second grade teacher was never hungry. She wouldn't come with us into any nice restaurants. She'd say, "Oh, no thanks. I'll just get a sandwich later." On Saturday, the third day of the seminar, Diane took the three nuns window-shopping at some fashionable stores in a nice section of Portland. They paused to look at this one elaborate storefront, and then started to go inside. But the second grade teacher said, "No, I don't have time. I have to get back to the hotel." So they all went back.

At the hotel, Diane asked her, "Why wouldn't you go into that lovely store with us? And why wouldn't you eat in those restaurants?" You know what the nun said? "They were too nice for me.

I don't belong in places like that. I don't need to eat expensive food, and I don't need to wear those kinds of clothes." See? When we stick to our environmental comfort zones, we don't allow ourselves to go into situations which, in our own minds, are either not good enough or too good for us. Subliminally, we build a restrictive zone—*"This is good enough for me"*—and we don't go outside of our own nine dots. Remember: *We limit ourselves by the way we think. We must learn to think outside of our limitations.* It's like those people in Columbus' time who "knew" that the earth was flat. They believed if you went any further, you'd fall off the edge and die.

12

ENVIRONMENTAL COMFORT ZONE:

Leaving Mental Prison

Stay with the Familiar

Up till now, I've been talking mostly about the *internal comfort zone*—the mechanism in each of us that regulates our emotions, making us feel either safe or afraid, competent or inept, happy or sad, loving or cold, disappointed or satisfied, meek or strong, proud or ashamed, aggressive or shy, smart or dumb, open-minded or locked-on. We have internal comfort zones that define what's good enough for us emotionally, ethically, spiritually. In effect, they control our internal "reality."

But did you know that we also define "the way things are supposed to be" *externally*, too—in our environmental "reality"? We have an idea, recorded on the subconscious level, about the way our whole environment should look—whether we should live in the city or country, mountains or shore, desert or rain forest. We know what our apartment or home should look like—the color, the size, whether single-family dwelling or apartment complex, wood or brick, old or modern, expensive or practical. We have an idea of the store where we should buy our food, the kind of shops where we should buy our clothes, the kind of car we should drive. We also have a picture of the right neighborhood for us—urban or suburban, rich or poor, with tree-lined sidewalks or subway grills. We know what races, creeds, and colors our neighbors should be. We know what our work environment should be like—the location of the office, the interior design, how our own office should look.

Environmental comfort zones aren't right or wrong. But once you get the picture in your mind, whenever you're out of place for you, that's when the negative tension occurs. Have you ever been

134

far away from home for a while and told yourself, "I'm homesick"? You probably got very creative finding ways to leave. Even if that vaction resort or home-away-from-home was a lot nicer, more fun, more relaxing, you were still driven to get back home "where I belong." It's like throwing kids into kindergarten for the first time, and wondering why they don't want to stay. School is good for them— it can be fun, they can meet new friends, they can have exciting learning adventures. So why don't they want to stay? Well, think about it. Before coming to school, what is the child's environmental reality? It's the house they live in, the houses next door, the familar trees, neighbors, cats, and dogs. They're used to that environment; it's where they feel most comfortable, most confident, most assured.

If you yank them away from home and drop them, unprepared, into a strange brick school building—even though it might be a more comfortable, secure, beneficial environment—they'll feel so out of place, they'll get very creative to get back home: "Whoops, wrong place! Nothing looks familiar! Let me out of here!" So they grab onto your skirt or your pants. Failing that, they run outside and attach themselves permanently to the bumper of your car. They don't want to stay in the wrong restroom for very long. *Nobody* does.

But what if you use imagery and visualization to prepare them for the kindergarten environment ahead of time? You could paint a picture for them of what the school experience will be like: "The school is a red brick building a mile from home with two big playgrounds; your classroom is yellow and blue with lots of pictures on the walls; all your friends will be there; the teacher is helpful and nice; you get to play with animals; you get to learn to spell; you get cookies and milk; it'll be so much fun!" You keep painting the picture for the child, over and over, adding positive imagery each time, so they visualize the school experience with positive expectancy.

Pretty soon, you've expanded their comfort zone. Now they can't wait for the school bus to pick them up for their first day at the new fun place. What a difference from throwing them into a strange environment and making them stay there until they get used to it. Painting them into it ahead of time removes the stress, and helps them get used to the new—beforehand. When they finally go there for the first time, they feel *school* is where they belong. Now, they're out of place at *home*: "I go to school now. I'm too big to stay home." See? They're safely at the next plateau.

You might ask, "What happens if you don't prepare ahead of time, and you're out of your environmental comfort zone, and the tension hits to get you back where you belong—but you *can't* get back?" In that case, your subconscious will remind you to *"Stay with the familiar."* In other words: Re-create your familiar environment to relieve the negative stress. When the Dutch left Holland, and the English left England, and the French left France, they came to America where they were completely out of their environmental comfort zones. What did they do? They re-created their picture here. That's why we have New Holland, New England, New Hampshire, New York, New Orleans, New—. The negative tension feedback—"There's no one like me here."—was so powerful, it drove them to re-create their houses, their shops, their streets, their whole culture in order to feel more "at home."

Look at Little Havana in Miami. Anti-Castro Cubans who fled their homeland for Florida clustered together in Miami and re-created it. They hung signs: "Spanish spoken here." They renamed the streets the same as those in Havana. They ate Cuban food, played Cuban music, sold Cuban goods. See? *Stay with the familiar.* When you're out of place, you either get back to where you belong, or you re-create "the way things are supposed to be" right where you are.

Now, that's okay; that's the way we're built. Environmental comfort zones help us adapt to anything new. But they can also become mental prisons; they can put bars on your potential. They may keep you from venturing too far away from the familiar to experience the new. They might deter you from exploring new languages, new foods, new cultural traditions, or people of different races, colors, and creeds. It's like Americans who travel abroad and stay at the Hilton or the Holiday Inn. They aren't comfortable staying at the local inns or hotels; they need to feel they have a familiar "home" base.

The American military understands the concept of environmental comfort zone as restrictive zone. One U.S. Army barracks in America looks like every other U.S. Army barracks in Germany, or Korea, or anyplace else abroad. Why? Because the military knows that, when you transfer troops to a new environment, you don't put them fifty stories high. What you do is, you take thousands of young soldiers with their Army barracks comfort zones, and you drop them into Germany where virtually nothing is "the way things are supposed to be," and you re-create the barracks they had at Fort Dix or Fort Bragg or Fort Campbell or—. That relieves much of the negative stress in adjusting to a new environmental comfort zone. Then you sell them American products at duplicate PXs; feed them hamburgers, hotdogs, and beans, and provide American movies, newspapers, and magazines.

It's funny. They advertise, "Join the Service and See the World." But you know what many of those kids see over there for two years? The Fort Dix, or Fort Bragg, or Fort Campbell barracks! And they seldom leave the barracks. When they do, they travel in packs of ten, fifteen, twenty kids exactly like themselves, they don't go very far away, and they hustle right back. They tell each other, "*Hostile* out there! Man, they don't even speak *English*!" See? Fear of stretching comfort zones.

That's why some of us still cling to our old high school friends; why we won't leave our hometown; why we always listen to the same kind of music; why we return, again and again, to the same vacation spots. *Stay with the familiar.* No negative stress. But remember, if you want to fulfill your potential, if you want more excellence, more success, more variety, more experience in life, you must continually shift your picture of "the way things are supposed to be."

"Easy Time"

My warden friends tell me that it only takes about six to eight weeks to make a good convict in a federal prison. When they arrest someone who's used to being free, and then incarcerate them in an environment of armed guards, hostility, and fear, these new prisoners experience enormous pressure, tension, and stress. Their pictures don't match anymore. They're so far out of their comfort zone, they might as well be stranded on the moon.

Immediately, their subconscious goes to work to adjust the picture to their situation, so they can feel more comfortable. When prisoners are trapped in that confining, regimented environment, their pictures gradually change to "This is the way it's supposed to be *from now on.*" Once that occurs, they can do *"easy time."* But watch what happens when they're released back into society. They're so far out of their presently dominant comfort zone, and the stress is so overwhelming, they have difficulty adapting back again.

That's one reason there's such a high recidivism rate in our prison system. After a person's been imprisoned for several years, they're doing "easy time." If they're suddenly set free again—and if they don't know the techniques to change their comfort zones— they're so uptight being free, they get very creative finding ways to get back to where they belong. Even if it's a prison cell! They'll do the dumbest things to get back, like pulling stickups in their own home town—without a mask. Some return to prison so fast after release, their friends think they just went to the infirmary. Does that make sense? Have you ever seen what happens to an elderly person who's lived in the same house for forty years, but then suddenly must live in a rest home? That's tragically hard on them. Nothing's familiar; they're way beyond their environmental comfort zone with no way back. Without visualization techniques—without a kind of "simulator" preparation period—the stress of the new environmental reality could literally kill them.

If we don't make the change *inside* first—like the smoker who can't quit, the soldiers who rush back to the barracks, the convicts who return to jail—we'll slip back to our currently dominant picture. Good leadership knows why people resist change and growth. Outmoded leadership doesn't know; all they do is fix the blame on their people for not growing.

Remember the programs to help the undeveloped nations? Back in the 1960s, they had high ideals and unselfish motives, but apparently no understanding of environmental comfort zones. In many cases, they searched the world and found all these cultures where people weren't using their potential—and they decided to show them how. They said, "Let's go down there and shape 'em up. Let's teach 'em our language, our economic system, our agricultural and sanitation techniques." In other words, "Let's go yank these people out of their environmental comfort zones, throw 'em into the wrong restroom, and see if they can use their potential."

So they went down and "shaped 'em up"—according to *their* picture—and then they left those poor people on their own. Ten years later, they returned to see the fruits of their efforts. Why, those ungrateful wretches! They kept their animals in the *houses* that were built for them! They had their oxen pulling the *tractors!* What's the matter with those people? Don't they want to change? "Quite frankly, no. This is good enough for us."

Lasting change cannot be imposed from the outside. You can *temporarily* change the environment, but the moment you let go of the wheel, the boat starts turning back again. So how can we change our comfort zones? It's a matter of imprinting in our subconscious the image of the new before we ever get there. We must be able to visualize ourselves into the new situation before it's part of our "reality." Only then will we develop the creative energy to change. So, growing and changing will largely be a matter of properly setting goals, writing affirmations, and correctly visualizing your goals as though they were already accomplished.

Before I teach you those techniques, you must first decide what you want for yourself in the future. How do you want things to be for you tomorrow, next month, next year, in ten years, in twenty? I want you to start imagining now the way you want your community to look, what kind of family you want, what type of house you want, the income level that's good enough for you—all your major future goals. Then I'll teach you how to change on the subconscious level before you go after the goal. When you can do that, you will no longer be content with the old environment, living the same old way, staying only with the familiar.

Remember: The old way to try to change and grow is to grab yourself by the seat of the pants, throw yourself into something, and force yourself to stay there—in the new job, with the new friends, in the new environment—until you get used to it. But we now know that you don't need to feel tense and uptight, you don't need to be nervous and sick, you don't need to stay with the familiar. You can do "easy time" without gutting it out. Because you can learn how to take yourself out of your comfort zone *safely and deliberately.*

Deliberately venturing beyond your comfort zone stimulates within your system the creative tension and energy to resolve conflicts, accomplish new goals, expand comfort zones, and grow. I'll show you how to change the picture in your mind *before* you have the interview, *before* you have to shoot the free throw, *before* you have to start your new job, *before* you move into your new home—without feeling uptight.

139

Deliberately taking yourself out of your comfort zone is called *adventure*. I promise you: If you learn the techniques I'm about to explain, you will be able to create so much positive change in your life that adventure will become "the way things are supposed to be" for you from now on.

So stay with me. Adventure on the way.

13

"CREATIVE DISSONANCE":
Controlling the Chaos in Your Life

"Buyer's Remorse"

Sometimes, you and I resist change because we tend to feel awkward, uptight, a little uncomfortable. It doesn't matter if the changes would be good for us or not. It's the *difference* that causes the negative tension in our system which drives us back to "where we belong." But our creative subconscious has the amazing ability to transform that same negative tension into the positive energy we need to solve problems, resolve conflicts, make changes without stress, and accomplish our goals.

In 1957, a psychologist by the name of Leon Festinger termed this inner tension *"cognitive dissonance."* "Cognitive" means idea, attitude, opinion, belief. In other words, your perception of "the truth." "Dissonance" means discord, tension, disharmony. Festinger found that human beings experience cognitive dissonance—anger, irritation, stress—whenever we hold two conflicting ideas, attitudes, opinions, or beliefs in our mind at the same time. That's why, when you hold a strong belief about something and somebody presents you with an opposite view, you get upset. In other words, you knew it was an old lady and, all of a sudden, somebody showed you it was a young lady, and, geez, that upsets you. The dissonance really stings. That's your subconscious saying, "The pictures don't match!"

The point is, once we lock on to what we believe, we actually lock out evidence to the contrary—and it almost makes us feel crazy. We're always trying to prove to ourselves that we're right to believe what we believe. That's why you missed the word "FLY" when it was staring at you amidst arrows and combs. That's also why you can't find your keys once you tell yourself, "I can't find them.

142

They're *lost*." Once you believe that, you're not so much looking for your keys as you are trying—subconsciously—to prove you aren't crazy for believing they are lost. So *finding* the keys would cause you discomfort: "Geez, that annoys me." Because finding them would be contrary to your belief.

There are too many opposing "truths" to what we believe, so our creative subconscious protects us from getting constantly stung by the dissonance. It does that by building scotomas to information that doesn't match our present beliefs. Our creative subconscious says, "I'll help you. I'll keep you from feeling crazy. I'll blind you to your keys." It does this to anything that doesn't match. That way, we don't have to walk down the street every day saying, "Geez, that makes me mad!" "Boy, that gets me upset!" "Darn, that bothers me!" That would be too much dissonance.

According to principles in Gestalt psychology, human beings are always striving for order in their minds. Order, very simply, is when our *internal* picture of "the way things are supposed to be"—in our environment, our social life, our business life, our home life—matches the *external* picture we perceive through our senses. When we perceive disorder, our system creates energy to bring us back to "where we belong." In other words, when the pictures don't match, we have a problem: "This doesn't taste right." "That doesn't look right." "This doesn't sound right." "Something doesn't feel right to me."

The anticipation of that dissonance makes some of us reluctant to make decisions in life. Ever been around people who can't make up their mind? You go shopping with them and they say, "I'm gonna buy a new pair of shoes." And they ask the salesperson to show them every shoe in the store. Then they're overwhelmed with the choice: "I don't know which I like the best. There's too many to choose from." They just don't want to feel the wave of discomfort later when they decide, "Well, I made the wrong choice."

Why do you think some people are so reluctant to make decisions? *Cognitive dissonance.* Subconsciously, they ask themselves, "Will I feel crazy for making this decision?" These people experience a kind of pre-dissonance: "What if I make the wrong decision? I'll feel terrible!" Consequently, they need lots of reassurance; they don't like to make decisions on their own. But to be a good leader today, or a good executive, or to just make things happen for yourself, you must recognize that it's all right to make a decision, even if it turns out to be wrong. If you are wrong, sometimes it will hurt. But it's okay to make mistakes. You just take the dissonance, tell yourself, "That isn't like me," and move ahead. That's how to excel.

There's also something called post-dissonance. That's when you've made a decision to do something—to take a new job, buy a new coat, sell your washing machine—and then, later, you worry, "Did I do a smart thing?" Ever hear of "buyer's remorse?" Same thing as post-dissonance: "Was I right to have bought this thing? Was this the right decision?" Did you ever go looking for a new car? You made up your mind which car you wanted, paid the money, signed the papers—and the moment the car was yours, you asked yourself, "Was I crazy for buying this car? Was this an absurd decision?" We all ask that.

Let's say that you and a friend are looking for new cars. You're sizing them up and you say, "I don't like this one. It'll burn too much gas." And your friend says, "Ah, very perceptive of you." You come to another car and you say, "I don't like this one either. It won't have any re-sale value." Your friend says, "Oh, I'm glad you saw that." You both see "the truth"—until, finally, you decide exactly what you want. Once you've decided, your subconscious starts to alter your perception. For example, say you decide, "The best car for me to buy is a Volvo." That's your opinion, that's "the truth." And you put thousands of dollars into that "truth." After you buy the car, you feel "buyer's remorse": "Was I smart to buy this Volvo?"

Then you start driving down the road and, suddenly, you start seeing Volvos all over the place. "There's one! There's one! There's one!" They've always been there. You just didn't need to see them. Now that you've *bought* a Volvo—now that you've commited your belief to it—your mind manipulates your senses to feed you information that verifies your belief. Remember: you're really not searching for truth now. You're just trying, subconsciously, to verify your own opinions and beliefs.

Let's say your friend buys a Chevrolet. He drives down the road and he starts seeing Chevrolets everywhere—and they're probably all the same color. "There's one! There's one! There's one!" In other words, "Wasn't I smart for buying a Chevrolet? *Everybody's* got 'em, and they're all the same color as *mine*! Thank God, thank God, thank God." See?

Now, what happens when your friend keeps coming to visit you with his terrific new Chevrolet? Every time he comes over, he brags about his darned new car. He tells you what a great deal he got. He tells you how much fun the Chevy is to drive. But you automatically lock out—build a scotoma to—anything positive about your friend's new car. Why? Because good news about his Chevrolet makes you feel disturbed about having bought your Volvo. What would make you feel good? Anything *bad* about your friend's Chevrolet. So *that's* the information your subconscious lets through. You allow the bad to get through, but you screen out the good. It's like, "Hey, I read in the paper where they recalled a whole *bunch* of Chevrolets like yours! Heh-heh-heh. Darn the bad luck."

Why do you think there's a maid of honor and best man at weddings? To help kill the pre-dissonance. "Am I doing a smart thing?" the bride says. And the maid of honor says, "Oh, yes. It will be wonderful." After the wedding, comes the post-dissonance, the "buyer's remorse." "Did I do such a smart thing?" And did you ever wonder why the reception line comes *after* the wedding? It's like buying the Volvo or the Chevrolet. Everybody comes by and says, "Congratulations, you'll make a lovely couple." And your subconscious says, "Oh, thank God, thank God, thank God."

"Straighten Up the Mess!"

Here's the good news. When the pictures are out of line, that stimulates enough dissonance within us to resolve the conflict. Have you ever had the urge to straighten a painting hanging crookedly on the wall? That's a response to the dissonance: "That painting doesn't look the way it's supposed to look." Or let's say you have an idea of how your living room should look. You come home and it's a mess—popcorn on the floor, melted ice cream on the TV, a chair overturned. You think, "Geez, that upsets me!" Why? Because it doesn't look the way it's supposed to look. So now you become a manager: "Find the kid who did this!" And when you find the culprit who messed up your picture, you say, "I won't live this way. *Straighten up the mess!*" As soon as it's straightened up, order is restored and you can relax.

Then you walk into the kitchen—and it looks like a garbage pit! That really ticks you off; it doesn't look the way it's supposed to look. As you roll your eyes in disgust, you see a jam sandwich stuck on the ceiling: "That's not where a jam sandwich is supposed to be!" Again, your subconscious provides the energy and drive to *"Straighten up the mess*! Restore order! Get it back to the way it should be!" I term that energy and drive *"creative dissonance."* It's the fuel that propels us to solve problems, resolve conflicts, achieve goals.

Now watch this. You have the creative dissonance to straighten up the mess—but once order is restored, what happens to your creative energy and drive? Why don't you start repainting the kitchen? Why don't you put new doors on the cupboards? Why don't you install a new sink? "Because this is good enough for me." See, you have a picture in your mind of the quantity and quality of excellence *necessary for you.* When the picture outside matches the picture inside, it shuts off your creative dissonance. In other words, your motivation stops, and you can go to sleep.

Have you ever told your kids, "Wash the dishes?" What do they do? They go in, start washing, and come back out. Then you go in and check: "Hey! What about the *silverware*?" And they say, "You didn't *say* to wash the silverware. You said to wash the *dishes!*" That's how your creative subconscious works when you try to solve problems or achieve goals. It does only what you tell it to do—but nothing more. That's why, once we achieve a goal—once we *straighten up the mess* so it's good enough for us—we "flatten out" emotionally and lose our motivation. The subconscious burns all the necessary fuel; there isn't any need for creative dissonance to do anything more.

So how much power, drive, and energy can you get out of yourself to achieve a goal? Very little beyond the picture of excellence you hold in your mind. Suppose you're a professional football coach and, at summer practice, you decide that the team goal for the coming season will be "TO GET TO THE SUPER BOWL." And let's say the team adopts that goal and *gets* to the Super Bowl. How do you think they'll do in the Super Bowl *game*? Put it this way: What if their *opponent's* goal is "TO *WIN* THE SUPER BOWL?"

Who's likely to have more creative dissonance—more energy, drive, and motivation—to win that game?

Getting Used to It

There's another way we lose our creative dissonance: We allow ourselves to get used to something. Some people get used to having no money in their savings account. They tell themselves, "I can't save money yet. There isn't enough to live on. I'll save when I earn more money." So their subconscious causes them to earn only enough money for what they need *right now*. Remember: Your subconscious does only what you tell it to do; it delivers what you expect of yourself—but no more.

How much money do you give to charity? "Well, I don't give to charity. I can't afford it. Someday, when I'm rich, I'll give a lot to charity." Will you? First of all, if you maintain the picture of "I can't afford it," you won't allow yourself to be rich. That would almost make you feel crazy for believing "I can't afford it." Secondly, if you've assimilated "I don't give to charity" into your self-image, then once you've cashed your usual paycheck, you won't have enough creative dissonance left to clean the silverware. See what I mean? It's not part of the picture.

So, what have you allowed yourself to get used to? What's good enough for you? Have you ever worked especially hard to clean your house for company because "I don't want them to see me living in a mess like this?" You vacuum, dust, polish, sweep, scrub, repair, rearrange, and clean that place until it sparkles like new. In other words, you clean it better than your own picture of how it should be! The question is: Why aren't you living in a house that nice *all the time*? "Oh no, that's too nice for me. Don't expect me to keep it that clean all the time. This was a special, one-time occasion."

And isn't it great when the company leaves? Now you can relax and go back to what you're used to. You can go back to being yourself. It really takes work, struggle, and effort to try to maintain a level of excellence that's *beyond* your own picture. You get your house unusually clean, but the moment the company leaves, you let things slide back to the way they're supposed to be: "There. That's more like the way I *really* live."

Did you ever move into a new residence to find certain things aren't fixed the way you expected? You find closet doors stacked in the hall, and maybe a leak in the roof. At first, you're really upset: "Boy, that makes me mad. That should've been fixed last week." Later, you tell yourself, "Well, I'll fix it myself while I'm living here." But while you're living there, you keep looking at things as they are. Pretty soon, without realizing it, you let your subconscious get used to it. A few days later, the dissonance is gone, and you're doing "easy time" with closet doors stacked in the hall and a leaky roof. You've lost the motivation and drive to straighten up the mess. You've adjusted your inside picture to match your environment.

What happens when you get a dent in your new car? At first, it gets you angry: "That dent doesn't look right. I gotta get it repaired." But you keep putting it off. Day after day, you continue looking at the dent, until the inside picture starts to match the outside environment. At that point, your car could have *fifty* dents in it, and you wouldn't see them. *Because you can get used to anything.*

So what is goal-setting? It's deliberately deciding what you'll allow yourself to get used to. As you raise the level of your expectation and your standards of personal excellence, you become increasingly discontent with the status quo. What was good enough for you last year will no longer satisfy you today: "That's not the way things are supposed to be. *Straighten up the mess!*" On the other hand, if you allow closet doors to stay stacked in the hall and you let the roof leak, you'll tolerate it, get used to it, and lose the motivation to change it. In fact, very soon you won't see the mess anymore.

One time, when I returned home from Cleveland, Diane was waiting for me with some company in the living room. When I came in, she gave me a glass of wine, and we sat in front of the fire. I started to sip my wine—and I almost spit it all over the company. I'd glanced at the floor and noticed that someone had charcoal-broiled a huge black *hole* in our rug! I didn't want to make a fuss in front of everybody, so I asked Diane if I could see her in the hall. We got out there and I said, "What the heck happened to our rug?" She said, "Didn't I tell you when you called?" Then she explained that the man who'd cleaned our fireplace the previous night didn't have a metal bucket for the ashes on the hearth. So he swept them into a plastic bucket, and the cinders burned through the plastic and seared a hole in the rug. She said, "But I called the carpet store and they said they would repair it tomorrow."

I thought, "Ah, good," because now I could see a resolution to the conflict. But I still couldn't sit there and sip my wine and look at that ugly black hole. So Diane got this tiny Oriental throw rug, brought it in, and placed it over the hole. How come? You know that old saying, "Out of sight, out of mind"? Well, she was helping me build a scotoma to the blemish. If you can't see the blemish, you still have a picture of order in your mind, and you can start getting used to the status quo. Keep in mind, we could've left that nice little throw rug there forever. Nobody would've known, except the company, Diane, and me.

The next day, I came home fully expecting to see the hole repaired. But the throw rug was still covering it. Made me madder than the dickens. I said, "Diane, I thought it was going to be fixed." She said, "So did I. But the man from the store called and said he couldn't do it today. He promised he'd fix it tomorrow." Now, Diane *always* says, "They'll fix it tomorrow." Why? Because it shuts me up. It closes down my creative dissonance to clean up the mess because I see a solution coming. Unless you allow yourself the feedback—unless you look at the *truth*—you'll never make the change.

The third day, I came home anticipating the repair. The darn hole was *still* there. But it didn't bother me nearly as much on the third day. Why not? Because I'd gotten used to the throw rug covering the blemish. If we can't change the environment to match our inner picture of what it should look like, then our picture will automatically change to match the environment. That way, order is restored, the creative dissonance stops, and we feel sane again.

We all do that, from time to time, in our emotional lives. Say you marry a wonderful person. Things are fine until your spouse starts yelling and screaming at you. At first, it annoys you; then you don't like it that much, but you expect it to pass; then you try to ignore it; pretty soon you lose your motivation to fix it. This also happens in the quality and quantity of excellence you get used to in your social life, your business life, your financial life, even with your health: "I felt dizzy every day this week. It's probably nothing. I'll go to the doctor next week." You allow yourself to tolerate the blemish, and you lose the drive to fix it. In other words, you get used to the hole in the carpet.

Did you ever know anybody who wouldn't bother to look at the truth? Ever know anybody who always wants to lose weight, but won't ever step on the scale? It takes the difference between the vision that you *want* and the reality of things *as they are* to cause you to create the energy to get the best out of yourself. My point to you is: What have you allowed yourself to get used to? You can allow yourself to get used to being in debt. You can allow yourself to get used to having no money in the bank. On the other hand, can you see yourself getting used to being $12,000 to the good? Can you imagine waking up and looking at your bank account and being down to only $75,000, and wondering who burned a hole in the carpet? Some people do that with a *million* dollars.

Remember: *Goal-setting is deliberately deciding what you'll allow yourself to get used to.* You are a very powerful person. You can learn how to use visualization to imprint the new picture of what you're willing to get used to into your consciousness first, so it can stimulate the creative dissonance you need to straighten up the mess. You make yourself discontent with the way things *are* by changing the way you *want* things to be in your mind. "How do you keep them down on the farm once they've seen Paris?" Remember that song? The answer is you can't. They don't want to stay on the farm anymore. Once they get used to the new, there's no way they'll stay with the old.

So where do you want to grow? As a person, wherever it is you want to grow, you've got to make yourself discontent with the present by visualizing the new. How much money is good enough for you? What quantity and quality of product service is good enough for your company? What kind of relationship with your parents is good enough for you? How much abuse do you take in your marriage before you decide, "This just isn't good enough"? You have the ability to create and accomplish almost anything. What stops you is that you allow your creative dissonance to shut off. But if you control it through imagery, you can boost yourself to any new plateau you choose.

Making the Extraordinary Ordinary

Some people say, "Thank goodness Christmas only comes once a year." Why? Because: "Wouldn't it be hard if I had to be this nice *all year 'round?"* If that's your picture, the answer is, "Yes, it *would* be hard. It would be extraordinary." On the other hand, suppose you saw yourself as an extraordinarily giving person. Suppose you repeatedly affirmed with your own self-talk, "I'm a very giving person. I enjoy giving of myself every day because I love feeling like every day is Christmas." Once that goal is burned into your subconscious, here comes the creative dissonance you need to be a giving person *all year 'round.*

That's what affirmations, visualization, and deliberate goal-setting do. What I've learned to do—and this is what I'm leading you to—is take the unusual, the special, the extraordinary, and assimilate it into my subconscious so it becomes usual, automatic, ordinary. I take a look at all the special occasions, all the exciting travel, all the adventurous styles of life that I once considered extraordinary and too hard to keep up, and I imprint them into my subconscious as if it were Christmas every day. Then *that's* what I get used to.

Let me give you an example of how Diane and I use this knowledge in fun ways to lift our lives to higher plateaus just by the way that we think. A few years ago, I decided that Diane and I should have a party on September 3 to celebrate our wedding anniversary. On past anniversaries, we'd had very nice parties with excellent entertainment—like famous country-western singer, Hoyt Axton. And we always invited a lot of people because that's what we'd allowed ourselves to get used to. But we hadn't decided on anything yet; all we started with was, "Let's have a party on September 3."

I asked Diane, "Well, what kind of party should we have?" She said, "I don't know. Let's just keep adding to it as we think about what we want." I said, "Okay. Why don't we invite Hoyt Axton again? He was terrific last year. Everybody loved him." We agreed and said, "Okay, what else?" And we quickly decided, "We'll invite our special friends and family members." Then we said, "Well, as long as we just moved into our new ranch in the Methow Valley, why don't we have the party there?" That sounded right. Sometime later, I thought, "Hey, won't our marketers and sales people from around the nation be up at the ranch about that time for our annual meeting? Let's invite *them* to the party." About a week later, we thought, "Why don't we invite a lot of our friends and neighbors in the valley?" And we just kept repeating, affirming, clarifying, and adding to the party. We didn't know *how* we would accommodate all those people with room, board, and events. But we knew the *what* comes first, and then you figure out the how.

Soon, we came up with, "As long as we're inviting the people in the valley, let's put up a frontier village, and some teepees, and have musket-shooting demonstrations. And let's invite people from the community to bring their pottery, their art works, and their handmade clothes, and they can sell them there." Then we figured, "As long as we're going to do that, we might as well have a big dinner." And we agreed we would roast a pig. Then we said, "No, better have two pigs." Then we said, "We better put some turkeys inside the pigs." Adding to our picture of the party.

Remember, we didn't start off with all that. We started off with just one affirmation: "We're going to have a party September 3." So then we thought, "Why not have some games and events, and give away prizes?" Great! We decided to have tee shirts with "TICE RANCH DAYS" printed on them, so we could give some away as prizes and put the rest up for sale. Then we figured, "Well, if the community shows up, let's have them all to dinner. So we agreed, "Better get a dozen kegs of beer and pop." I said, "Some of our guests will be there overnight. Let's have a nice breakfast for them."

Finally, we ended up with about 1500 people, 18 kegs of beer, teepees, horses, covered wagons, mule rides, musket shooting, wine, roasted pigs, chili, and popcorn wagons, Hoyt Axton, community singers—and a two-day family "happening." But all we started with was, "I think we'll have a party." The point is, we planned, we affirmed, we visualized, and ultimately had the type of party that we would have originally considered to be extraordinary—especially for an "ordinary" anniversary celebration. Yet, in our minds, as we repeatedly affirmed and visualized its reality, that extraordinary party became ordinary for us. And that's what you want to do when you set your goals. Keep assimilating the extraordinary so it becomes what's ordinary *for you.*

It isn't just wishful thinking. It isn't just having positive thoughts; it isn't just hoping that, some day, the Fairy Godmother will zap you with a wand and transform you from a frog into a prince or princess. What you must do is change your inner image of "reality" first. Remember: *All meaningful and lasting change starts first on the inside, and works its way out.* It does not start on the outside and work its way in.

That's how TV commercials work. Millions of dollars are spent on producing imagery to get you so discontent with the old, that you feel the dissonance to buy the new. In a good car commercial, the camera slides you behind the wheel so you can visualize vividly what it would feel like if you were driving this elegant, sleek new car. If the imagery is repeated often enough, your subconscious won't know the difference between *pretending* that you're driving the car, and actually driving it. It will record your vision as if it's real. And then, like walking from tee to tee on the golf course, thinking about the slice in your swing, you'll drive that car a hundred more times in your mind. Pretty soon, you'll have a new internal image of "reality"—a new picture of the kind of car that's "good enough for me."

You might say, "But there's no motivation to actually go out and buy one of those cars." That's right, there isn't. Until you compare your *new* image of "reality"—the elegant, sleek new car—with your *old* image of "reality"—your "ugly," "crummy," "falling-apart," last year's model. Once you compare the image of the new with the image of the old, you throw your system out of order and you become discontent with the old. Anything except the sleek, elegant new car that you visualized will almost drive you nuts.

That's the energy of creative dissonance propelling you toward the new. The longer you struggle with the stress of staying with the old, the longer you'll feel like you're fifty stories high. And your subconscious will keep hammering, *"Straighten up the mess!"* Eventually, you will invent a way to get the new. You'll rationalize, "Well, with the money I save from the new tires I'll need to buy next year, and with the better gas mileage, and the better resale value of the new car, it'll pay for itself. In fact, I'd be stupid *not* to buy it!" See how it works?

So I'm going to teach you how to mentally paint your own commercials. From now on, goal-setting will be a matter of deliberately throwing your system out of order to stimulate the creative dissonance energy you need to resolve the conflict or achieve the goal. But you must imprint the vision of the new into your subconscious so vividly that it is stronger than the way things presently are. The vision must be strong enough so you absolutely can't stand the "old car" anymore. If it isn't strong enough, you'll start smoking again, you'll take out your bad golf ball, you'll eat the whole cake. In other words, you'll return to your currently dominant picture of you.

It's going to take a lot of fortitude, a lot of self-esteem, and a lot more knowledge to change your picture because the process takes time. It's like prenatal development of an embryo. You see no evidence at first, and yet that infant is growing. In goal-setting, when you use imprinting, affirmations, and visualizations, it can take a few days, a few weeks, or even a few months for your picture to change. It's like preparing those kids for kindergarten. You start talking about it months in advance, not the day before. You get the kids to visualize the kindergarten environment so vividly, they start to feel as though they've already been there. Then you can't keep them home. That's how you will feel when you goal-set properly: "I've *been* there. This goal is *mine.*"

No Back Door

Current reality is the key to helping you realize your visions and achieve your goals. It's the combination of looking squarely at current reality (the way things are right now) and holding a vivid mental picture of your goal that stimulates the creative dissonance energy you need. Some people will set a vision or a goal, and then build a scotoma to current reality. Then they'll wonder why they aren't getting there. They won't look at the *real* score of the game; they won't check the chart to see how their sales are *really* going; they won't step on the scale to see their *real* weight. "Don't tell me the truth. It stings too much." Just like when I saw my beautiful carpet charcoal-broiled: "Geez, that makes me mad!" I had to look at the burned carpet to feel the dissonance sting.

So we must be aware that once we set a vision of how we'd *like* things to be, and we look squarely at the way they really *are*, we're going to experience the sting of negative feedback—the sense of incompletion or contradiction. And, quite frankly, that's a big reason why most people are reluctant to venture out of their comfort zone to change. When you're in the wrong restroom, the feedback makes you feel like throwing up. What does a manager, trainer, mother, coach do? They give us feedback: "You're not hitting your goal." We might say, "Boy, you're negative." Why would we say that? Because every time someone gives us information contrary to what we believe, we feel like throwing up. So people get labeled "negative" for giving you the feedback. But keep in mind that feedback isn't necessarily negative. It's just opposite "truth." Without seeing the opposite "truth," there is no dissonance. And without the dissonance to create motivation, energy, and drive, you're merely wishing for things without aggressively going after them.

What happens if you set a goal and you don't get it? You feel uptight, you want to throw up, you can't sleep, you can't face people. "Well geez, I don't want to feel that way." Fine—then don't set any goals. If you do set a goal, go get it. If you don't get it now, get it the next time. You've heard people say, "Be happy with what you have, dear. That's good enough for you. If you start wanting things you don't have, you'll just make yourself sick. I only tell you this because I love you." In other words, "Don't bite off more than you can chew. Don't reach beyond your grasp." People say this to their children to protect them from getting hurt. They won't allow them to set their vision far enough away to make a change because, "My gosh, if they don't succeed, they won't be able to handle the disappointment."

That's why it's essential to control your self-talk through positive affirmations about your goal, and stay on course. This isn't magic; it takes concentrated effort. But you can do it—if you have the guts to take the heat and stand the sting. You must tell yourself you are absolutely committed to achieving your goal. People say, "Let's not get married. Let's just live together in case it doesn't work out." When they feel the slightest dissonance, they break up and say, "It's a good thing we didn't get married." But remember: *We move toward, and we become like, that which we think about.* If you do get married, you're fully committed because there are no easy "outs." When the dissonance hits, instead of giving up on the goal, you will most likely work at straightening up the mess. That's the way you must be when you set your goals: *No "outs," no back door.*

Before I teach you how to visualize, I want to re-emphasize one key fact: Once you arrive at your goal, you "flatten out" and lose your drive and motivation. So you're at your best when you have "a problem." But let's not call it a problem; let's call it a challenge. Let's say we've got challenges to improve ourselves. But once you run out of those challenges, your system shuts down. Some people can't take the stress of challenges. They set their goals so close that they can't feel the sting of the creative dissonance. If you set goals that are too easy to attain, you won't grow very much. Say a youngster sets a goal to get out of school. Once they're out, they can't find a job. That's like, "Well, you didn't *say* to wash the silverware. You only said to wash the *dishes!*" Remember that? Same thing. Some people set a goal to get to college. Once they make it, they can't study effectively. Why? Because their goal was only to *get* to the Super Bowl, not to *win* it. Their creative dissonance shut off.

What happens if a parent sets a goal to see the kids grown and out of the house—and then the kids finally leave? The parent stagnates, gets depressed, loses energy and motivation. And they wonder, "What's the matter with me?" What about someone who goalsets to get hired by a company? They connive and invent and dress well and act bright to get the job. Then they're hired, but the company can't get them to work. What was their goal? To get *hired*. After that, it's "I *did* it. Now I can relax." See how we trap ourselves by setting our goals too short?

"Through, Not Up To"

Ever hear of "The Peter Principle"? It suggests that people tend to reach the highest level of their incompetence. In other words, when our pictures match, we lose our motivation to excel and achieve. Everybody does. We have boundless creativity, drive, energy, and competence as long as we have a conflict. But when we resolve the conflict, we shut right down. Years ago, I used to teach a three-and-a-half day seminar every month. My goal was to just get through that seminar and get home. One time, my second-grader, Nancy, won a poster contest at her school with her drawing of what her dad did for a living. I went to school to receive the award with her. You know what the drawing was? Honest to God—*her dad asleep on the couch!* "What does your dad do?" "He sleeps on the couch." That was her picture of her old man. Because, at the time, my only goal was to get home and crash. When I saw Nancy's drawing, I realized that if I wanted to have dinner with my family, and enjoy them after dinner, I had to learn how to goal-set *through* getting home, not just *up to* it. That kind of goal-setting—"*through, not up to*"—has become a style of life for me today.

Do you know anybody who goal-sets through their work week? They get up on the weekend and they can't get out of the house. They can't even get up to get a snack: "Bring me a sandwich. I'm too exhausted. I don't know what it is. I must be working too hard." Their goal was to get *to* the weekend, not *through* it. Once they get there, their creative dissonance runs out. I once worked with this large airplane manufacturing company on the east coast, and they told me they gave their retiring executives ninety percent of their last three years' salary averaged out monthly for their retirement fund. I said, "My goodness, that must cost you a great deal." They said, "No. We know we'll only need to make about sixteen payments." You see, when you goal-set to retire, and you neglect to set new goals, you may die very soon afterwards. You don't need to go into the same line of work, but you must set bigger and better goals than "I want to retire and just do nothing." Remember Bear Bryant, the legendary Alabama football coach? He died less than a month after his retirement. That man was notorious for his boundless energy and drive right to the end of his long career—but he apparently had nothing left after football.

The same can happen to you and me. Goal-setting is so powerful. You must learn to create and endure the creative dissonance, and ride it to higher plateaus of happiness, excellence, and success. You must continually use the principles I'm going to teach you to create innovative, dynamic new goals for yourself. You have a tremendous capacity for creative resolution of conflicts. You have a tremendous capacity for motivation to excel and improve. You have a tremendous capacity for positive energy and drive. You can achieve what you want, if you accept the accountability to go out and accomplish it. In these final chapters, I'm going to give you all the tools you need to make that happen.

14

SELF-ESTEEM AND PERFORMANCE:

Archie Bunker or Elite Commando?

"Credit Where Credit Is Due"

It's fine to understand how you can use creative dissonance to help you solve problems and achieve goals—if you're tough enough to take the heat. But what if you lack the self-assurance to *try*? A lot of us have felt devalued, insignificant, powerless to control what happens to us. If you feel that way, you'll find it difficult to reach the next plateau because you think, "I can't make it. I'm no good. I don't have what it takes."

Self-esteem is what it takes—and you can improve that the same way you can improve your self-image: through your own self-talk. Remember when I said, *"We limit ourselves by the way that we think"*? Well, if your attitude about yourself is devaluative and limiting—"I'm not smart enough." "I can't do anything really well." "No one would like me if they really knew me." —then you limit your ability to change and grow. Remember the attitudinal balance scale, and the premise that *we move toward, and become like, that which we think about*? Well, if we dwell on being powerless and insignificant, our subconscious—the perfect servant—says, "Okay, whatever you say." It adds heavy weight to your negative bucket, so you start leaning toward—what? A negative, locked-on, limiting view of yourself as ineffective and powerless. On the other hand, what do high-performance people think about themselves? How do they feel about themselves? What are they leaning toward?

High-performance people have high self-esteem. What *is* that? Self-esteem is your confidence, satisfaction, and respect for yourself. It's how *good* you feel about being you; it's your positive feeling of

160

dignity and worth. And it affects what you can achieve. We find that the better we feel about ourselves, the better we perform and behave. So you can talk yourself into being very positive, strong, firm, committed, powerful, assured. You can talk yourself into taking risks, trying new adventures, learning new skills, extending yourself to new people, and new places. In fact, everything you do corresponds to your self-esteem.

Remember when I said we all start off life with empty attitudinal buckets, and that our own self-talk starts filling the positive and negative buckets until we lean one way or the other? Well, when we were young, we may have run into negative wizards who loaded us down with heavy negative weights. We didn't know any better, so we accepted the weights and started leaning toward the negative. Some people—like some of my adopted children—were raised by parents who had low self-esteem themselves, which caused them to chip away their children's self-respect and self-worth. The children then blocked themselves with careless, negative self-talk simply because they believed the observations of someone else.

If you continue that pattern into adulthood, you find it very difficult to elevate your self-esteem, because you don't respect your own opinion. To elevate your opinion, you think you need the applause, approval, and compliments of someone else: "Please tell me: Do I look all right?" "Please tell me: Do you think I can get that job?" "Please tell me: Am I doing the right thing?" You'll sanction someone else to give you the go-ahead to change and grow, which damages your self-image: "I know I'm not my own person." Whereas if you have high self-esteem, you respect your own opinion as equal to anyone else's, and you do not need the approval of others.

So let's talk about what takes self-esteem away and what enhances it. One problem is that some of us have developed a mistaken idea about humility. Many of us were raised to believe psychologically, religiously, socially, educationally, even athletically, that thinking well of ourselves is wrong. We were taught, "Don't get a swelled head. Nobody likes a braggart." In other words, "If you start thinking you're too good, I'll point out a hundred things that are wrong with you." It's like, "Daddy, I did good in baseball today! I got a hit!" "What did you do the *other* times you were up, son?" "I struck out once and walked once and—" "Well, that's not as good as Joe DiMaggio. And I saw Babe Ruth play, too, you know." In the kid's mind, his dad is really saying, "Someday, kid, you might be good. But right now, you aren't worth a darn."

As a result, we might have a tendency to reject what's good in ourselves. Keep in mind that the subconscious is a literal recording device. If you think, "Oh, I'm no good," it can't decipher your spirit of intent. It doesn't question: "Well, are you kidding or serious?" Your subconscious doesn't know you mean *only right now* and *only in baseball*. It accepts literally whatever you affirm, and then *interprets* it. It could record this affirmation to mean, "I'm lousy in everything, forever and ever, Amen." The good side of that coin is that we know that when we excel at any one thing, it tends to improve our performance in all other areas. Our subconscious picks up the *positive* message, too.

Now, humility doesn't mean, "Think less of yourself." It means "truth." To high-performance people, humility simply means *"Credit where credit is due."* If somebody helped you to succeed, give them credit. If you succeeded with the help of God, give credit to God. If you succeed on your own, give *yourself* credit. If you elevate your self-esteem through your own self-talk, your performance in life will follow. The opposite brings the opposite.

Not too long ago, I was working with the staff in a federal penitentiary, and I met this young man of about twenty who had been behind bars for a long time, but who was scheduled to be released. I asked him, "What kind of job will you get?" He said, *"Anything."* In his mind, he was saying, "I've been in prison. I'm a bad person. I don't deserve a good job." It was as if I'd asked him, "What's good enough for you?" So then I said, "How much do you think you ought to get paid?" Honest to God, he said, *"Whatever."* See what I mean? He'd been beaten down, psychologically, by so many people throughout his life, and for so long in prison, he'd lost his own self-worth. So he told himself, "Whatever people are willing to pay me is all I deserve." This applies to everyone, because we are all drawn to the jobs and incomes and opportunities that, in our minds, we've allowed ourselves to get used to.

Then I said to this kid, "You'll probably be looking for a car to get around in, right?" He said, "Yeah, probably." I said, "What kind of car?" He said, "Just some wheels." In other words, "Any old junker is good enough for me." Do you see what can happen when you have a diminished sense of self-esteem? *Anything* will be good enough. Then I said, "Some day, you'll want to find a girl and get married, won't you?" He said, "I suppose so." I said, "What kind of a girl are you hoping to find?" You can guess his answer. He said, *"Anything."* It's sad and tragic. Because what kind of girl would most likely be drawn to him? A girl looking for "anything," too.

We draw ourselves to the relationships, the jobs, the incomes, the material goods that we feel worthy of receiving. Not *consciously*; I'm talking about our subconscious self-image behind our self-esteem. That's why it's going to be so important that you continually work at building your self-esteem, and building your children's self-esteem. You must continually upgrade their self-talk, too, by telling them, "You're a good person," "You're a brave swimmer," "You're really nice to your sister," "You're smart." But beware. They will go out to the playground and the streets, and somebody else will tell them they aren't worth anything, and they might get careless with their self-talk: "They're right. I'm not worth very much." Be aware that other people will try to take away their heart, their brains, and their guts. You must stay strong and constructive, and continue to bolster their self-esteem. Of course, to do that, you will need to build high self-esteem in yourself.

Archie Bunker Self-Esteem

People with low self-esteem are frightened of change and risk. They wait for somebody else to step out first, and then maybe they'll follow their footsteps. Diane and I have traveled to some of the world's finest resorts, and we used to observe the youngsters there. We'd never see the high self-esteem kids. They'd be out having fun, taking adventures, meeting new friends. The low self-esteem kids would spend days sitting in front of the television. Their parents would say, "Why don't you go to the pool and meet some of the other kids?" "No, I can't. I have to watch this program." "Why do you have to watch that program? You're in a different country." "Because I have to." "Why won't you go out and meet some new people?" "I don't want to."

Those kids are thinking, "Who would want to play with me? Nobody likes me at home, so who would want to be my friend here?" Even if they want to meet new friends, they think, "I can't.

My self-esteem is so soft that one more blow will kill me. If I go out and you tell me I'm not worthy, I can't take the hit. So I'll stay here and protect myself." You'll find people in your companies, in your offices, on your teams, who think and act like that. They say, "I could've taken on that other company, but I didn't want to. They aren't worth my time." "I could've told the boss about the new product, but I didn't want to. She wouldn't've cared." "I could've played with that team on the weekend, but I didn't want to. They're a lousy team."

You ever hear that stuff? *"I don't want to."* The real reason—and they won't say this out loud—is, "I'm frightened to death." So instead, you may see them criticizing those who *do* take risks and try the new. That's because people with low self-esteem are threatened by people with high self-esteem. They need to rip and tear at them to put them in their place. And where is that? *"Below me!"*

Prison is full of low self-esteem people. Out in the yard, at meals, even in the cell blocks, they rip and tear and devalue. You never hear a good word said about anybody. Do you know what the life expectancy of a child molester is inside a maximum security penitentiary in America? Not very long. If they're not in protective custody, someone will try to kill them. When they succeed, everybody struts around thinking, "Look at the noble thing we did. We rid the earth of this scum." But do you think they did it for the enoblement of mankind? No. The prison population has selected child molesters as the scum of the earth in order to elevate their own self-esteem. They're so down on themselves, they have to find *someone* to squash. The child molester fills that role: "Rape's okay with us. Murder's fine. But child molesting? The *worst!*" So they kill child molesters almost as soon as they walk through the gates, and they tell themselves, "Look at the noble thing we did."

So if you have low self-esteem, you look for somebody else to squash. A husband with low self-esteem can't stand to have a wife who thinks highly of herself. If she has a job that he considers better than his, he might comment to her, "You'll never hold that job. You can't even organize the house." In other words, "Get back down where you belong." Parents with low self-esteem won't allow their children to rise above them. They'll say to their child, "What makes you think you're so good? You can't even do your chores right at home." Low self-esteem managers are threatened by employees with high self-esteem. They become the most fault-finding, sarcastic, belittling, angry managers to work for. Teachers with low self-esteem won't let kids in their classroom think better of themselves than they do of the teacher: "Don't be a 'Know-It-All.' If I need your help, I'll ask for it."

Did you ever watch Archie Bunker on "All in the Family"? Great example of low self-esteem. Edith, "Meathead," Gloria, the blacks, the Catholics, the Jews, the Poles, the Republicans, the Democrats, teachers, lawyers, doctors, cops—everybody caught it from Archie Bunker. Nobody could do anything right, except him. He was really telling everyone, "Get back down where you belong." "Where's that?" "*Below me.*" So it's important to be cognizant of conditions in your family, at your job, in your relationships, in your community. Because the self-esteem of those around you can also have a profound effect on you.

"Send Me Anywhere!"

If you have high self-esteem, you're not afraid to take risks. It takes high self-esteem to get out of your comfort zone, and to attack life as though it's an *adventure*. If someone tells a high self-esteem person, "You can't do it. You don't have the skill." They'll respond, "I'm good enough to learn it." "Maybe, but you've never done it before." "It'll be fun learning how." "Maybe, but look at the competition." "I didn't even think about the competition. I don't need to."

High self-esteem people don't consider situations as "risks." They think they can handle anything, an attitude that helps them build scotomas to risk. In doing some research on high-performance thinking, I had the opportunity to spend time with some of America's elite commandos. I helped debrief some of them when they came back to the United States from the Vietnam war. They were in the same kind of elite strike force as the Israeli commandos who raided Entebbe to save hostages from a hijacked airliner; the same kind of commandos as those in the SAS of Great Britain who scaled an embassy wall, crashed through the windows, and rescued hostages as though they were simply going out to dinner. The question I was interested in was, "How do they *think*?"

Finding out how these people were trained was an "I'll be darned!" revelation to me. Before that, my concept of military training was people going in the Service and being bullied, belittled, embarrassed, demeaned. In fact, that's the way I used to coach football. I'd run my players down, tell them how wimpy and cowardly they were, hoping to motivate them—and then I'd say, "Now go out and win!" I'd humiliate them all week, and then on Saturday, they'd go out and perform in the game like the humiliated wimps they *believed* they were. That was the kind of team self-esteem I'd inspired.

At that time, I was totally ignorant of how to train high-performance people. When I dealt with our commandos, I found out for the first time that when they're in training, no one ever devalues, criticizes negatively, belittles, or demeans them. Their goal is to elevate self-esteem in the individual and in the group. So they instill pride, worthiness, excellence, capability, and success. To these commandos, no assignment is too tough. They think they can do anything they're asked to do. I discovered that because of their exceptionally positive training, these elite commandos were willing to take risks commensurate with their high self-esteem. In other words, the better they felt about themselves, the more likely they were to attack hell with a bucket of water.

As a result of their training, elite commandos come to expect the highest performance out of their equipment, the utmost support from their staff, and continual success from themselves. They have the self-assurance and high self-esteem of royalty: "I am the best." It makes sense, doesn't it? You know why children of royalty are treated royally? Because some day, they'll be king or queen. Can you imagine raising a future king or queen, and running them down, telling them how unworthy they are, and then saying, "Go out and act like royalty"? It doesn't work that way. That's why the people around those commandos are constantly putting them up, positively affirming and re-affirming, "You are the world's finest. You've got what it takes." So these people think, "I can do anything. Send me anywhere!"

This may give you an idea of how to treat your spouse, your children, your employees, your teammates. Think about it: Are your people treated like wimps or like elite commandos? Do they expect excellence from themselves? Are they willing to take risks? Whom do you surround yourself with—people with high self-esteem or people whose self-esteem is lower than yours? Does your family or your company have a "Flat World Mentality of the Greatest Magnitude"? Or do they think, "I can do anything"? Do they believe they're outer-directed and dependent on "lucky breaks," or do they attack conflicts and problems like elite commandos?

The way to go is to raise your self-esteem, and then allow the people around you to have high self-esteem as well. You do that through controlling your own self-talk, as well as the way you talk to others. You must look for ways to put yourself up with your self-talk, and ways to catch your people in the act of doing things right. From here forward, you must tell them, "Hey, you're really good. You're one of the best. I like the way you do things." By positively affirming, you become a powerful, significant, positive wizard to the people around you.

But you start first by elevating your own self-esteem. That is a *must*. The rest of this goal-setting stuff isn't worth anything without that. So let me conclude this chapter with a little story that illustrates why elevating your self-esteem must be a continual project throughout your life. Several years ago, I was selected to address a prestigious, high-powered group called the "Young Presidents Organization." To belong, you have to be either a president or owner of a corporation that does millions of dollars worth of business before you're forty. By the time you're fifty, you're out of the club.

The various chapters of the "Young Presidents Organization" get together all over the world to seek out the best people in business, in politics, in economics, in banking, and so on, to regularly update themselves with cutting-edge information. They meet for a week at a time in exotic locations, bringing in the best resources in the world. I happened to be selected as one of those resources to come to their conference in Madrid, Spain to talk about "Human Potential."

To give you an idea of the magnitude of the other speakers who came to the meeting, they had, among others, Henry Kissinger, King Juan Carlos of Spain, and Father Hesburgh, the former president of Notre Dame. And the 1500 members who came to the meeting could choose whom they wanted to hear. So here I was, a former high school coach from Seattle, among all these internationally known speakers, wondering, "Will anybody show up to hear *me* talk?" Which was not exactly a boost to my self-esteem.

I was scheduled to deliver four talks of an hour-and-a-half each on four afternoons—Monday, Tuesday, Thursday, Friday. I told myself, "The best time would have been in the morning." I was thinking, "After a big lunch and maybe a glass or two of wine, people might get sleepy." Already, I was thinking negatively and diminishing my self-confidence. On Monday, three hundred people arrived to hear my first talk, which surprised me. The organization had arranged to televise the talk, so there were hot lights in a stuffy room, and I noticed that some people did fall asleep. I started to develop a negative picture, so I tried to bolster my self-esteem by telling myself, "That has nothing to do with your talk. It's the lights, the food, the wine. . ."

I taught as hard as I could teach, but something still didn't feel right. I just didn't think people should be that drowsy. The next day, I had the biggest room—it accommodated more than three thousand people—but only about two hundred showed up. "Only" two hundred, of course, was my negative perception, because I kept telling myself, "There should have been a lot *more*." Again, I taught as well as I could teach. But it still didn't feel right because, as I talked, I kept noticing the empty seats staring back at me from all around the room. The whole next day, which everybody had off, I walked around thinking, "I could be doing much better."

At about 1:00 A.M., Diane, myself, and some friends came out of the restaurant at the Palace Hotel, and a fellow who had worked for us in California came up to me and said, "Lou, could I speak with you a minute?" He seemed a little boozy, but I said sure. And he said, "I'd like to talk to you in private, if I could." I figured he had something personal he needed to resolve, so I excused myself, and went with him to the corner of the lobby where we sat down. He said to me, "Lou, I wouldn't tell you this if I wasn't your friend. Frankly, I think you're going a little too slow for these people. They're different than the companies you talk to all the time because they are unique. Actually," he said, "I think you're boring them to death."

I assimilated that, and got up to leave. He added, "By the way, did the committee find you?" I said, "No, why?" He said, "They were looking for you all day yesterday." I thanked him for all of his "constructive" criticism, and I went upstairs for the night. But I couldn't fall asleep. I rationalized, "It's early in Seattle, and my body is still on Seattle time." As if it couldn't possibly have anything to do with what that guy had just told me. Finally, I woke up Diane and I said, "Tell me, Diane. Am I on the right track?" I didn't tell her what that guy had said. She said, "Yes. Your talks have been very insightful. Why do you doubt yourself?" I said, "Just wondering." She said, "If you see these people as any different from anyone else, you will miss their basic needs. Don't change a thing."

I got up early the next morning and went down to the conference to hear some of the other presentations. At ten o'clock, everybody hit the lobby for coffee, juice, and rolls. I started dwelling on why the committee was looking for me. I was anticipating the worst, when suddenly I heard, "Lou! Lou!" I turned around and it was Jim Hesburgh, Father Hesburgh's brother, who'd come out from Los Angeles. He was one of "the committee." I thought, "Man, how could he find me with 1500 people in the lobby?" He said, "Lou, I was looking all over for you yesterday. I'd like to talk to you in our office." I'll be honest with you; one word went through my mind at that moment: "Shit."

We went into the committee office and sat down, and Jim said, "We've gone over every evaluation of every session for every speaker so far, and we've gone over yours." I was waiting for the blade to fall. "We wanted to know," he said, "if you would give the closing address to the whole conference on Friday." What went through my mind right then was, "Oh you of little faith!" At one in the morning, one person whom I'd suspected had a little too much to drink, gave me *his* evaluation of me, and I'd listened to him instead of to what I *knew* about myself. I'd allowed that guy to become a negative wizard for me, and to almost take away my heart, my brains, and my guts.

You might be thinking, "You *teach* this stuff. Don't *you* have high self-esteem?" Yes, I do have high self-esteem. But, in *that* incident, apparently only when I stayed in Seattle, teaching the same material to the same people. The lesson was: Be aware of what can happen to your self-esteem when you get away from the familiar and tackle a situation that's unique for you. In my case, that was a high-powered conference with acclaimed people from all over the world. If we're not careful, we might allow ourselves to become susceptible to negative criticism. And then self-doubt brings on hesitation, which can bring on failure.

169

Later, I reflected back on the hundreds of people in my life who'd told me I'd delivered excellent talks, add how much they'd enjoyed listening. Why hadn't I recalled their compliments when this guy told me, "You're boring them?" Remember: You can reject compliments or accept them. The choice is yours. Sometiems, when you're out of your comfort zone and feeling vulnerable, you build scotomas to the positive about yourself. What I'm saying is, I'm no different from you. Unless I continually elevate my own self-esteem from within, I can be vulnerable in risk situations. Just like you, I need to constantly bolster my self-esteem so that, whenever I move into something unique, I'm thinking like the world's greatest elite commando: "I can do it. Send me anywhere!"

15

MOTIVATION:

Adjusting the Rules

The Picture of Hell

I've emphasized the importance of self-esteem in helping us achieve our goals. But self-esteem alone isn't enough to guide us consistently toward excellence and success. Something else inside us can still block our way. I'm speaking about our *motivation*. Now that we know so much more about how our mind operates, it's absolutely essential to also understand why we act the way we do. Otherwise, we won't know why we keep getting in our own way, or how to get out of our way when it counts.

Motivation means incentive and drive. It's the key component in the fuel that propels us toward either failure or success. Much like our self-image, we motivate ourselves internally with our own self-talk. Depending on our self-talk, we are either constructively or restrictively motivated. Constructive motivation is on an *"I want to, I choose to, I like to"* basis. Restrictive motivation is on an *"I have-to . . . or else"* basis. A good way to start examining our own internal motivation is by asking ourselves these important questions: "Am I my own person?" "Am I living the way I live because I choose to, or because I'm afraid to live any other way?" "Do I move optionally, creatively, free-flowingly through life, or am I constantly restricted, afraid, uptight?" "Do I assume personal accountability for my own actions, or do I think someone else is responsible?"

One way to answer these questions is by noticing how you feel when you set out to accomplish your goals. Positive, constructive motivation throws your system out of order, causing you to feel energetic and creative about solving the problem. Under the restrictive form of motivation, you don't accomplish things for the pleasure of enjoying the end result, you accomplish them because you're afraid of the consequences. If you clean the jam sandwich off the kitchen ceiling because you're looking forward to the pleasure of a clean kitchen again, you are constructively motivated to straighten up the mess. If you feel you *have to* clean the sandwich off the ceiling *or else* be punished by your parents, you'll become very creative about finding ways to *add* to the mess while you're cleaning it up. So the differences between constructive and restrictive motivation can mean the difference between joyful achievement and unhappy failure.

Constructive motivation means visualizing, in your mind, what you *want* in life. You talk to yourself about why you'd *like* the new job, why you *want* the new salary, why you'd *enjoy* the new skill, the new boat, the new adventure. Then you'll be more likely to act on a "want-to, choose-to, like-to" basis. You'll do things because you naturally see their *benefits.* Constructively motivated people constantly imprint positive imagery into their subconscious—*solutions* to problems, *resolutions* to conflicts, *satisfying end results.* When you're constructively motivated, you look forward to the end results with feelings of pleasure, joy, fulfillment: "What if I take that promotion? How good will I feel?" "What if I run for that seat on the Board of Education, and win? How much good I can do for my community. How much good I can do for students and their parents. How much good I can do for the schools." Constructive motivation creates a positive expectancy of joy and success.

Restrictive motivation creates exactly the opposite—fear of rejection, of failure, of punishment. Instead of seeing the benefits, you see only the awful consequences: "What if I ask her out and she says no? I'll be humiliated." "What if I apply for that job and they turn me down? I'll feel sick." "What if I don't meet my quota? I'll be fired." Whereas constructive thinking is seeing the way around the rock, restrictive thinking is dwelling on the rock until you crash right into it. Remember: *We move toward, and become like, that which we think about.* If you dwell on what you *don't* want to happen, you unconsciously help bring it about. When you picture *awful consequences,* your knees buckle, you sweat profusely, your stomach churns like a washing machine—and what happens? Fear makes you so uptight, you slip off the beam and topple over the edge fifty stories down.

How do we get trapped like that? Many of us were raised, habitually, on restrictive motivation. Our parents, teachers, spiritual mentors found it was an effective way to get us to "toe the line." So they instilled fear-based thinking in us that repeatedly set up "*I can't*" situations: "I can't go there." "I can't buy that." "I can't do that." As a result, we didn't allow ourselves to apply for that job, ask for that date, run for that seat on the Board. Instead of looking forward to the benefits, we feared the awful consequences: "Go up there in front of the class and read your paper, or else I'll flunk you."

"But I don't *want* to get up there."

"You *better* get up there, or else you'll not only flunk this paper, but I'll flunk you in this course. If you flunk the course, you won't graduate. Will you do it now?"

"No."

"If you don't graduate, you'll miss college and you'll never get a job. Without a job, you'll end up rolling in the gutter for the rest of your life. *Now* do you want to get up there?"

"Since you put it that way—yes."

"Why? Because you *like* to read in front of the class?"

"No. I can't stand it."

"Then why would you do it?"

"Because I don't want to end up rolling in the gutter!"

Fear works. But it motivates us to do things for the wrong reasons. When we're fear-motivated, we don't embrace the adventure of life; instead, we weakly accept its burdens. Now, many of us absorbed plenty of theological, fear-based motivation as kids. We learned to be good, not so much because we *enjoyed* being good, or *chose* to be good, but because we were told, "Either be good, or else you'll to to hell. And let me paint *the picture of hell* for you. Have you ever been thirsty?"

"Yeah."

"In hell, there's no water. You'll be thirsty forever and ever, Amen. Did you ever burn your hand on a hot plate?"

"Yeah."

"Your whole body will feel like that all through eternity. *Now* will you be good?"

"You bet I will."

"How come? Because you *want* to?"

"No. Because I'm afraid to burn in hell!"

So we've trained ourselves to be good, not because it's personally beneficial, but because we're constantly trying to outrun the flames of hell licking at our rear ends.

I remember when I went to my junior high school dances, the girls stood on one side of the gym and the boys on the other. We looked across at all these girls we wanted to dance with, but we knew if we walked over and asked, they'd probably say no. We dwelled on the fear of rejection, instead of the joy of success. And whenever we *did* go across, we stepped out of our comfort zones. We'd ask the girl to dance, and nothing would come out: "Uhh, er—." Sure enough, the girl would say, "No!" and we'd walk away thinking, "I *knew* she'd say no." To cover our embarrassment, we'd say to our friends, "She was ugly anyway. Who wants to dance? Let's go have some *real* fun."

That's how restrictive motivation prevents us from doing things we really want to do. Some of us run our whole lives that way. Fun, isn't it?

"I Have to . . . or Else"

How in the world can we tell when we're being restrictively motivated with fear images? By understanding the two most common forms of restrictive motivation: *coercive* and *inhibitive*. Coercive motivation is when you tell yourself *"I have to . . . or else."* Your self-talk is, "I have to behave or else I have to pay the price." And when someone else tries to coerce you, they're saying, "Do it or else something awful will happen to you. And let me paint the picture of hell for you." It's like, "Shape up or else ship out!" or "It's my way or else the highway." Those are classic coercive demands designed to restrict your behavior and keep you in line.

I want you to examine all the *"I have to . . . or else's"* in your life: "I have to do my work or else I won't get paid." "I have to go to the show or else my friend will be mad." "I have to clean the house or else the guests will think I'm a slob." "I have to increase my sales or else my boss will fire me." You know what happens when you tell yourself, "I have to"? The same thing as when you're physically pushed. When someone tries to push you, you automatically resist by pushing back. It's a reflex action. Similarly, whenever you feel you "have to" do something, you feel you're being "pushed" into it, and, subconsciously, you push right back. You tell yourself, "I have to do this. I have no choice. But if I had my way, I wouldn't do it." Your subconscious chimes in, "Oh, but you *can* have your way. Let me show you how to get out of it or how to screw it up." And your subconscious works very hard to get you to push back through procrastination, slovenly work, and creative avoidance.

If you're a supervisor, are you interested in productivity in your outfit? Do you use coercion to try to shove people into better performance? Do you know you're not only *not* eliciting better performance, you're actually setting your people up for *worse* performance? They slow down. They resist. They screw it up. If you keep pushing, they unconsciously push back. *Anyone* with high self-esteem will find themselves pushing back. They get infinitely creative finding ways to do *less* and to do it *poorly*. You can push them right into absenteeism, into being late, into being ill on the job, into breaking equipment, and making other unintentionally careless mistakes. You can push them so hard with "have to, or else" motivation, they'll slow to a standstill just to get you to shut up. It'll drive you absolutely nuts—and maybe out of business.

Parents, you can do the same thing to your kids. I used to tell my kids, "Get out there and rake those leaves. I'm not going to tell you again. Do it, or else!" It would take them forty-five minutes to get started. *Procrastination.* I'd get aggravated and yell, "What's taking so long?" They'd say, "We can't find the rake." And they weren't lying. In reaction to being "pushed," they unconsciously built scotomas to the rake so they wouldn't *have to* do the work. I'd go out and immediately find the rake, and I'd say, "Now get to work. And do it right!" They'd take five swipes at the leaves and fall down, exhausted. *Slovenly work.* Then they'd check behind them to see if the "or else factor" was still there, and they'd say loud enough for me to hear, "Boy, I'm really bushed!" Now, how can you possibly get bushed searching for a rake? *Creative avoidance.* If you *have to* find it, you get bushed.

What happens when you demand that the kids wash the dishes after a big dinner? It's the last thing they want to do, but you figure,

"It's my house. As long as they're living under my roof, they'll play by my rules." That's how some parents motivate their kids to be cooperative at home. It's coercion, and it doesn't work very well: "Do the dishes, or else you're grounded for a month. And do them right!" The kids will say, "I thought you wanted me to do my home-work." *Procrastination.* They didn't even *think* about homework until you said, "Wash the dishes." They'll do the dishes, but they'll take an hour to do a ten-minute job: "I was just watching the birds on the feeder. We have some baby cardinals, you know." *Creative avoidance.* And they won't do *all* the dishes; they'll leave crusty globs of food on the edges. *Slovenly work.* And they'll break two of your best china plates, and hide the frying pan you cooked the fish in by dumping it on the closet shelf above your cashmere coat—which, two days later, smells like dead trout. They're *pushing back.* Isn't that a wonderful way to work together? Everybody loses—but nobody knows why.

You get the same negative response when you push *yourself.* Some habitual smokers tell themselves, "You *have to* stop smoking!" Then they innovatively, creatively, unconsciously get into a pressure situation, or cause someone to get mad at them, or disappoint some-one they respect, just so they have an excuse to smoke again. When you push yourself, even if it's for your own good, your creative sub-conscious tries to stall, delay, and get you out of it. When you feel you *have to* grow, *have to* change, *have to* learn, *have to* make more money, your conscious willpower is at odds with your creative subconscious, and your creative subconscious will win every time. However, when your willpower and your subconscious creativity *team up*, you are absolutely unbeatable.

Wouldn't it be ridiculous to tell your sixteen-year-old, "All right, I'll be gone for a week. Here are the keys to the car, and here are all my gas station credit cards. When I get back, I want to see a thousand miles on that car. I'm not taking no for an answer. You do it, *or else!*" That would be silly. Because they already see the value, the profitability, the fun in doing something they want to do. In fact, to prevent them from driving that car, we would not only need to leave town with the keys, we would need to take the *distributor cap*, too. I'm talking from experience.

You want to see constructive motivation at work? Try chaper-oning an overnight co-ed teenage party sometime. About two in the morning, try keeping the sexes apart. They've been visualizing the pleasure and profitability of being together for weeks, so they start sneaking through the windows, the vents, even cracks in the walls, just to be with each other. They walk through doors without *opening* them. Why? Because we get very inventive and creative when we *want to* do something. We feel as though nothing can stop us. But if we feel we *have* to do something *"or else,"* we get just as inventive and creative to get *out* of it.

You don't need to coerce people into doing their best at things they *want* to do—and you can't coerce people into doing their best at something they *don't* want to do. You can't coerce *yourself* into it, either. In areas where you can't get yourself to do things—lose weight, stop smoking, quit drinking, earn more money—I guarantee you, for the most part you're trying to coerce yourself into it. You're telling yourself, *"I have to . . . or else."*

So don't force yourself to change. Don't grow until you want to, because you won't do it anyway. All your goals must be on a "want-to, choose-to, like-to" basis. It must be your idea; you must envision the value of achieving the goal or it will be like trying to run with somebody holding onto your pockets—pushing and pulling at the same time, unconsciously sabotaging your own success.

You "Get To"

What you must learn to do is eliminate, as best as you can, all the "have to's" in your life. And you must banish "have to" from your self-talk. From now on, it will be imperative that you don't allow yourself to think, "I have to get up in the morning." "I have to eat." "I have to go to work." Because it's really not true. There's only one "have to" in life: You have to die. Everything else is a matter of free choice, to the degree that you want to exercise it. Sometimes the choices aren't great, but they *are* choices.

I often fly to Australia on business. It takes me twenty-three hours to get from Seattle to Perth, sitting up the entire time in an airplane seat. I love being in Perth, but I get uncomfortable on the flight over. So when somebody asks me if I'm going to Perth, I say, "Yeah, I'm going," but my subconscious tries to get me out of it: "You have to go, but maybe you'll get sick so you won't have to go." Isn't that self-defeating? And I hold a sort of inner dialogue about it:

"Why don't you just call and tell them you're sick?"

"I can't do that. I've already committed myself. Besides, if I don't go, I might lose important business. People won't respect me."

"That's all very true. So shut up and go."

"But the flight over is murder."

"You could always take a boat."

"That's silly. A boat would take too long."

"True. Flying would be much better, wouldn't it?"

"Now that you put it that way, I *would* rather fly."

"Good. Quit complaining and enjoy your flight."

And then I realize, "You don't '*have to*' go to Perth, you '*get to*' go." And that's the way you must learn to talk to yourself. Most losers conduct their lives on a "have to" basis. They give up the accountability for everything they do. Whenever you tell yourself "I have to," you're not only giving up personal accountability, you're also tearing down your self-esteem. "I have to" means "I am not my own person. Someone else is controlling me." In "have-to" situations, you're constantly telling yourself, "I'll do it. But if I had my way, I'd rather be doing something else." That really means, "I'm being forced to do this against my will." It's like telling your spouse, "I have to stay late at work. The boss is making me finish my report." That means, "*They* are making me do it." Who are "*they*"? When you allow "*they*" to be in control, you lose self-respect: "I have no power over my own life." Instead, you must tell yourself, "I'm not going home yet. I choose to stay and finish my report so that, when I leave, my mind will be free."

Stop lying to yourself. You don't *have to* do anything. You don't *have to* change your kids' diapers. Leave them on; they'll eventually fall off by themselves. You don't *have to* turn on the heat in winter. You can wear heavy coats around the house, and you can buy new pipes when the old ones freeze. You don't even *have to* pay your taxes. "Of course, I do," you say. "Or they'll throw me in jail."

"Possibly. Or you could go on welfare."

"I don't want to go on welfare."

"Then leave the country and work overseas."

"I can't uproot my whole life like that."

"Then hang around here and see what happens. Maybe they won't catch you."

"But if they do, I'll end up in prison."

"That's true. But you don't have to *stay* in prison."

"Are you nuts? Of course, I do."

"No. You can get out of it anytime you want. Escape."

"They'd shoot me!"

"Probably."

"I don't want to *die*!"

"It's your choice, though, isn't it?"

"Well, yes. I choose to pay my taxes then."

"Good. Quit complaining and pay your taxes."

See? You just choose to pay your taxes rather than die. The point is: You can do whatever you want in life—as long as you're prepared to accept the consequences. Your kids might say, "I have to study. If I don't study, the teacher will flunk me. I don't have a choice." Tell them, "Yes, you do have a choice. You can choose *not* to study. Maybe you can scrape by on what you already know or maybe you'll flunk. They're not great choices, but they *are* choices." The point is: Let's look at what's best for us and, instead of telling ourselves, "I have to," let's say, "I *choose* to, I *want* to, I *get* to." That way, *we* call the shots, not somebody else. And our subconscious says, "I'm in control. I have the power."

One time, a famous distance runner who was preparing for the Montreal Olympics came to me to help him resolve a serious problem. In recent races, whenever he reached the last quarter-mile, he suddenly felt excruciating pain in his lungs. They burned so badly, he felt like he was dying as he ran. He said, "I wonder if there's something I can do, psychologically, to beat the pain." I said, "Sure, but you might not like it." He said, "What do you mean?" I said, "Tell me what you think about when you run." He said, "I block out everything. But when I reach the last quarter-mile, my lungs start burning and I tell myself, 'You have to run! You have to finish the last quarter-mile!'" I said, "Here's the answer. When you get to the last quarter-mile and you feel like you 'have to' keep running, stop right there and sit on the curb." He looked at me like I was nuts. "That's ridiculous," he said. "If I sit on the curb, I lose the race." I said, "Yes. But your lungs stop burning." He said, "Why do you think I run?" I said, "I haven't the slightest idea. I don't have that problem. I *never* run." He said, "I run because my family sacrificed to send me to college in America. I want my family and my country to be proud of me. And if I win the gold medal in Montreal, I'll go back to Kenya and they'll give me a cow. That will make me rich in my country."

I said, "Man, then quit complaining and run! Realize that you're not running because you *have to*. You *choose to* run, you *want to* run, you *love to* run. It's your idea, your free choice. You can anticipate the *joy* in winning—focus on that. You can feel the *pride* in winning—focus on that. You can see the *cow*—focus on that. Nobody is holding a gun to your head. Nobody is coercing you. So you don't really *have to* run, you *get to* run." Then I said, "Here's what you do. When you get to that last quarter-mile, and your lungs start to burn, remind yourself, 'I don't have to, I don't have to, I don't have to. I choose to, I love to, I get to.' And, man, you will eat that race alive!"

That's the way I want you to start living *your* life. Throw away all the "have to" situations, and watch the tremendous surge of power that comes over you. You'll have greater energy, greater joy, a better marriage, a better family, a better career, a better life. You will radiate self-esteem and confidence from within, and you will attack life like the little kid looking forward to opening birthday gifts: "I can hardly wait!" Realize that you will want to be tough in this motivation business because life is tough stuff. Maybe you'd like to believe there's a magic formula to help you make choices. Lou Tice has no magic formula. Visualization and affirmations aren't magic. The only magic formula is inside of you; it's called personal accountability. So take charge of your own future—not because you *have to*, but because you *get to*.

The Flood of Fear

The second kind of restrictive motivation is called *inhibitive*—which means discouraging, restraining, prohibitive. Like coercive motivation, inhibitive motivation is fueled on fear. Whereas the trigger words for coercive motivation are *"I have to,"* the trigger words for inhibitive motivation are *"I can't."* So the thrust of inhibitive self-talk is, "I can't misbehave or else something awful will happen."

Inhibitive motivation is restrictive because it blocks option-thinking and choice. In athletics, a coach will train the team in certain techniques, and if the players fail to execute those techniques, the coach will impose punishment: "Two hundred push-ups! Then run laps till you puke!" As a result, those players learn, "I can't misbehave, or else I'll feel terrible." The military sometimes uses restrictive training tactics: "March this way." "Carry your weapon that way." "Say 'Yes Sir,' or else you'll pay the penalty." So what do you learn? "I can't do things any other way or else I'll be punished."

For many of us, the command "You can't" is so powerful that sometimes we don't even question *why not*. We just experience an overwhelming flood of fear, and we obey. Remember the fear associated with "I can't eat meat on Friday?" At first, we told ourselves, "I can't eat meat on Friday or else I'll burn in hell!" But, eventually, we didn't need to remember the specific "or else" anymore. As soon as we thought about eating meat on Friday—or doing anything else we were told we couldn't do—the flood of fear washed over us, and we got uptight: "I don't feel right about this." We no longer needed to know the specific consequences; we just knew, inside, that something awful would happen if we disobeyed.

This ties in with my discussion earlier on the process of thought. First we *perceive* the situation through our senses. Then we *associate*: "Have I experienced anything like it before?" Then we *evaluate*: "What is this leading me toward?" If we're inhibitively motivated, the pattern of fear from our childhood, our religious training, our athletic training, our military training, is recorded as "I can't"—and, bang, we get that sudden flood of fear. And we conclude, "Nothing good!" Finally, we *decide*, "You can't change. Stay in line. Don't make waves." It's the same decision ten or twenty or thirty years later when we think, "This company can't change. They can't violate policy." In other words: You can't get outside of your nine dots or else something terrible will happen.

So, for example, how might you inhibitively prevent a six-year-old girl from falling off her bike? Simple. Every time she falls off, just step on her hand, grind your heel into her fingers, and kick her hard in the ribs. Of course, I'm exaggerating here to make this point. What is that little girl going to learn? She'll learn, "I can't fall off my bike or else!" So she gets the inhibition down perfectly, and she doesn't fall off the bike. The problem arises when you say one day,

"Okay honey, now I want you to try something new." She'll say, "No! I can't!" You have any people like that in your family, on your team, in your company? They're scared to death to try anything new. It might be because they were inhibitively punished—physically and psychologically— so often in the past that they know it hurts too much to learn something new. So they think, "I can't make a mistake! I can't make a mistake!"

When you have people in a company, for example, who've been grooved through inhibitive fear to be afraid of making mistakes, they'll fight change in the company to the death, if necessary. They'll think, "Don't try to mess with my responsibilities. Don't try to make a change. It'll *hurt* too much." That's the same thing as "I can't eat meat on Friday." They're responding to the flames of hell. Only it isn't the flames of hell; it's the fear of screwing up the new task and having their hands crunched and their ribs kicked, and then having to run laps till they puke. So things remain the same. Even if the change would be advantageous, their resistance rushes up in a flood of fear: "That's not in my job description! It's out of my area! I don't do that!" That kind of motivation breeds inhibition to options, change, and growth. Instead, you get stagnation and rigidity.

You and I must recognize that it's all right to make mistakes. You don't *want* to make them, you don't *choose* to make them, you don't like to make them—but you don't get your hands crunched or your ribs kicked every time it happens. When you make a mistake, take responsibility for it and tell yourself, "That's not like me. I'll correct it the next time." Then, through visualization and affirmations, try again with commitment and assurance—and *allow* yourself to change.

"Captain of the World"

A big problem with restrictive motivation is that once the fear feedback loop is conditioned in, whenever you violate your restrictive zones, you get irritated, anxious, upset. You not only feel upset when *you* violate your restrictive zones, but also when *somebody else* does, too: "Why are they smoking in this restaurant? I can't stand that. Do they have a nonsmoking area?" You sit down to eat, and somebody puffs a cigarette clear across the room, and you can't enjoy yourself: "Geez, that ticks me off. I have to leave. I can't take this anymore."

We may have one restrictive zone or thousands. And the wide variety of restrictive patterns that were conditioned into us by our parents, teachers, coaches, bosses, and mentors, are like exposed nerve endings. Every violation hurts: "Get your hand away from your face. You'll spread germs. Why do you think I bother to tell you this? I tell you for your own good. So stop it!" You ever know anyone like that? They're always shaping you up for your own good. They end up irritated with other people all day long: "How can anyone *breathe* so loud? That really annoys me. Boy, I always have to shape *everyone* up for their own good!"

What happens when you have a parent, teacher, or supervisor who has dozens of restrictive zones? They think, "I'm the boss now. I'm sure glad I finally got this command because I'm gonna shape everybody up. From now on, everyone toes the mark. I'm instituting some very serious rules. To begin with, no long hair and no short skirts. And don't let me catch you using pencils instead of pens, or else it's off with your head! And everybody signs in when they arrive, and out when they leave."

See, now that you're the boss, you'll do to your employees exactly what your parents, teachers, and supervisors did to you—try to force conformity to restrictive zones that have nothing to do with the tasks at hand. In fact, the cause of many employee strikes is not that employees aren't getting enough benefits, but that some rigid, dictatorial, dogmatic boss has a whole load of "garbaged-in" restrictive zones which they feel compelled to pass along to everyone else. They're not happy at their job; it irritates them. So they decide to shape *you* up or ship *you* out.

One way to become cognizant of your own restrictive zones is to consider your habits and attitudes, and ask yourself: "In what ways do I act *compulsively*? Does that behavior make much sense?" For example, suppose you're compulsively punctual. How did you get that way? Probably through fear feedback: "I can't be late or else." Maybe when you were young, daddy trained you to always be on time by scolding or spanking you whenever you were late. When that didn't work he grounded you, socially, for a month. What did you learn? "I can't be late or else awful things happen."

So here you are at twenty-seven, thirty-seven, or even forty-seven, and you're running a little late, and you start to think, "Man, I can't be late!" You don't think, "Or else daddy's gonna punish me"—because you're an adult and anyway, daddy died five years ago. All you know is "I can't be late or else." That compulsive, restrictive behavior can prevent you from acting sensibly and realizing your potential, because it limits your behavior to a conditioned, "or else" response.

In fact, a punctuality compulsion can cause you to do irrational things. For example, say you're a compulsively punctual person and you're running late for an appointment. You're driving along fine until you see a train about to head you off at a crossing. You get the feedback: "I can't be late!"—so you race the train to the crossing. Recklessly, you risk your own life and the lives of everyone else in the car, just because you're afraid of being late. And if the train *beats* you to the crossing, you almost feel like you're going crazy: "It's *illegal* for a train to take this long at a crossing! I'll report this to the authorities!" You are so annoyed, you can't think straight. When the train passes, you get even more compulsive, more reckless. You punch the gas pedal and drive seventy in a thirty zone. Even though daddy is dead, you're still trying to avoid his punishment.

And remember: Compulsively punctual people will get upset not only when *they're* late, but also when *anybody else* is late. "Geez, that gets me mad! Can't you be on time?" *Anybody's* lateness can drive them almost to distraction. So they try to control everybody's behavior by becoming a self-appointed "Captain of the World." They take it upon themselves to shape up the whole world—for the world's own good. By the way, I once held that position when I was a high school teacher. I had about thirty-five rules for my classroom alone—all for the kids' own good, of course. "Don't chew gum!" "Sit up straight!" "Didn't I say to write your name on the *left* side of the page?" Every time a kid violated one of my rules, it made me so mad that I couldn't think straight. I knew I had to shape those kids up. Man, I was so busy trying to beat the train to the crossing, I hardly had any time left to teach.

Why was I so upset? Not because those kids were behaving badly, but because they were irritating me by violating my restrictive zones. Were my rules constructive? Were they conducive to running a good class? Did they have anything to do with teaching school? Absolutely not. They were silly, unnecessary rules. Why did I impose them? "Oh, I can justify it. These kids have to learn how to behave when they get out into the *real* world. That's what I'm teaching them, you know." No, I wasn't. I was teaching them to stay the heck out of Lou Tice's restrictive zones—*or else!* You ever know anybody like that?

Do you think my job as "Captain of the World" ended with the 3:00 P.M.. bell? Not at all. There was plenty of time left to shape up more people in my other job as football coach: "Pick up the towels." "Put your pads on right." "Run this way." "Pass that way." "Darn kids!" I loved that job, too, though. And it didn't end at 6:00 P.M. There was still plenty of time to shape up people on the way home, in traffic. After all, somebody was always violating my restrictive zone when I was driving: "Hey man, who taught *you* how to drive? Who's crowding in? *Get* them! Where are the cops? *Get* that guy!" I couldn't even drive home without becoming a nervous wreck.

And I'd go out of my way to get irritated at strangers. I'd be in my community of Burien, and I'd spot some kids leaning against their car, smoking cigarettes. I'd pull up beside them, and I'd get out, chase them down the block, grab their cigarettes, and throw them away. I'd say, "Go on home. Where are your parents? Don't they care? Nobody cares but me!" And, boy, I'd get home exhausted after a hard day's work. Diane would say, "What's wrong with you?" I'd say, "You can't imagine what I go through all day. I caught those same two kids smoking again tonight. Can you believe that? I don't even know who they are. It's a tough job shaping up the whole darned world."

But let me point out right now that I resigned from the post of "Captain of the World" many years ago. And I want to thank those of you who have taken up that burden and responsibility. Because the world sure runs a whole bunch better since I quit.

"Button Your Button!"

It's important to realize that you don't need to feel accountable for everybody else's behavior. You don't need to allow other people to make you feel miserable and ruin your day. If you choose to, you can change the fear feedback loop through visualization and affirmations—and I will show you how. But first, ask yourself, "What rules are necessary?" Examine the way you conduct your family life, your career, and your social life by trying to identify rules you enforce that exist for no other reason than to make you feel good.

Why should you bother? Because if you don't change your restrictive zones, you may never use your full potential as a human being—and you may inadvertantly block someone you love from using theirs. When we adopted children and had foster kids as well, I wanted all of them to feel happy and loving around me. But I would come into the living room with all the kids there and, at one point or another, somebody would violate one of my restrictive zones. I would scold, "Get your feet off the couch!" "Get the dog out of here!" "Don't eat ice cream in that chair!"

Zip, those kids would start filtering out of that room one at a time: "I think I'll take out the garbage, dad." "And I'll help him, dad." "Gee, I almost forgot, dad. It's my turn to mow the lawn." I'd say, "No, it isn't. And anyhow, it's *raining*!" See, they suddenly got very creative finding things to do. Soon, I'd be sitting there alone, wanting to be a loving father but feeling as though everyone *hated* me. To justify it to myself, I'd say, "That's just the consequence of being a good father."

So there will most likely be consequences whenever you impose your will upon someone else, especially when you try to imprison them in your restrictive zone. What happens in a marriage when you argue over restrictive zones? You start off loving each other, and you end up trying to strangle each other. Because "Don't slurp your soup!" and "Don't let me catch you squeezing the toothpaste in the middle!" and "Don't chew that ice around me!" are the kinds of unnecessary restrictive rules that can break up marriages. Think about all the silly things you start fights over. Why do they upset you in the first place? "Well, because I can't be late or else daddy will punish me!" Remember: Your parents passed on some of these prohibitions to you. Be assured, unless you are aware you have them, you will pass some of them on to *your* kids, too.

Another problem is recognizing how we sometimes retaliate against people who violate our restrictive zones. In the days of the "Wild West," when people felt hostile, they could solve the problem by taking out a six-gun and shooting. In medieval Europe, they could express their hostility by wielding a sword: "Off with their heads!" But in our very sophisticated, modern society, we've gone into the banking business to vent our hostility. We build up "IOU" accounts. When people irritate us, we tell ourselves, "I won't let that bother me." But, subconsciously, every time we think about it, we make a deposit in our "IOU" account: "I owe you one for that." And pretty soon, when our account gets full, it's time to start paying people back what we owe them.

One way you do that is you find out what upsets them, and then—consciously or unconsciously—you do it. "I didn't know that bothered you, dear. Heh-heh-heh. I'm sorry." No, you're not. Husbands and wives know how to irritate each other, kids and parents know how, employers and employees know how. It's a safe way of paying someone back for upsetting you. For example, I used to say to my kids, "Take out the garbage. I'm not going to tell you again." To maintain my restrictive zone, I *pushed* them. Well, they automatically pushed back.

But how? They couldn't say, "All right, I'll take out the garbage. But, first, I'll dump it over your fat head!" Yet that's probably what they were *thinking* all the way out to the garbage can. So they waited for an icy, winter Sunday afternoon, when I was watching my third football game on TV—and they knew I wasn't getting up for *anything.* Those kids went outside and left the door wide open. I thought, "Geez, that bothers me." So I yelled, *"Close the door!"* That's all they were waiting for. They grabbed the door and *slammed* it shut. And I said, *"Don't slam the door!"* See? They got me *twice:* once by leaving it open, and once by slamming it shut. Then they said, "Sorry dad. The wind caught it." Well, there *was* no wind. There were just some long overdue IOU's.

A friend of mine is a warden in a federal penitentiary. He told me that, in the old days, convicts had to keep the top button of their uniforms buttoned at all times. He said if a convict ever really wanted to annoy a guard, all he had to do was get up early in the morning, rip the top button off his uniform, and throw it away. The guard would spot the wide-open collar before breakfast, and he'd get upset: *"Button your button!"* The convict would say, "Can't. Lost it." The guard would get so mad, he'd stomp around muttering angrily all day long. The cons would keep it up all year 'round.

Now, can you imagine torturing yourself every day over *"Button your button"*? Some of us do that for most of our lives.

Another hostile response to the imposition of someone else's restrictive zones is *"witholding."* When you make people feel hostile, they find out what you want or need, and they withhold it from you. Little kids withhold their toys or their cooperation: "I won't talk." In a company, when one department gets mad at another department, they withold cooperation. People who are habitually late to business meetings could very well be hostile people withholding their very presence from the meeting. One of our clients is a National Basketball Association team which started a recent season with a great surge, but finished with a predictable crash. I called the coach—a good friend of mine—and I asked him, "What's the matter?" He said, "A few players thought some of their teammates were getting too much publicity, so they stopped passing them the ball. They'd just say, 'I didn't *see* him.' " In other words: withhold, withhold, withhold.

So, how is it in your family? How is it where you work? Do you see why it's important to dissolve all those restrictive zones? You can have the best superstars in the NBA, but if they develop hostility they will start violating each other's restrictive zones—which only compounds the problem and creates a mess. So what's the advantage to you of knowing this information? You can now see some of the underlying causes of anger and hostility. And you realize that if you don't know how to treat the problems, you might very well fall back on age-old "remedies" like divorce, firing people, benching them, "pushing" them back, withholding, imposing more rules. The point is, unless we recognize some of the things that are bothering us, and reprogram ourselves inside, we will keep producing conditions which are tremendously unhealthy.

The way to avoid that is to start setting your goals on a "want-to, choose-to, like-to, get-to" basis. Visualize the profitability in the goal and why it will be advantageous for you. It's not just a matter of looking forward to something; it's *how* you look forward that makes the difference. You don't want to look forward with trepidation and fear. That's worrying—or negative goal-setting. Even if you have unappealing choices, try to see the advantages in one over the other, and tell yourself why it's in your best interest to go that way. Then move aggressively into it. Focus on the *value.* Flying to Perth may be tedious, but it's faster and more convenient than taking a boat. Studying for an exam won't be as much fun as going to a movie, but it's better than flunking and going to summer school.

So, from now on, try to place your whole life on a value-oriented basis. That's what creates the inventiveness and creativity to succeed. That's what makes you start attacking life as though it's an Adventure of the Greatest Magnitude.

16

GOAL-SETTING:

Target Practice

Teleological

Human beings think *teleological*—which means we think in terms of purpose, or are goal-oriented. When we function properly, we are directed toward and shaped by our goals. Our teleological thoughts and ways of perceiving are like the guidance system of a missile; they direct us toward our target. Our guidance system is our inner picture of how things are supposed to be: "I have a picture of the way I want my family to be." "I have a picture of the way I want my company to be." "I have a picture of where I'm going on my vacation." "I have a picture of how much money I want to earn this year." In other words, our guidance system targets our future goals and keeps us on course as we work to achieve them.

It is absolutely vital that we have goals. To change and grow, we need to look forward to something in the future. Otherwise, just like missiles without targets, we will fizzle out and self-destruct. Our goals can be anything. For some, it might be the next episode of a favorite soap opera: "I can hardly wait for tomorrow's 'General Hospital,' " Or it might be, "I can hardly wait for Friday." Or, "I can hardly wait to finish work and go out for a beer." Others look forward to building a new skyscraper, developing a cure for cancer, founding a new nation. We all need targets. What are yours? Do they cause you to linger in the past, or float in the present, or leap into the future? The point is, once we learn how to program this mechanism—this teleological way of perceiving—inside us, it can guide us anywhere we choose to go.

What is most significant about this mechanism is its feedback system. A missile doesn't move in a straight line. It pitches and yaws from side to side and up and down for a very important reason. The reason is: If the target moves, the missile must still be able to track. So when the missile is off-target, its sensory impulses and scanning devices send feedback to the guidance system—"We're too high! We're too low! We're a mile wide!"—and the guidance system immediately adjusts the missile's course.

The same kind of feedback is necessary for human beings so that we can adjust direction on the way to our goals. We get the feedback from our senses. Once we target a goal in our mind, our senses alert us to where we are in relationship to the goal: "Where am I? How am I doing?" If we are off-target, we get negative feedback in the form of tension or dissonance: "It doesn't look right." "It doesn't smell right." "It doesn't taste right." "It doesn't sound right." "It doesn't feel right." In other words, "You're off-course for the income you've planned." "You're off-course for the way you want to behave." "You're off-course for—." *Then* you can make adjustments.

You might say, "I don't know about this feedback stuff. I can do fine without it." If you think so, try this. Get a 500-piece jigsaw puzzle and empty the pieces in front of you. Throw away the box cover with the picture of the completed puzzle. Now try to put the puzzle together. You can probably do the perimeter, but the rest will be very difficult. Why? Because the picture is your feedback. Without it, you can't accurately gauge: "Where am I? How am I doing?" You need the picture—the target—to adjust your progress on the way to it: "Am I too high? Am I too low? Am I too wide?"

But feedback alone isn't enough. To reach a target or goal, you must also be able to *accept* the feedback. People with low self-esteem can't stand the tension. They don't want to set goals because when they veer off-course, the feedback stings too much. So they build scotomas to it. For instance, a heavy smoker who doesn't really want to stop smoking, might think, "I'm not short of breath because I smoke too much. I'm short of breath because it's too hot." So, let's say you're struggling to lose twenty pounds. You must be able to step on the scale and accept the feedback: "Hey! You're not losing any weight!" That triggers the creative dissonance to correct for the mistake: "I'll add exercise to my diet and make *sure* I lose the weight." Otherwise, your subconscious will blind you to the numbers on the scale, and continue to maintain your present picture of yourself as twenty pounds overweight.

Once you target, in your mind, the way you want things to be—the business merger that you want, the income that you want, the respect that you want, the environment that you want—you must now allow yourself to look at the way things really *are*: "We said we were going to deliver quality in our product, and we aren't delivering it." "We said the project would be completed by now, and it isn't finished." "I said I would stop yelling at home, and I haven't stopped." "How are we doing in our family relationships?" "How are we doing as a team?" "How is our marriage doing?" "Hey, you're out of line! You're off the target!" When you feel the anxiety and tension of being "off-target," that triggers your subconscious creativity: "Line it up! Line it up! Line it up!"

Here's something else of concern. What happens if we don't set any goals—if we don't have anything to keep us looking forward, with positive expectancy, to the future? Quite frankly, we can waste away and die. Research on the plight of prisoners of war has revealed that many of the younger prisoners between the ages of eighteen and twenty-three are unable to cope with the mental torture inflicted by their captors. They just waste away. At first, this phenomenon was labeled "give-up-itis." Later, it was identified as "clostermorastis"—a withdrawal behavior usually observed in children.

Captors usually initiate this process by destroying their prisoners' goal-orientation through relentless, specific kinds of mental torture: constantly painting a bleak future; rewarding prisoners for ratting on each other; providing "Dear John" letters, divorce subpoenas, bill collection notices; brainwashing with false versions of history. They so thoroughly obliterate their prisoners' hopes for the future that a lot of those young kids just crawl into a corner, pull a blanket over their head, and die. Remember: *When you give up on your goals, or when you have no goals at all, your whole system shuts down.*

So having goals is absolutely essential to your existence. Keep in mind also: *We move toward, and we become like, that which we think about.* So if you don't deliberately anticipate the way you want your life to be, the way you want your family to be, the way you want your career to be next week, next month, next year, then, for survival, your subconscious will duplicate your presently dominant picture. Like a copy machine, you might end up repeating last year's goals again and again. That's what happens when people allow themselves to stay in a routine job, repeating the same tasks day after day. We commonly call that a "rut."

Another pitfall of not setting your own new goals is that you can become extremely open to the suggestions of others. Then it's very easy to get caught up in doing what the crowd does. You become too lazy, or afraid, to think for yourself: "Let's drop that client." "Oh, that's a good idea." "Let's go to that new movie." "Oh, that's a good idea." "Why don't we sell our car?" "Oh, that's a good idea." See, *anything's* a good idea—and you move toward whatever anybody triggers in your mind. "My minister inspires me." "My coach really gets me up." "My parents guide me." That's fine—but high-performance people also find their own goals, their own motivation, their own inspiration. Once you know what you want to achieve, you can learn to affirm, visualize, and imprint, and then let your goal-oriented mechanism—your teleological way of perceiving—guide you to your goal.

The Finished Product

We are approaching the most important phase of this curriculum: learning the techniques for writing affirmations, and learning how to effectively visualize and imprint your goals to assure success. That's coming up in the final chapters. But first, I want to emphasize the importance of deliberate preparation for personal change and growth. Change, or goal-setting, will be a process of familiarization: familiarizing yourself *beforehand* with the upcoming job interview; familiarizing yourself *beforehand* with a new environment; familiarizing yourself *beforehand* with the new way you want to behave. The key premise here is "*All meaningful and lasting change starts on the inside first, and works its way out.* Change starts first in the imagination, and *then* manifests itself externally. If you don't change your picture inside first, you will have the tendency to go back to the familiar. That's what happens, for example, if you consciously force yourself to lose weight without first changing your picture. If your picture remains "I see myself as twenty pounds overweight," your belief system will keep you there until you change the picture. Even though you can *temporarily* lose weight, as soon as you let go of conscious control, you will return automatically to your currently dominant picture. So, unless we learn how to correctly alter our picture internally first, we will unconsciously prevent ourselves from growing by returning automatically to the way things are presently "supposed to be." As you'll soon see, we can alter our picture effectively and lastingly through affirmations and visualization.

This sort of goal-setting is not new to you. It's not unlike cooking from a recipe. When you open a cookbook to a specific recipe, what do you see? The ingredients. But what do you see in your mind's eye? *The finished product.* Well, writing and visualizing goals is like reading the recipe for a cake, and then envisioning it as if it is already baked.

The recipe for change is this: *Deliberately throw your system out of order.* Remember when I discussed creative dissonance? That's what I want you to do when you start setting goals: Create dissonance inside yourself so you will have the energy and drive to change your picture. Suppose you know you're usually in debt for only five hundred dollars, and then bills suddenly come rolling in to put you in debt for five *thousand* dollars. You think, "I've got a problem. This is more debt than I'm used to." That turns on your creative energy and drive to "straighten up the mess." You stop spending foolishly; you start saving money; you get an extra job—whatever it takes to get the two pictures to match.

But that's the easy part. We must then watch out for the dangerous trap of "flattening out." Goal-setting is not static; it must be a continuous process. Because once we achieve a goal, once we make the pictures match, our motivation "flattens out," and we relax and float. The mind is very tricky and powerful. As soon as you get back to the level of indebtedness that you're used to, you no longer have the motivation to get a *better* job or to make *more* money. You only do "what's good enough" to relieve the tension, and no more. Once you've returned to "what's good enough" for you, your system will shut right down.

So don't join the "Thank God It's Friday" club. Goal-set *through, not up to.* Visualize the next day, the next week, the next month, or as far beyond as you can reasonably imagine for yourself. But keep in mind that deliberately throwing your system out of order is like going out of your comfort zone. And what happens when you feel out of place? You unconsciously start correcting for the mistake to get back where you belong. You think, "It's a mistake for me to make this much money." "It's a mistake for me to be a nonsmoker." "It's a mistake for my business to go this well." But if you use affirmations and visualization to upgrade "where you belong" *before* you go out of your comfort zone, you won't feel the tension when you actually get there. If the child visualizes kindergarten in advance, and affirms "I'm going to have a great time," that child will comfortably adapt to kindergarten *beforehand*.

Don't get me wrong; you can change without this particular method. You have already done it many times. But I'm talking about deliberately preparing to be a better father, mother, son, or daughter; deliberately preparing to be a more dynamic leader; deliberately preparing to have a more free-flowing memory; deliberately preparing to become financially secure; deliberately preparing to do all those things you want to do, but which, for some reason, keep eluding you. Using this method properly, you will experience more deliberate growth over the next five years than in all the previous years of your life. I'm talking about taking giant strides—and it isn't magic.

Inside, you have a powerful creative genius capable of making almost any picture materialize in your life over a period of time. But to engage that creative genius, you must constantly upgrade the picture of "what's good enough" for you. If you believe you're a "C" student in school, and then you surprise yourself by getting an "A" on one exam, why is it so hard to get another "A" after that? Because you think, "Hey, look how good I did. That isn't like me,"—and your subconscious finds a way to correct for the mistake. It might convince you that, "I can flunk the next two tests and still get my 'C.' " Why would you think like that? Because your expectations are "I'm a 'C' student, not an 'A' student. Don't expect me to get 'A's' all the time. That's too tough for me." The point is: It's almost impossible to motivate yourself beyond your own expectations. *But if you know how to subconsciously raise the level of your expectations, you can raise the level of your performance.* This also applies to setting goals. Change your picture of what you deserve, and you will automatically change what you achieve. It's just a matter of what target you're aiming at.

17

AFFIRMATIONS AND VISUALIZATION:

Building a Better You

A "Do-it-Yourself" Project

We have all heard people proclaim, "Change is impossible!" They're wrong; change *is* possible. But before I show you how to do it, step by step, I want to explain about the process of creating *meaningful and lasting* change. Because, remember, you might be able to change your attitudes and habits *temporarily* but, if you don't also change your inner picture, the stress will eventually drive you back to "where you belong." So you must learn how to change naturally, effortlessly, safely, without tension or stress.

That can be accomplished by setting goals through the use of affirmations and visualization. But first you must learn how to prepare mentally so that when you write goal statements in the form of affirmations—statements of fact which we can imagine—and then visualize them, they will imprint in your subconscious. Otherwise, you will end up with something like New Year's Eve resolutions—vague, half-hearted intentions that are easily forgotten. How many times have you started out on January 1 with well-meaning intentions—"This is the year I'm gonna make those big changes"—and then, by the third week in January, you've forgotten what they were? Well, unless you learn to consciously control the goal-setting process, that's the way you will always be.

Why will you be that way? Because our belief system resists change. It fights hard to keep us the same as we are right now. That's what allows us to always be ourselves. It keeps you from being me, and me from being you. I can go anywhere and be myself. I can go to Australia and be me, I can go to Japan and be me, I can go home and be me. And I can pretty well count on being me tomorrow. I don't need to write a list of my attitudes and habits, because my belief system keeps that list. When a situation occurs, I know I'll act like myself. In fact, our subconscious checks-and-balances system— our self-image—is so deeply imprinted that, for some people, even reading about change in a book can cause tremendous tension and fear: "Hold it! This Tice guy says, 'Change is possible?' That sounds too good to be true. Don't read on. Don't mess with it. Stay the same!" So keep in mind that when you set new goals to grow and change, you are up against the present you.

The good news is you can use affirmations and visualization to stretch the present you. By writing affirmations in the form of goal statements ("I am my own expert, and I am not affected by the negative attitudes of others." "I am logical and decisive in making important decisions.") you are programming your subconscious to stretch its present image of you by "leaning" toward what you now see yourself to be. It's the same process you have used all your life, though you didn't know how to control it. It's the same way you "leaned" toward your first big date. You deliberately visualized what it would be like, and you got very creative finding ways to make it happen. It's the same way you looked forward to high school in your final year of junior high. You visualized what it would be like, over and over, until you were ready to *attack* high school. It's the same thing kids do when they start looking forward to Christmas in November. They can hardly wait to possess that day.

Something happens to us inside when we start visualizing, and looking forward to, anything we want. We become discontent with the old, while we keep vividly "experiencing" the possession of the new. There is nothing mysterious or unique about this. Imagery is a natural part of our total life process. I'm just going to show you how to control it.

Remember the example of the DC-10 pilot who controlled the airplane when the tires blew out? I've explained how pilots train in simulators to anticipate emergency situations, in their minds, before the situations occur. When they're in the simulator, they teach themselves, "If this happens, here's what you do. If that happens, here's what you do." They visualize situations vividly, then rehearse them over and over until their reactions become routine: *"Got it!"* But they don't rehearse the accident; they rehearse the recovery. Remember that. You don't visualize *running into* the rock, you visualize *steering around* it. If you do that often enough, with the right kind of imagery, the imagined event becomes your new present reality. Then, when the event actually happens, you will act like your present picture of yourself: *"Got it!"* Why? Because your belief system forces you to always act like your picture—the present you.

If you use the tool of affirmations and visualization correctly, you can deliberately change your inner picture. But just as pilots don't merely "talk" their way through simulated emergencies, you don't merely "say" your affirmations. You write them down in a particular manner—which I'll teach you in the next chapter—and then you visualize them vividly as though they are actually happening now. Remember: Every time we imprint "how things are supposed to be" into our subconscious, we behave like that automatically, free-flowingly. If we record "That's like me" often and vividly enough, eventually we will not have to *think about* how to behave. We'll automatically act the way we believe ourselves to be. It's a matter of taking the controls by consciously using affirmations and visualization to change your picture in your mental simulator.

Suppose you think of yourself as a $2000 a month person. You need more money to pay bills, so you decide to work harder to become a $3000 a month person. What happens? You feel the tremendous strain of *trying hard* to change. Then, subconsciously, you get very innovative and creative to bail out and return to your presently dominant picture of "I earn $2000 a month." However, if you use affirmations and visualization, you can consciously alter your self-image so that now you believe "I earn $3000 a month." How? Remember: Once you perceive yourself acting differently from your presently dominant self-image—in this case, earning only $2000— your subconscious automatically corrects for the mistake: "It's a *mistake* for you to earn only $2000." See? It's the same as "It's a *mistake* for you to be this nice." "It's a *mistake* for you to strike out with men on base." "It's a *mistake* for you to lose weight." Unconsciously, you then get very creative to get back to sanity, back to your presently dominant image of you. *That's* how you stimulate change.

Keep in mind that, at first, the change will only be internal. You might have a new picture of you in your mind—but don't spend that extra $1000 a month because you haven't changed the reality *outside*. In other words, you haven't started *earning* it yet. So when

202

does the change occur outside? It occurs after you've repeatedly read your affirmation ("I enjoy earning an extra $1000 each month."), vividly pictured yourself cashing your $3000 check, and felt the joy and satisfaction of having the extra cash. Once that picture imprints, you get the tension feedback. For instance, the next time you cash your usual $2000 check, your belief system will say "What's this crummy *$2000*? That's not good enough for you. You're a *$3000* person now!" See? And the dissonance in your system drives you to go out and actually earn $3000 a month to "straighten up the mess. "It's like visualizing yourself driving the new car, over and over, and then getting into your old car again. Once you get the tension feedback ("This old car's not good enough for me.") you can't stand the mess. So your system develops enough creative energy, drive, and motivation to straighten it up: "I will find a way to buy the *new* car now."

That's why you don't have to quit the old job, for example, before you are mentally ready to leave. You can simply visualize yourself working the new job, and temporarily maintain the status quo until your picture changes to "This old job isn't good enough for me." Once your new picture imprints in your belief system, you feel so discontent with the old job, you can't stand the mess. You have visualized the new job so often that you've already changed *inside*. You then become very creative, subconsciously, in finding ways to change things *outside*. When it comes, it's like déjà vu: "I've done this before." That's how you make change safely, effortlessly, under control, without tension or stress.

Change is a do-it-yourself project. You must take accountability for, and control of, your own goal-setting. If you don't constantly control your affirmations and visualization, you might set your goals too short. That would be like looking forward to getting home from work so you can just enjoy dinner with your family. That's fine, but as soon as the pictures match, you'll fall asleep on the couch. You won't even have enough energy left to get up and go to bed: "Throw a blanket over me, honey. I'll sleep right here. Must be tired blood." No—you just set your goal too short and "flattened out."

I want to remind you about the importance of self-talk in goal-setting. Let's say we prepare our kids for the first day of kindergarten by helping them affirm and visualize it weeks in advance, and by bringing them to the school beforehand to show them around. What if we then send the kids off for their first day by saying, "And by the way, your teacher is a monster"? Those little kids will think, "Uh-uh, I'm not going! No way!" So it isn't just a matter of *looking forward* to the new; it's *how* we look forward to it. We must control not only the imagery we visualize, but also the emotions which that imagery triggers. Otherwise, when we start setting goals for new lifestyles or careers, for instance, we might end up with the right goals but the wrong emotions: "I heard about two other people who worked there, and they didn't come back alive! You couldn't *pay* me to apply for a job over there." So when we set goals, we must be very cognizant of our self-talk because we don't want to look forward with apprehension or fear. We want to always look forward with positive expectancy and joy: "I can hardly wait!"

Lastly, keep in mind that your creative subconscious considers it more important to maintain sanity than health or safety or happiness or success. For example, you'd like to have more money, but you know you're poor right now, and your expectation for the future is continued poverty. What happens, then, if you are suddenly flooded with prosperity? You will subconsciously correct for the mistake by carelessly spending, losing, or giving away the money to maintain your present picture of yourself as poor. So, if you just *wish* to be different, or *want* to change, or *intend* to change, and you don't correctly alter your picture first, the tension in your system will drive you back to "where you belong." That's why it's so vital to *consciously control* the process of changing your picuture of "where you belong."

The tools I'm leading you to—affirmations and visualization—will help you avoid these roadblocks on the route to growth and success. They will provide the key step up to the next plateau: *deliberate preparation for a predetermined outcome*. You will use them to help deliberately anticipate the way you want your life to be—working the new job; living in the new house; enjoying the new marriage, the new friends, the new outlook on health, the new—. So start looking ahead a little bit. How would you envision your life in the near future? What would constitute the best fall for you? The best winter? The best spring? The best summer? How would you imagine the ideal job for you? If you could design the ideal day, what would it be like? How about the ideal week? The ideal weekend? What kind of people would you have around you? What sort of conversations? What kind of entertainment? How would you imagine your ideal relationships—family-wise, socially, spiritually? Where would you like to live? How would you like to feel every day?

Think about all this as you prepare to invent your future and build a better you.

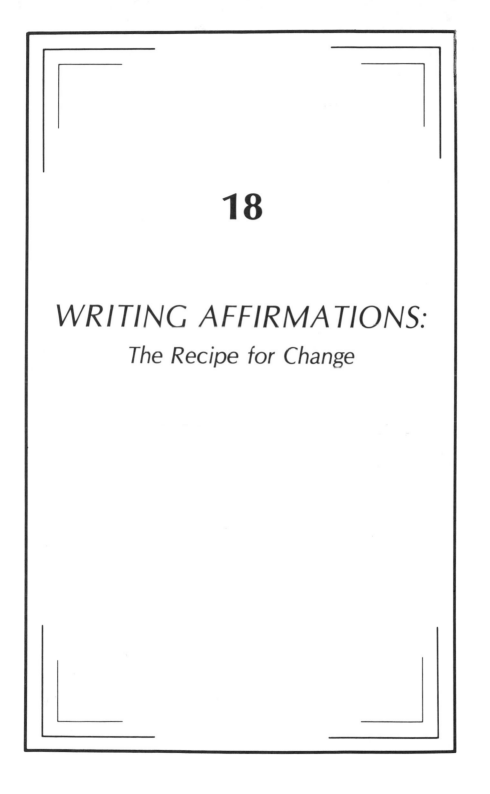

18

WRITING AFFIRMATIONS:

The Recipe for Change

Now we come to the tools that millions of people have used to enhance their lives. This is where all the principles and techniques in the book come together. Now that you understand the importance of your self-image and how it is formed, the significance of self-talk, how comfort zones work, the keys to restrictive and constructive motivation, the importance of changing your picture, and the need to set goals constantly for the future, you are ready to start building a better you.

The decision to set goals for growth and change is the first step. The next step is to consciously visualize your goals in your mind. The third step is to write your goals down as affirmations—statements of fact or belief. The last, and most important, step is to correctly imprint the goals into your subconscious belief system, often and vividly, until your future goal becomes your present reality. That is the effortless, safe way to grow and change.

Written affirmations are simply a blueprint for growth and change. Remember: This isn't magic; there is nothing exotic about it. Goal-setting is a natural part of the life process. It's as practical as balancing your checkbook. Transforming imagery into written affirmations is a reliable way of deliberately programming your subconscious mind to anticipate desired changes as if they have already happened.

Here are my step-by-step guidelines for how it's done.

1. *Where to Change*
Before setting goals, you must consider the areas in which you would like to grow and change. Maybe you're already good at something, but you'd like to be better. Maybe you've never done something, and you're eager to try it. Maybe you want to alter some

characteristics in your personality, some habits you don't like, or some outdated attitudes. Or maybe you'd like to adopt totally new habits and attitudes—naturally and free-flowingly—so they're part of your new picture of you. You might want to improve your financial situation. Or you might just want to adjust your attitude about prosperity—deciding whether you deserve it or not. Maybe you want to improve your memory, your concentration, or your stamina at work. You might want to change your views on education, politics, religion. Maybe you'd like to get into the habit of cooking for yourself, exercising regularly, reading more books, or mowing the lawn. Or maybe you'd just like to change your attitude about having a gardener. It could be a change in the way you treat your family, like your attitude about showing love to your kids. In any case, the first step is to give some thought to *where* you would like to grow and change.

2. *Writing Goals Down*

Why should you write your goals down in the form of affirmations? First, so you don't forget them. Second, to remove them from the realm of chance. Rather than passively wishing, hoping, or intending to change, and leaving it to circumstance, you write down affirmations to start *deliberately* changing "the way things are supposed to be" for you. Third, by writing affirmations to change your picture, you can achieve goals effortlessly and safely, without the stress of "trying hard."

A written goal, like a recipe, prompts vivid imagery of an end result. That imagery—along with the emotions it stimulates—imprint in the subconscious as if the goal is already accomplished. Remember: The subconscious doesn't know the difference between something real and something vividly imagined. It works like this: First you set a goal—for example, baking a cake. Next, you read the recipe. Then, in your mind's eye, you visualize the end result: the baked cake. Next, through repetition and anticipation, you imprint the vivid image of the baked cake so powerfully in your subconscious that you can almost smell and taste it. Now you start anticipating the joy of eating it: "I can hardly wait to eat that cake." At this point, even though you have only changed your picture *inside*, you feel as if you've just baked the actual cake. Then, when you perceive that you don't *have* a baked cake yet, you've got a problem.

That causes the dissonance, so you need to tell yourself, "Straighten up the mess!" That process, which starts with just a *written affirmation*, creates the energy and motivation you need to make the pictures match. So you bake the cake and achieve your goal.

Now, the emotion—the "I can hardly wait" anticipation—stimulated by looking forward to the goal, is essential to this process. Without that anticipation, your goals might turn into half-hearted intentions that never happen—like those New Year's Eve resolutions. If you don't vividly target the end result, your belief system can't trigger the Gestalt to accomplish it. So, *writing goals down* initiates the process of targeting your goals by imagining them vividly. Keep in mind that wishing, hoping, or intending to change is like waiting for the Fairy Godmother to transform you into a prince or princess. She isn't coming, and neither are your desired changes—unless you deliberately follow through on them. And the first step is disciplining yourself to write your goals down.

3. *Brief Definition*

Written affirmations are goals about "the way things are supposed to be" in the future: "This is the way my life is supposed to be," "This is the way my family is supposed to be," "This is the way I am supposed to look." An affirmation is a way of stretching present reality by imagining a new "supposed to be." If you have a lot of areas in which you want to grow, you might feel overwhelmed. Then you might end up setting goals haphazardly, leaving them to chance. One way to commit yourself to setting new goals regularly is to write them down in clear, concise, one- or two-sentence definitions.

A one- or two-sentence goal statement, as opposed to a paragraph or a whole page, provides a manageable definition that is easy to visualize and imprint into your subconscious mind. Remember: It isn't the writing that makes the change; it's the process of visualizing with feeling, and then imprinting. So it is essential that each goal, or each aspect of a goal, be written simply, clearly, concretely. But you don't need to limit yourself to just *one* brief affirmation per goal, because some goals will be more complex than others. If you are working on an elaborate change in one area of your life, you may need *several* brief affirmations, each one covering a particular quality or characteristic.

For example, let's say you want to affirm an overall improvement in your personal relationships. You can write a broad, general affirmation like "I am receptive and friendly toward all the people I meet. I treat everyone with consideration and respect." If you want to set more specific goals within that category, you can write additional affirmations for each one. For instance, "I am thoughtful and patient with my mother." I am sensitive to my brother." "I listen to my daughter with care and interest, especially when she talks about herself." Or suppose you want to improve your golf game. You might want one affirmation for your short game, another one for your long game, another one for handling pressure. . . and so on. And how could you fully describe, in just one brief goal-statement, what kind of parent you want to be? You might need one affirmation to cover your overall attitude on parenting, another on improving your relationship with your son, another on relating to your daughter, another for the kind of education you want for your kids, another for the emotional support you want to provide at home. If each aspect of the overall goal is written in a one- or two-sentence definition, it will aid in the imprinting process because each one will imprint separately and distinctly.

4. *Experiential Imagery*

In an earlier chapter, I suggested that you should remember the formula $I \times V = R$—Imagination times Vividness equals Reality (on the subconscious level). Well, here is where use of that formula is most critical. In writing affirmations, you want to trigger, in your subconscious, an experiential image of you doing, having, being something, as though it's actually happening right now. Remember: Whenever we vividly imagine something, and we hold it long enough in our mind, it becomes reality on the subconscious level. So you want to visualize your goal in such vivid imagery that it creates a new "R"—a new reality—in your belief system.

When you trigger experiential imagery, your mind becomes a simulator in which, like the DC 10 pilot, you can actually *hear* the tires blowing out, and *feel* the plane skidding down the runway, and *smell* the rubber burning, and *see* yourself grabbing the controls to bring the plane safely to a halt: "*Got it!*" You've created such powerful imagery in your mind that you actually feel as though you're

211

living the experience. Only then will your subconscious record the imagined event, or goal, as if it is actually *happening*.

That's what you're after when you write your affirmations. A properly written affirmation triggers experiential images which stimulate the right emotions, which eventually imprint in your belief system as your new present reality. It works like the TV car commercials where the camera places you almost literally in the driver's seat. You "experience" the feeling of driving, and you record, "This is *my* car. I own it." When you record that imagery repeatedly in your mind, and then you later drive your old car again, your subconscious triggers the Gestalt that says, "You have a problem. Straighten up the mess!" At that point, your picture has changed, because now you see yourself driving the *new* car.

An important guideline here is that the experiential imagery must feature *you* at the center. In visualizing your own goals, you don't see someone else achieving them, you see yourself achieving them. Did you ever point out to your kid, "Look at how those other children behave. Why can't you behave like them?" Well, one reason might be, "Oh, I can see how *they* behave. But I can't see *me* doing that." In other words, I can see somebody else parachute-jumping from an airplane but, quite frankly, I can't see *me* jumping out of an airplane.

If you don't see yourself at the center, your goal imagery won't trigger the Gestalt to make the pictures match. What would happen if the TV car commercial showed *someone else* driving the car? Instead of feeling "It's *my* car," you'd feel "It's *their* new car"—and that wouldn't create the motivation for you to buy the new car. That's why the imagery must be personal and experiential. If just any image worked, all we would do is observe someone, and we'd immediately become just like them. That doesn't happen. If I just watch Bill Cosby on TV and think "Gee, I'd like to be like him," I won't suddenly become just like him. If somebody living in poverty watches a "Dynasty" or a "Dallas," and thinks, "Gee, I'd like to live like that," they won't suddenly become rich and powerful just by watching a TV show about the rich and powerful.

Years ago, I was in Arizona visiting a friend who had just bought a beautiful new home at the edge of a golf course in Phoenix. We went to see this house and I said, "I'm happy for you. I'm really glad you have this new home." But as I was driving away, I told myself, "I will never have a house like that if I keep talking this way." I realized that I could see my *friend* in that kind of house, but not myself. I had always wanted to live like that, but I couldn't see myself into that situation yet. So I knew I had to work on seeing *me* into my goals, not somebody else. Otherwise, instead of creating the Gestalt for change, I'd end up creating envy, wishes, or idle dreams.

So the imagery triggered by your affirmations must stimulate strong experiential emotion that tells your subconscious, "This is happening to *me*." Until you see *you* doing, having, being something, it doesn't affect your present image of reality.

5. *Specific Details*

Your goal-setting affirmations must convey specific and detailed imagery, so your subconscious can record the goal as concretely as the image of the baked cake. You can set a goal, for example, to wake up in the morning. But that goal is too narrow. You can improve it by adding small details: "I am going to awaken full of energy and enthusiasm." Or "I am going to awaken full of energy and enthusiasm, feeling strong, and looking forward to getting to work." In other words, keep adding to the party. Remember: Once you arrive at the specific goal you set, you "flatten out" until you set another goal.

Keep in mind, too, that you must set clear, concrete goals. If you say, "I am a nice person," that will be difficult for you to visualize. If you say, "I am a strong leader," that still isn't specific enough. Pinpoint exactly what you choose to be, and how you choose to be it. Otherwise, it will be like telling the waiter in a restaurant, "Bring me some food." The waiter has no idea what you want because *you* don't know. But what happens when you pin it down and say, "Bring me a double cheeseburger, slice of pickle, onions on the side, wheat bun, glass of iced tea with a lemon wedge?" Now the waiter knows exactly what to bring. And you can almost taste it, can't you?

Having an accurately defined target is essential for both individual and group goal-setting. You and your people could goal-set for your company to have "a good year." But why would you only want to have a "good" year? If you are vague about your target, you won't get any *feedback*, and if you don't get feedback, your system won't know when you're off-target. Of course, if you don't have feedback, you don't get the uncomfortable dissonance. On the other hand, you also don't get the *motivation* to attain your goal. That's why coaches say, "It's going to be a building year." Or someone asks a supervisor, "How do you think business will be this year?" and the supervisor says, "Oh, better." These statements mean *"Keep the heat off me."* It's like someone who doesn't really want to exercise saying, "I'll do a little jogging." You know how much "a little" is? Maybe fifty feet. Maybe less. You think your subconscious isn't that precise? You must pinpoint what you want—the exact distance, the exact amount of new business, the exact income, the exact career—because then your subconscious holds you accountable, gives you feedback, and makes you act as you believe yourself to be.

So, effective goal-setting means deliberately determining what is important. As soon as you determine that, you become very "lucky." Your Reticular Activating System opens up and filters through the pertinent information. The less specific the visualization, the less information that gets through. For example, if you go out looking just for "something" for your children for Christmas, you probably won't find anything. Because how do you visualize *"something"*? But if you're looking for a 24-inch trail bike with quick-release wheels, zap, they'll scream through everywhere: "There's one! There's one! There's one!"

One time, years ago, I decided I wanted a swimming pool. But I was a teacher and football coach; I couldn't afford it. So I decided to get a swimming pool *for free*. As soon as I decided, click, swimming pools started screaming through like the baby's cry. I saw them, I heard about them, I read about them—but none were free. So I asked an informed friend, "Where can I get a swimming pool for free?" He immediately took me to the north end of the Seattle-Tacoma Airport where they were extending the runway. Workers were preparing to move a big brick home, which had a great big, old swimming pool. My friend said, "You can probably get that one for nothing."

Now, I know what you're thinking, "How do you move a swimming pool?" That's another story. But, believe me, I found a way.

6. Positive
A key to effective goal-setting is affirming your goals in the

positive. Always write your goals based upon what you *want*, not what you don't want. It's a process of moving away from the negative, away from restrictive and coercive motivation, away from the flames of hell. The images in your goal statements must be positive images of something you want to possess. Instead of visualizing your old impatience, you visualize distinct situations in which you act patient; instead of visualizing short, bitten fingernails, you visualize long, elegant fingernails; instead of affirming, "I don't want to drop the football when the pressure is on," you affirm, "I always catch the football when the pressure is on." Remember: When you have a problem, you don't dwell on the problem because that's what your subconscious will record. You don't visualize the rock; you visualize the way *around* the rock.

So, if you have problems or conflicts, before writing your affirmations ask yourself this key question: *"How would it be if I didn't have the problem?"* The answer to that becomes your written goal statement. For example, suppose you think, "I've got this terrible temper." That is your problem. So you ask yourself, "How would it be if I didn't have my terrible temper?" And you might answer, "I would remain cool, calm, and poised under pressure." From that, you develop your positive goal statement for any given circumstance: "Whenever the kids fight with each other, I am always cool, calm, and poised." "Whenever a crisis at the office occurs, I am always cool, calm, and poised." It's that easy. Or suppose your problem is "I don't have any money." If you affirm the problem, what happens? Your subconscious confirms that reality—"Okay, if that's the way you want it"—and it keeps you in poverty. But suppose you ask yourself, "What would it be like if I had enough money to live happily for a few years?" Then, instead of affirming the *problem*: "I'm broke. I only have thirty cents to my name," you affirm the *solution*: "Money flows toward me like water out of a faucet. I have a hundred grand in the bank."

It's the difference between negatively affirming the *problem*: "My teenage sister and I don't get along"—and positively affirming the *solution*: "Because of the caring way I treat my teenage sister, we get along like best friends." The key is to trigger positive images of what you want, not negative images of what you don't want. Even though you haven't the slightest idea *how* you will accomplish the goal, you have already created the Gestalt to accomplish it. It's the combination of creating the positive image of what you want, and looking at "the way things *"is"* now, that creates the motivation to make the pictures match. So goal-setting negatively to lose weight—"I'm too heavy for my own good"—and then refusing to step on the scale for feedback, will do nothing. It will merely extend today's reality into tomorrow. Because remember: *We move toward, and we become like, that which we think about.*

7. Realistic

One important reminder: You must always set *realistic* goals. What is "realistic"? If you can vividly see and feel yourself experientially attaining the goal, then it's realistic for you. If not, then you need to back it up a little closer to your vision. Say you're only in kindergarten and someone says, "Won't it be great to be in college?" At that age, you can't realistically visualize what college would be like. If you're thirty pounds overweight at age fifty, you probably can't realistically imagine yourself being as slim as you were at seventeen. It's the same as me not being able to visualize myself parachuting from a plane. I can't envision what that would be like. If you can't imagine your goal vividly, *experientially*, with the right emotion, your subconscious will know it's unrealistic, and the goal won't imprint in your mind.

So how far into the future can you see yourself doing, having, or being what you want? Why not just say, "If all this goal-setting stuff works, I'll just goal-set to be a billionare and save time"? It isn't that simple. You can't just say you want to be something and change your picture. If you can't realistically visualize yourself as a billionaire, you won't create the dissonance, so nothing will happen. How do billionaires think and act? What do their homes look like inside? Where do they shop? Where do they eat? Who are their friends? Can you really see yourself as a billionaire? I can't. I don't know what they do or how they live. But I *can* see myuself maybe doubling my present income. Like a lot of people, I feel as though I'm *spending* that much now!

The idea is to visualize your goal close enough so you can see yourself into it. But be careful; if you set your goals *too* close, you will lose motivation, energy, drive. So set your goals with about fifty percent believability for now. Later, when you are more proficient at it, you will be able to gauge how far into your future you really can see. Keep in mind that setting realistic goals doesn't mean your goals can't be quite a ways out there. I have been affirming and changing my lifestyle drastically for years. But back when I left high school teaching, I couldn't imagine myself living or thinking the way I do now. It would have been way out of my comfort zone, and much too unrealistic.

I grew up in poverty. My dad died when I was twelve, so I had to help raise our family. I sold holly, I sold newspapers, I did all kinds of odd jobs just to eat and stay alive. By the time I left teaching to start my own business, quite frankly, my vision of the future was very narrow. In fact, all I could imagine at the time was making enough money to survive. Diane and I had $1000 in the bank, bills to pay, nine kids to feed, and one seminar with seven people—and most of them were relatives. I thought, "If I can just make twice as much as when I was teaching, I can run my business and feed my family." But because I learned the information in this curriculum and started building a better me by stretching my comfort zone and setting bigger goals, I have continually managed to expand what is "realistic" for me. Remember that, because once you get the handle on this kind of adventurous goal-setting, the same thing will happen to you.

Now, being realistic when visualizing the future may seem contradictory. But remember: It's the gap between the two which creates the internal disharmony that you need to stimulate change. The gap between current reality and your vision causes your system to say, "You've got a problem!" The problem might be the difference between your vision of the career you want and the career you currently have; between your vision of the income you *want* and the income you currently have; between your vision of the way you *want* to get along with your family and the way you get along with them now. That gap, or feeling of disharmony, is the dissonance in your system that eventually drives you to "straighten up the mess." But because of that same uncomfortable tension, people sometimes won't set goals much further than their current reality. They can't stand the dissonance.

Be honest with yourself; did you ever dream about having, doing, or being something new, and feel miserable just thinking about it? That's the dissonance of current reality—that's the problem. But remember: Don't shut it off. You *want* the problem. That's what will bring out the best in you. What you must do is learn how to hold the vision in your imagination *stronger* than the sting of current reality. If you can do that—through affirmations, visualization, and proper imprinting of your goal—eventually you will attain your goal. But if you shut it off, if you can't stand the dissonance of current reality, you won't be able to realistically see yourself into the change.

8. *First Person, Present Tense*

In first-person, present-tense goal-setting, you write all of your goals with you at the center: "*I* am a warm, compassionate mother." "*I* am a decisive father." "*I* treat everybody fairly." "*I* am a leader in my company." It will sound selfish because you will always be talking about you. But that's absolutely necessary if you want to change your picture. Keep in mind also that you cannot affirm to change someone else; you can only affirm to change yourself. While writing this book, I could have affirmed, "Because of the clarity, the logic, the convincing examples, and the spirit in which this information is being delivered, readers will easily understand and apply the concepts I'm teaching in this book." It wouldn't have made any difference. Because I only have the power to affirm changes in *me*, not in you. If I want the information in this book to have a positive affect on you, I can only affirm that I will write clearly, sensibly, colorfully, and forcefully enough to make it easy for you to learn. The rest is up to each individual reader.

There's a second step. If you want your personal goals to imprint in your belief system, you must affirm them in the present tense—in the "now"—as though you already *are* that person: "I *am* the new department manager." "I *am* friendly and outgoing." "I *am* a .300 hitter." You affirm that you already live in the new house, even though you still live in the old one; that you've already won the game before it's played; that you have enough money to take that vacation, even though you only have twenty dollars in the bank. If you weigh 140 pounds and you want to weigh 120, you might write an affirmation like "I look young and feel confident and attractive at 120 pounds." You write the goal as though it is already achieved, even though it isn't. If you trigger the right imagery and emotion, your subconscious will believe you.

You might wonder "Am I lying to myself?" The answer is no. You are simply altering your image of reality. Affirmations are neither moral nor immoral. They are neutral. They are just the trigger tools for creating the right imagery for change. By using first-person, present-tense affirmations, you're deliberately triggering a conflict to stimulate the Gestalt to "straighten up the mess" and make the pictures match. That's what drives you to accomplish your goal. Why Because once your picture changes—"I *am* 120 pounds." I *live* in the new neighborhood." "I *love* my job."—and you perceive that, presently, you don't actually *have* what you've affirmed, your system says, "You've got a problem." Immediately, it starts correcting for this mistake by providing the motivation you need to act "just like me." So goal-setting is simply a process of constantly stretching what is presently "just like me."

Another key reason why you must write your affirmations in the present tense is because, otherwise, you might end up affirming *ability* or *potential* instead of accomplishment. For example, if instead of affirming, "I *am* patient with my kids," you affirm, "I *can be* patient with my kids", nothing happens inside of you. Your subconscious has nothing to change because you already possess the ability to be patient with your kids. The same is true if you affirm, "I *can be* brave," or "I *intend to be* rich," or "I'd *like to be* a dynamic leader." In affirming your potential, you don't create any Gestalt for change. Keep in mind that when you think, "I *can be*" or "I *intend to be*" or "I'd *like to be*," you are also thinking, "*but right now, I'm not.*" And since the subconscious is a literal mechanism, when you affirm, "I *can be* a nice person," it records, "I *can be* a nice person, *but right now I'm a jerk.*" See? "I *can be* rich, *but right now I'm poor.*" "I'd *like to be* brave, *but right now I'm scared.*"

So affirming your ability or potential doesn't alter your present reality. You must affirm *achievement*: "I *am* a loving father." "I *am* a winning athlete." "I *am* a dynamic leader." "I *am*—" If you don't affirm in the present tense—"It's over, it's done, I've got it." —you won't create the motivation to achieve the end result that you want. And you will end up wondering, "Why can't I change?"

Lastly, you must affirm in the present tense because otherwise you might get trapped affirming the past. Remember: "*Our present thoughts determine our future.*" So, what happens if you sit around thinking past tense—"the way things *used to be*"—while you're immersed in present reality—the way things *is*"? The pictures don't match, so you become discontent with the present. But you don't long to improve it, you long to go back. That's like some elderly people who like to complain, "Ain't things awful? I remember the good old days when—." They live every day not in the present, but in "the way things used to be." If you are around people like that, you need to be careful not to start unconsciously affirming *their* self-talk: "Things are crummy. People are mean. Values are dead. The world has gone to hell." What will your tomorrow look like if this is how you describe today? It will look the same.

That's what blocks most change. People keep reproducing, in their minds, the way things look right now, or "the way things used to be." Some retired athletes like to talk about the big game twenty years ago because, when they quit sports, they didn't goal-set to accomplish much else. So they get trapped talking constantly about history. Even some astronauts get trapped. Wherever they appear— at speeches, at parties, in TV interviews—people keep asking them about the past: "What was it like to walk on the moon?" They're always signing autographs for what they did, not for what they are going to do. They constantly dwell on history, so it's tough for them to grow, even though they once accomplished something great.

That's why you must be cognizant of how you are talking and thinking. And what about the people around you—family, friends, business associates? What are *they* talking and thinking about? History or the future? High-performance people—who are constantly growing and changing—think future tense as though it's done: "The money's earned." "The game is won." "The house is built." They continually invent their own future *before* it happens. Remember: The future is *now*. So affirm all your goals in the present tense—or your tomorrows will look like yesterday.

9. No Comparisons

If you feel you can only grow by comparing yourself to somebody else, you will always think that somebody else is better than you or worse than you. If you feel they're better, that's like adding a negative weight to your attitudinal balance scale: "I am not as handsome as him." "I'm not as pretty as her." "He's a better hitter."

"She's a better doctor." That's restrictive motivation. Instead of feeling, "I *choose to* set this goal for my own personal growth," you always feel you *"have to"* become better than someone else. Or, if you feel they're worse, you relieve your dissonance, not by getting what you want, but by finding someone who has even less. Comparing is like saying, "I'll achieve *their* goal, only I have to do it better than them." It's negative, ineffective goal-setting.

So you don't grow by comparisons. First of all, why would you want, or need, to be better than somebody else? You have your own unique visions, fears, comfort zones, attitudes, and "Who-Saids" of the Greatest Magnitude which other people don't know about. So it doesn't do any good to compare yourself with somebody else when it is you who must do the growing and changing. You must choose to grow for more significant reasons than just to beat somebody else.

There is a place for a healthy competitiveness. For example, I work a lot with college and professional athletes. They need a competitive, attack mentality to achieve their personal and team goals— to be better than their opponents so they can win. That's different than competing with family members, with friends, or with fellow employees. The very nature of putting together a winning athletic team demands competition with other teams, whereas competing against family members produces only disharmony and discontent. Competing against friends might ruin friendships. Competing against fellow employees in a company can breed selfish attitudes and habits that will be counterproductive to the overall company goals. Keep in mind that the best salesperson in any particular company may not be very good. So if you are better than that person, you might still be mediocre. Yet, if your goal is not to be the best salesperson you can possibly be, but rather to merely be better than the *company's* best salesperson, you might feel satisfied with beating the company's best. The danger in that kind of goal-setting is that you can "flatten out" in mediocrity, thinking you're the best.

You are in the business of personal growth and change—for your *own* reasons. You already have enough *internal* competition that can detour your growth: Your own restrictive motivation; your own flat worlds; your own blocks, traps, and lids. You are trying to become the best possible you, and to improve your personal relationships with everyone in your own world. So a healthy, personal goal-setting attitude would be "I am trying to build a better world and a better me."

There is a healthy, positive way to incorporate in your own goal-setting whatever you admire in others. You can observe people you admire and try to emulate them. You tell yourself, "I like the way she treats her family." "I like the way they run their company." "I like that quality." "I like that attitude." "I like—." That is not comparing yourself to anyone else. You are not telling yourself that you're better or worse than somebody else. You are just observing qualities you like, and making affirmations to assimilate them into your own belief system.

I am a good teacher and public speaker, but I am continually working to improve. So I have studied other people who I think are excellent, too. I studied Jack Benny for his timing. I studied Bill Cosby for his gentle, insightful humor. I studied Bishop Fulton Sheen for his emotional magnetism on TV. I studied Martin Luther King, Sir Winston Churchill, and Billy Graham for their remarkable ability to captivate and move an audience. I studied flamenco dancers for their ability to gather eyes to their hands. I studied Tai Chi to learn how to channel an inner sense of power and control. I studied French singers—even though I didn't know French—because of their extraordinarily powerful use of body langauge.

I would always reflect later: "I like this and I like that," and I would lay back and visualize how I would integrate all those different elements into my own personal speaking style. I didn't compare myself to any of them, and I didn't create a competition for myself. Even though there are others in the same business as mine, you know who my only competition is? *Me.* I want to be more capable, more creative, more dynamic and clear and interesting in presenting these concepts. I want to improve *me*, so I can become a better delivery system for this information so other people can improve their lives. And that's the way *you* want to feel when you set *your* goals.

10. *Spirit of Intent*

Written affirmations will have no power to change your belief system unless they are buttressed by a strong spirit of commitment. Just as when you compliment someone else with genuine feeling, it is the spirit of genuine and deliberate intent in your own affirmations which creates the dynamic change inside of you. Words that are empty of commitment are merely worthless platitudes. Remember the wizard concept? Well, when you invest as much credibility in your own word to yourself as you invested in the word of wizards in your life, you will not need to keep repeating your affirmations until your picture changes. When you really get good at this, one affirmation—like the "I do" wedding vow—will be enough to make the change.

Affirmations make you more aware of the immense power of words. You will discover that sometimes, when you set a goal, you will be unconsciously kidding yourself. You won't be seriously committed to your goal. Eventually, if you really want to grow and change, you will stop using words idly both to yourself and to others. Remember that words are only seeds. They have to be nourished with your intent in order to transform you from within. Some people will need to repeat their affirmations often to talk themselves into it. Some will visualize and affirm often to build up their sense of worthiness before they are willing to believe, "It's over, it's done." Some already feel worthy enough to immediately believe, "It's mine." It is all a matter of how good your word is to you and to everyone else.

I have affirmed my goals for years and made drastic changes in all areas of my life. My word is pretty strong now. If I give my word in an affirmation, it's done, it's over, it's mine. Years ago, I was about thirty pounds overweight, but I didn't really care. Every so often, I would half-heartedly make an affirmation about losing some weight, but nothing would happen. Sometimes, I would get up in the morning and glance in the mirror and say to myself, "Today's the day." Of course, what I really meant was, "Today's the day—if nothing gets in the way." You know what got in the way? Lunch. Or, if I skipped lunch, two dinners would get in the way to correct for the mistake. It was funny. I could make all kinds of things happen in my personal and professional worlds with just one affirmation, yet when it came to losing weight, I had affirmation cards stacked as high as a table. I wonder why.

Obviously, my word on that issue was worthless to me. Yet there I was at the office, talking about bouncing information off satellites, and doing business in Great Britain and Asia and South America, and starting this and venturing into that. I had to sometimes ask myself, "Hey, is this nonsense, too?" Finally, a few summers ago, I decided to quit fooling around. I said, "Okay, that's it.

No more." And I lost forty pounds in six weeks. I wasn't hungry even once. What was the difference between fifteen years of affirming, "Today's the day," and one morning of affirming, "No more fooling myself"? *My spirit of intent.*

So be aware that all of your well-meaning goals are garbage without the spirit of total commitment behind them. But if you combine real intent with properly written affirmations, nothing can get in your way. You can change belief and you can change your life. It's that easy. You know why I finally decided to lose that weight? I wanted to make myself tougher so I could move on to bigger accomplishments in life—like helping millions of other people build a better world. That one affirmation about fooling myself improved my word so powerfully, I now believe I can do just about anything.

So when you say, "I think I'll quit smoking," or "I think I'll be a better person," I say, "Save your breath." One thing you might consider, in fact, is affirming the power of your own word to yourself. That could be your first affirmation: granting yourself the ability to do what you say you will do.

11. *Private*

Lastly, when you set your private goals, I suggest you keep them to yourself. You might want to share some mutual goals with family members, teammates, or fellow employees. If so, share them only with those people who will help you achieve them. Do not share your goals with people who will work against you. Only you know who those people are.

Sometimes, when we tell people about our goals, we start to feel as though we can't back out: "Well, I said it. Now I *have to* do it." You don't need that kind of restrictive motivation. Set all your goals on a "want-to, like-to, choose-to" basis. Otherwise, you will feel coerced into achieving them. Another pitfall might be losing your flexibility to attain the goal. I remember when we told our children that we were moving to a new home—*before* we found one. We sold the old one and prepared to move out. Our daughter, Nancy, was only in second grade at the time, and we thought she would be unhappy about having to move away from her friends. So we assured her that we would rent a house in the neighborhood until we found a house to buy, and she could stay in her old school. I will never forget her reaction. She said, "No! I'll run away!" I said, "Run away? The kids *love* you at school." She said, "I'm running away!" I said, "Why?" She said, "I told everyone we were moving, and they gave me a going-away party. I can't go back!" See, once we shared the goal, we lost our flexibility in terms of the timing. When you keep your goal to yourself, you have greater flexibility, and the timing is always in your control.

There is also the possibility that the people with whom you share your goal might not be very supportive. Suppose you affirm a goal about being more patient with your spouse, and you tell them about it. If you have a temporary setback, your spouse might say, "Well, this stuff isn't working, is it? I thought you were going to be patient." Then *your* attitude might change to, "Well, I was. But I'll be darned if I will now!"

A further possibility is that people who love you might try to talk you out of your goals because, as you change, you are changing *their* reality, too: "What are you moving for?" "Are you studying French so you can be better than me?" "Why did you invest in that business? You should save the money to fix up the house." Change can threaten people who have grown accustomed to "the way things are supposed to be" for you. Those closest to you may give you all kinds of advice: "Why don't you just be satisfied with what you've got? Don't try to reach too high or you'll get hurt. I'm just trying to protect you because I love you." See? You don't want that kind of aggravation. They don't mean to do it, but you are changing their comfort zones, so they're fighting for their own sanity. That's why it might be best to set your goals silently, and let the changes speak for themselves.

Remember what this is all about: You are embarking on the adventure of building a better you. Writing affirmations is not magic. It is only the first step in a conscious, deliberate process of change. The *imprinting* of your goals is what makes the difference.

So hang on, because that comes next.

19

IMPRINTING:

The New Reality

Meaningful and Lasting Change

Written affirmations initiate the goal-setting process by triggering images *now* of "the way things are supposed to be" for you in the *future*. But the next step—imprinting—is the real key to change. Because it is imprinting that constantly activates the new reality in your life.

The subconscious imprinting of a goal, vividly and with powerful emotion, creates the energy, drive, and motivation you need to attain it. Remember: Only when you imprint the image of you as having already attained the goal does your inner picture—your self-image—change. And once you change the picture *inside*, your creative subconscious has the job of making sure the new picture happens *outside* consistently in your life. Whenever it doesn't happen outside, your subconscious corrects for the mistake so you can continually act "just like me." For example, to change your picture from that of a cigarette smoker to that of a nonsmoker, you must first affirm that you don't smoke ("I love feeling healthy and vigorous now that I am a nonsmoker."), then vividly visualize yourself as a nonsmoker. Pretty soon, when someone offers you a cigarette, you will automatically say, "No thanks. I don't smoke." If you have imprinted the goal correctly, you now *see* yourself as a nonsmoker.

I'm not talking about changing your picture temporarily by *forcing* yourself to change, and holding on through the dissonance. I'm talking about meaningful and lasting change. I'm talking about natural, automatic, free-flowing, effortless change. I am not asking you to go out and try hard to be what you affirm. Just affirm and imprint the picture you want, and then go out and continue to be yourself. If you imprint the goal properly, eventually the new picture will record in your subconscious and you will start acting like it automatically. You don't want to *remember* to be brave, you don't want to *remember* to be more assertive, you don't want to *remember* to be a nonsmoker. You want to do it *automatically*.

So, in effect, you use affirmations, visualization, and imprinting to change your subconscious reality in order to behave automatically the way you *want* to behave. That's the way change should occur—automatically, safely, without tension or stress. So you are really not trying to alter the way you *act*; you are trying to alter the way you *think about you*. Once you change your picture of you, the automatic process takes over and keeps you acting like your new picture. That's the way it happens every time—once you master the imprinting technique.

Here's how it works.

Read, Picture, Feel

Once you have written your goal in the form of an affirmation, there's a simple, three-step process of imprinting that goal in your subconscious mind as if it's actually happening to you now. Let's try an experiment to illustrate how this process works. Read this and then try it.

1. Close your eyes and relax.
2. Imagine yourself going purposefully into your kitchen to find a fresh lemon. Start walking to the refrigerator.
3. Open the refrigerator door and pull out the fruit bin. Reach into the bin for a firm, yellow lemon.
4. Close the door and take the lemon to the counter.
5. Roll the lemon back and forth until it starts to soften.
6. Reach in the cutlery drawer for a knife, and slice the juicy lemon in half.
7. Take one half of the lemon and slowly bring it to your mouth. It's coming closer; you can smell the juice. It's almost in your mouth. You can practically *taste* it. . . .
8. Now take a big bite.

Okay, open your eyes. Do you actually taste the lemon in your mouth? Can you feel the tartness on your tongue? Yet *there is no lemon*. What made it so real was your vivid visualization of finding, rolling, slicing, and biting into a juicy lemon. As I pointed out earlier, an event need not actually occur for you to "experience" and record it subconsciously. You must simply imagine it vividly, as if it *were* occurring. The vividly imagined experience of biting into a lemon is recorded in your subconscious *as if it really happened* because your subconscious can't tell the difference. And, in the future, every time you summon this same imagery in your mind, you will react physiologically, as if you were biting into a real lemon.

That is the imprinting process. It is the actualization of the $I \times V = R$ (Imagination times Vividness equals Reality) formula. A written affirmation creates clear, vivid images, which stimulate the correct emotions, which imprints in your subconscious as the new reality. Every time you write your affirmations correctly, with vivid, experiential imagery, and then go through the imprinting process, you record the imagined event in your subconscious as if it is actually happening to you right now. That imprinting process really takes three steps:

1. *Read* the words of your affirmation to trigger the imagery in your mind.
2. *Picture* the images triggered by the words.
3. *Feel* the emotion stirred by the images, and "experience" the affirmation as if it were actually happening to you right now.

After you've written the proper affirmation, the *kind* of imagery you visualize becomes vitally important. Remember how the camera in a car commercial slides you behind the steering wheel to help you see yourself driving the car? That makes a very powerful imprint—even though you may not know it's happening. But it wouldn't make an imprint if you didn't see *yourself* behind the wheel. The television term, *"subjective camera angle,"* applies here. To imprint properly, you must visualize your goal from a *subjective camera angle*, as if it is happening to *you*, not somebody else. That's why just watching TV or a movie, or merely observing people doing something, won't change you. That's why I can watch *other* people parachute from a plane, without it causing me to want jump, too. For my reality to be affected, I must vividly visualize myself jumping from a plane—I must see the chute unfurling above me; feel the tug of the lines and the wind blasting into me; see my feet dangling beneath me, the clouds above, and the earth coming up fast. If I just write down an affirmation to jump from a plane and then read its words without visualizing the situation experientially, it won't record in my subconscious mind.

That's why the angle at which you visualize yourself into your goal situation is vital to the imprinting process. You must imagine the event exactly the way you would actually experience it. That means you must see yourself, not from a detached, objective, "outside-looking-in" angle, but from a close-up, subjective, "inside-looking-out" angle. In other words, exactly as you see the world right now. For example, if you imagined yourself biting into a lemon exactly the way you would really do it, you wouldn't see your back, or your face, or the refrigerator behind you. In fact, unless you observed yourself in a mirror, you wouldn't even see the lemon going into your mouth. You'd only see your hands raising the lemon toward your face. That's the *"subjective camera angle;"* you see only what you would see if you were participating in the actual event.

Let's say you visualized yourself delivering a talk to an audience from behind a podium. You would not see yourself from the audience's point of view, as though you were watching yourself in a movie. You would see everything as if you were actually standing at a podium facing an audience: the podium, the microphone, the audience, your upper body, your hands. Maybe I shouldn't say *"Visualize* yourself in the situation," because that may be misleading. Maybe I should say, *"Experience* yourself in the situation." See what I mean? Suppose you set a goal to improve your skiing. First you write an affirmation like, "It's easy and exhilarating for me to ski on my new skis." Then you close your eyes and try to mentally "experience" skiing on the new skis. What would you see if you were actually skiing? You would see the slope, the surrounding scenery, perhaps other skiers around you, your chest, arms, legs, boots, and the front of your skis. You would feel the wind on your face, you would smell the trees, you would hear the snow crunching beneath you, you would feel yourself shifting your weight and working your poles as you slice down the slopes. In other words, you would experience the kinesthetic feel of skiing, as if you were really doing it.

Remember when I talked about how difficult it was for me to demonstrate my love for my sons? Well, how did I imprint this affirmation: "It's easy and deeply fulfilling for me to show my sons how much I love them"? I would "experience" in my imagination an actual situation in which I am demonstrating love to one of my sons. So I would see myself entering a room—from *my* point of view. I would only see the room, my son, maybe a chair or the couch, and part of the rug. I would feel myself walking toward my son, and see my arms extending around him. Then I would feel the embrace and the warm, loving emotions it would stir inside me. In my mind, I would be right *in* the situation, close-up, "experiencing" it as if it were taking place right now. And soon it was happening naturally in my life.

You might be wondering, "What if I have trouble picturing, or 'experiencing,' affirmations in my mind?" One thing you can do is talk yourself through it. Explain to yourself where you are, vividly describe your surroundings, tell yourself why you're there. Ask yourself, "Who am I with? What am I doing? How do I feel?" If you still have difficulty painting clear images, it may be because you aren't relaxed enough. If you are under tension or stress, the picture will be fuzzy. Or perhaps your words are too general. You must be very specific and concrete. You don't want to affirm something vague like, "I am a good leader." How can you paint a picture of that? Instead, you want to affirm something specific like, "I am a calm and resourceful leader whenever my teammates lose their composure on the field." Or you could be even more precise: "I always make the big defensive play or get the crucial hit when my teammates are down and the game is on the line." Then you envision a specific crisis in a game, and picture yourself leading your team through it. See the difference?

The most vital aspect of imprinting is *feeling the emotion* triggered by the words. If you've written your affirmation correctly, with descriptive, experiential words, you will *feel* the excitement; you will *feel* the joy; you will *feel* the anticipation; you will *feel* the love; you will *feel* the thrill that your affirmation triggers. Remember: The correct words will stimulate that *"I can hardly wait!"* emotion—like the anticipation kids feel when they look forward to opening gifts. But keep in mind that just *any* old emotion won't work. You must imprint the *correct* emotion. Otherwise, like preparing the five-year-old for the first day of kindergarten by saying, "Your teacher's a monster," you will record the *wrong* emotion, and block yourself from attaining your goal. That's why your affirmations must provide positive, "emotion" words: "I *love to*—," "I *proudly*—," "I *enthusiastically*—," "I *eagerly*—." You want to imprint the love, the pride, the enthusiasm, the eagerness, not the tension, anxiety, or fear.

"Flick Back-Flick Up"

There is a special technique for building the specific emotion that you want when imprinting a goal. I call it the *"Borrowing Technique,"* or *"Flick Back-Flick Up."* This technique is especially useful when fear feedback—fear of heights, fear of public speaking, fear of meeting new people—blocks you from trying new situations. Remember how your subconscious works when you perceive a new situation? You *associate*, "Have I experienced anything like this before?" If so, you say, "Uh-huh." Then you *evaluate*, "What is this probably leading me toward?" If the past experience was negative, you think, "Nothing good"—and you get inventive finding ways to avoid raking the leaves.

Let's say I'm going to give a talk at someplace unfamiliar. What would keep me from getting up there and sweating profusely, forgetting my speech, losing my voice? How can I prepare myself *beforehand* for going into the wrong restroom? Well, mentally, I can "flick back" to a triumphant situation in my past, "borrow" the positive feelings that it recorded in my subconscious, and "flick up" those same feelings into my current situation. For example, in preparing to give a speech in an unfamiliar environment, I might reflect back to an experience I had in third grade when my teacher left me in charge of the whole class. At that time, it was the biggest responsibility I'd ever had. I really felt important, powerful, confident; I was boss of everybody in the class! And I did a pretty good job of keeping things under control. After that, every time the teacher left the room, he would put me in charge of the class again.

233

At the time, that feeling of being in charge welled up inside of me so powerfully, it boosted my self-esteem right through the roof. So whenever I need a boost of self-esteem and confidence *now*, I can reflect back to what I felt like when I was boss of my third grade class. I then project those positive emotions of esteem, power, confidence, and success forward, into my present situation. I see myself giving the upcoming talk, and I "borrow" the emotions I had when I was in charge of my third grade class.

Now, the best way to prepare, of course, is to "borrow" *beforehand*. I wouldn't wait until the moment I was about to face the audience, because that wouldn't give me enough time to firmly imprint the emotions in my subconscious. Instead, like pilots using a simulator, I would simulate the anticipated experience as concretely as possible at least a couple of days in advance. In this case, I got ahold of a photograph of the room in which I was to give my talk, and I projected that image into my visualization a week before I arrived. So I had plenty of time to meld the image of the room with the "borrowed" emotions which I wanted to feel when I actually got up there to give my talk. First, I wrote an affirmation like, "Whenever I give a talk in unfamiliar surroundings, I feel as confident and in control as when I was boss of my third grade class." Next, I visualized myself giving the speech in the unfamiliar room as if I were doing it right now. Lastly, I imprinted the emotions of esteem, confidence, control, and success that I'd "flicked up" from my experience in school. A couple of days later, when I actually delivered my speech, sure enough, it felt like déjà vu: "This is easy. I've done it before. It's over. It's mine."

In other instances, I've reflected back to other positive situations in my past: back to the sixth grade when I was captain of the safety patrol and president of the boys club; to seventh grade, when I was captain of the football team; to great successes in college; to some of my previously successful talks. The point is: With this technique, you don't leave the outcome to chance. You deliberately program it in beforehand. You just "flick back" and "flick up"—maybe ten times, maybe twenty times, maybe fifty—whatever works best for you through trial and error. You can use this method to prepare for a new social event, traveling to a new country, or having an important talk with your children—anything new for you. You just "borrow" from the old and drop it into the new to create that feeling of positive anticipation: "I can hardly wait. I'll blow them away. It's easy. It's over. It's mine."

Of course, there's a flip side to this technique. I didn't mention all the *negative* things that happened to me in the past—all the emotionally traumatic situations; the disappointments, embarrassments, failures, mistakes. Like most people, I've experienced my share of tragedy—awful events that I couldn't control. For instance, when I was coaching one time, I had a little boy drop dead right in front of me. And I remember breaking the news to his father. It was devastating for both of us. I have other traumas recorded in my subconscious. Sometimes, inadvertantly, I'll lock out options by anticipating a traumatic situation and telling myself, "No thanks. I've had my share of hell." So it can work against you, too.

Instead of locking out options, you must learn to lock out the disappointments, the embarrassments, the failures, the mistakes. You take the hit, learn, and move on. Lock out all the jobs you didn't get, all the failed relationships, all the times you fell on your face. Otherwise, without realizing it, you might prepare yourself for an upcoming situation by "borrowing" a negative emotion. So, like high-performance people, you learn to control your emotional preparation by disciplining yourself to dwell only on past successes. And *that's* what you project into the new event.

The idea is to always prepare to be at your best. When we work with college athletes, we use *"Flick Back-Flick Up"* to prepare a whole team for a winning outcome. For example, suppose we're trying to prepare the University of Texas to beat Oklahoma next week in the Cotton Bowl. First, we will have all the players set their winning goals and write them down in clear, specific, convincing affirmations. Then we'll have them visualize those affirmations all week prior to the game. We'll have the offensive linemen visualizing the best blocks they ever made; the defensive linemen, the best tackles they ever made; the quarterbacks, the best passes they ever threw; the ends, the best catches they ever made; the defensive secondary, the best interceptions; the halfbacks, the best runs. Then we'll have them "flick back" to the past triumphs and allow those old feelings to well up inside. Next, we'll have them "flick up" to the present situation with the same aggression, the same confidence, the same enthusiastic expectancy that they had in those past situations.

By game day, that Texas team will come into the stadium sub-consciously expecting to win. They'll associate, "Have I experienced anything like this before?" "Uh-huh." And they'll evaluate, "What is this leading me toward?" "*Nothing but a win!* It's over. It's done. Got 'em. It's ours!" They'll be ready to play deadly football—cool, poised, coiled to strike, *elite*. Subconsciously, they will feel absolutely assured and confident that they can blow their opponent away.

The beauty of *"Flick Back-Flick Up"* is that you can use it to deliberately prepare, emotionally, for any situation coming up next week, next month, even next year. It will allow you to go into new situations with confidence and poise. And once you master it yourself, you can help people you love to do it, too. For example, you parents can use it to help your young children. At night, before your kids fall asleep, sit on their bed and ask them, "Tell me what you did today that was great fun. What did you do that made you feel proud of yourself?" Then let them talk about it and feel the emotions all over again. Then you say, "And what are you looking forward to tomorrow?"

See what you're doing? You're helping them to unconsciously affirm a tomorrow that will be just as much fun as today. We know that's how high-performance people think; one vital thought pattern is *"I have pride in my past performance and a positive expectancy of winning big in the future."* And that's how you can train your children to think. If you do that for them every day, you will help them develop that high-performance pattern for adulthood. As adults, they will be more inclined to attack life every day with that positive expectancy. They will be ready to go places in life they would have never considered before. And when they get there, they'll think, "This is déjà vu!" They will absolutely *own* the situation.

Now, that's what you want to do for yourself, too. It's great for building a storehouse of self-esteem. Every day, take some time, privately, to dwell on something you did well in the past, and relive that experience. What you will be doing is re-recording all those positive emotions, as if they're happening again right now. Then you just "borrow" those emotions and "flick" them forward into an anticipated situation in the future. It's a way of looking forward constructively in an "I can, I want to, I will" mode.

Imprinting and Intent

You might ask, "How long should I take to visualize my affirmations?" If you're affirming and visualizing internal changes in your attitudes or habits, or the enhancement of character traits, it shouldn't take longer than twenty or thirty seconds. But if you're affirming and visualizing external changes, like a new income level, a merger in your company, an athletic performance, or a new skill or routine that has multiple affirmations, you may need to spend more time.

"How many affirmations should I make?" I recommend that you make no more than about thirty affirmations. There's no magic number; the determinant is how much time you're willing to spend on each one. If it takes thirty seconds an affirmation, thirty affirmations will take fifteen minutes. And I suggest that you go through the whole process—"Read - Picture - Feel"—at least twice a day. That would be a total of thirty minutes. That may not seem like much, but you will want to keep it up on a regualr basis.

"How often should I repeat my affirmations before seeing a change?" For the most part, it will take many repetitions—possibly a hundred or two hundred—before the goal imprints and changes your picture. But don't be discouraged; the actual change takes time. Remember how the process activates change: Each time you imprint a goal in your subconscious, you are recording it once as if it's actually happened. And since your subconscious can't tell the difference between a vividly imagined experience and the real thing, eventually, through repetition—with the proper imagery and spirit of intent—your inner picture will change. And even though you are only changing the picture *inside* at first, once you perceive that you haven't changed *outside* yet, your subconscious will automatically correct for the mistake: "You're too high! You're too low! Straighten up the mess!"

So if you are twenty pounds overweight at 180, you might affirm, "I feel attractive and energetic at 160 pounds." Then you repeatedly read the affirmation, close your eyes, and "experience" how you'd feel, physically and emotionally, at 160 pounds. You would picture yourself at 160—wearing new clothes, doing new activities, looking great. You would hear people telling you how great you look. You might even imagine stepping on the scale and watching the numbers roll back. Or looking at yourself in the mirror to see how slim you are. Once that slimmed down image imprints, and you *really* step on the scale, and you realize you *haven't* lost the weight, your system creates the dissonance that keeps you on target until you *do*. It keeps you acting like the person you believe yourself to be—someone who now weighs 160, not 180. So don't be impatient. Through repetition over time, the new picture assimilates into your subconscious mind.

Let me point out, however, that mere repetition will not be enough to imprint affirmations. There's much more to it. In the first place, regimented repetition can become hypnotic, which causes it to lose its power. You might end up reading your goals indifferently, like reciting from rote. There's very little conviction in that. Remember: Words alone are empty of value or power. It is the *intent* behind the words that makes the difference.

If you lack genuine intent, you might find that you are repeating your affirmations because you've become dependent on them: "Well, I don't really mean it, but I better say it anyway because I know I should change." That's what happened when, for so many years, I kept affirming to lose weight. The repetition was worthless because I didn't really mean it. For all those years, I just repeated the affirmation because I was dependent on it. I told myself, "Well, at least I'm *trying*." But I wasn't trying. I never *intended* to lose weight at the time. I just repeated the affirmation in case it might work like magic.

So let me caution you that in repeating your affirmations over time, you must continually clarify them with more specific details and a fresh investment of emotion. In other words, when you read and visualize your affirmations—just like when Diane and I kept inventing new events for our "Ranch Days" celebration—you must keep "adding to the party." That way, the repetition becomes a means of more finely focusing your goals, and achieving greater clarity and power. If you only repeat for repetition's sake, you are wasting your time. Don't forget: It sometimes takes only one heart-felt affirmation—like a sincere "I do"—to change your belief system. So repetition in and of itself has no value. As you continue to improve your imprinting technique, you will learn which of your affirmations you are most sincere about, and which require more commitment and repetition.

Also, if your affirmations aren't bolstered by a strong desire and commitment, the repetition may actually imply *doubt* to your subconscious. You might be repeating an affirmation only to convince yourself that you really want it, or that you can really attain it. At first, you might start off affirming, "I am a nonsmoker?"—almost like a question—because you're not quite sure you want it. And your self-talk will kill you: "No, you're not. You're lying. You don't really want to stop smoking." And you'll keep trying to affirm it: "I look better when I don't smoke. And I feel better. And I—." But your self-talk will battle back: "You don't really care about that. You really want to smoke." So sometimes you must use repetition— "I *am* a nonsmoker because—," "I *am* a nonsmoker because—," "I *am* a nonsmoker because—" to keep convincing yourself that you are the kind of person you're *affirming* you are. Or that you really *want* what you're affirming.

Another reason to repeat affirmations is because, at first, you may not feel you're worthy of your affirmations: "Am I really *worthy* of that new job?" "Am I really *worthy* of earning more money?" "Am I really *worthy* of a new house like that?" I've done that myself: "Am I worthy of teaching this curriculum?" "Am I worthy of implementing this program in government, in business, in athletics, in—?" See? Those thoughts once troubled me, too. When you first start using this technique, it's like you're trying on a new fashion: "Geez, I'm not sure I look right in this." It takes time to get comfortable with it. Until then, though, some doubt can creep in. You might laugh at yourself, "No, no, no. This is ridiculous." But the more you keep repeating your affirmations—"I *am* a nonsmoker." "I *am* a strong teacher." "I *am* a good parent."—the more you believe, "I *can* attain that goal." But once you decide you *are* worthy, then you declare, "That's it. I've got it. It's mine." And you won't ever need to affirm for those things again. So an affirmation that you are worthy of your goal may be one of the most important affirmations you make.

"When is the best time to do my affirmations?" Just before you fall asleep at night, and again upon awakening in the morning. That's when your brain is most susceptible to suggestion. It would also be wise to do your affirmations during some quiet, private time when you won't be disturbed. And it might be a good idea to make one of your first affirmations, "I enjoy writing and visualizing my affirmations daily because of the positive results." I recommend writing your affirmations on 3 × 5 cards; and keeping one set with you, and one set at home. When you read them, just close your eyes and visualize. Or you could use a tape recorder or tape deck in your car to better use your time. On the way to your job in the morning, instead of listening to another "poor me" cowboy song, listen to your work affirmations. On the way home at night, listen to your family affirmations. Of course, if you do the imprinting process while driving, don't close your eyes!

"How long do I keep affirming for something I want?" Internal goals might only take a couple of weeks. External goals will probably take longer because they involve other internal changes as well. But don't be impatient. If you affirm, visualize, and imprint correctly, I guarantee you that in a relatively short time, you will notice a change. It's like planting a seed and waiting for the flower to grow. When you plant a seed, you trust and believe that the flower will grow from it. You know that this growth will begin with the roots in the soil, out of sight. You trust that the shoot will soon appear; you don't keep digging up the soil to see if the roots are growing.

20

"LONGER LEGS FOR BIGGER STRIDES":

Diane's Story

Some people have goal-set to read this book, but not to apply the information to their lives. Keep in mind that this curriculum is of little value to you until you make it a daily part of your life. Merely knowing this information means nothing. You must live it every day. If you constantly apply the concepts and techniques, you can do and become almost anything you envision. But you better know what you're doing—and how to do it *intentionally*.

With that in mind, both Diane and I will now relate our most significant example of how to live this information. It's a story of life and death. It's Diane's story about how she persistently applied the principles and techniques of this curriculum to help her fight off a deadly form of cancer. But it's much more than Diane's story; it's also the story of how everyone around her applied these principles to create an environment of wellness and hope. In reading this, you will pick up insights on how you might apply these techniques to your own future, and to the future of the people around you. You will see why it is absolutely essential that you leave nothing in life to chance. And you will better understand the value of mastering this curriculum as you strive to become—at the very least—a better you.

Diane's Story

LOU TICE: In August a few years ago, our family celebrated Diane's fiftieth birthday. She was happy, vibrant, upbeat. She had devoted so much of her time over the years to doing things for her family, and for others, that she hadn't really taken enough time for herself. She was eagerly anticipating that opportunity.

Every year, after her birthday, Diane takes a complete physical. Because she had just turned fifty, her doctor recommended that she also see a gynecologist for a pap smear. She decided she would. After the results came in, she was asked to return for a "D and C." She had that done, too—by a young doctor who seemed a little unsure of himself. Afterwards, Diane forgot all about the test. Quite frankly, she considered it routine.

Then suddenly, in September, our lives changed forever.

DIANE TICE: To me, my fiftieth birthday was a halfway point in my life. I was looking forward to, and planning for, the second half. I thought, "Now I can really begin. The kids have all grown and our company is really building, so now I'll have time to do all the things I really want to do." I was ready to enjoy my next fifty years.

I have a firm faith in God and His presence within me. And I believe that the locus of control in my life comes from within, not from other people outside myself. I believe in the immortality of my soul. But I never thought too much about these beliefs until the afternoon, a week after my tests, when I received a call at home from the doctor who had done my "D and C." In a quavering voice, he said, "I have the results of your test." I said, "Oh, good." I assumed everything was fine. Then he said, very abruptly, "You definitely have uterine cancer. It's in the third stage and there are only four stages. So you'll have to have a total hysterectomy right away. And, of course, I will assist at the surgery." I was stunned. I held the phone away from my ear, looked at it, and thought, "Like hell, you will."

I was upset about the cancer, but I was so angry with the way this man told me about it that I automatically resisted him. To me, his cold, matter-of-fact tone was saying, "You don't stand a chance. But I'll do you the favor of assisting in your surgery anyway." I thought, "No, you won't. Who do you think you are?" So I hung up and called my regular doctor and told him I was enraged at the way this other doctor had broken the news. I said, "It was so inappropriate. He didn't prepare me. He didn't even ask if anyone else

243

was there with me. What if I had taken it badly? I might've fainted dead away on the floor."

Of course, it had never occurred to me to faint. I just thought, "I am not going to let a doctor determine my future. Especially *this* doctor." I found out later, in my own research, that many people don't react assertively with doctors. They tend to believe everything that doctors say, and blindly follow their advice. I am not in awe of doctors—maybe because I've had serious ailments in the past. That attitude turned out to be an important factor in my recovery process.

This is the kind of event that makes you realize where the locus of control really is. You decide very quickly whether you're going to determine your own life, or sit back and say, "Yes doctor"—or, for that matter, "Yes teacher," "Yes boss," "Yes family," "Yes everybody else but me." Psychologically, when confronted with a serious threat, people will either flee, fight, or just give in. Reflecting back now, I can say that because of the inappropriate way I found out about my cancer and because of my self-confidence and my beliefs, I subconsciously decided to fight. And I'm glad it happened that way because it solidified, in my mind, my belief that we are all responsible for our own lives.

Though I do have a firm faith in God's strength within me, I know I must also do my part and use my free will responsibly.

LOU: See how Diane was thinking? Even though she'd taken a devastating hit, she was already visualizing the way around the rock. Immediately, her Reticular Activating System started screening out threats and filtering in important information. Instead of thinking, "I'm dying. Doctor, tell me what to do," she was thinking, "There's no way this doctor will participate in my surgery." Because Diane had that assertive, "I'm going to fight" attitude, the important information—that this guy was a locked-on, "flat world" thinker who locked out options—screamed right through. So Diane "knew," that he should not be involved in her case.

By deciding that this doctor would not participate, and also that she would fight, Diane made the first important decision in her battle to recover. The day after she decided to have surgery, she informed her regular doctor that she wanted to find the best surgeon qualified for the operation. He sent her to a highly regarded surgeon who was extremely competent. He, too, recommended surgery as the best first step. But Diane researched further. She considered not just the operation, but the *total process of recovery*. Only after she reviewed the opinions of respected surgeons from the best cancer centers in the world, did she decide that surgery was the proper way to go for the first step.

But with this unnerving intrusion into our lives, and all the uncertainty, I felt it was important to relax and have some fun first. So we agreed that it would be a good idea to get away for a few days before the surgery. We went to our ranch in the Cascade Mountains with two close friends, and we had a wonderful weekend. We didn't discuss the operation or the uncertainty; we conducted ourselves normally, having fun with people we liked. That, too, is part of our curriculum: When you are under duress, you can control the dissonance by staying in your comfort zone and conducting your affairs as normally as possible.

After the relaxing weekend, Diane felt more assured. The following Thursday, she checked into the hospital in Seattle, and the surgery was scheduled for Friday afternoon. I had already begun a four-day seminar for about two hundred people at the Four Seasons Hotel, so I needed to focus and concentrate on that, too. On Friday, after I finished teaching the afternoon seminar session, I went to my hotel room to await the call from the doctor at the hospital. I had a strangely troubling feeling. Events were out of our hands for the moment, and I had never been in this kind of traumatic situation before. I felt terribly uneasy.

My imagination and my self-talk were going both ways; I was letting in the positive *and* the negative. I had faith that the operation would be successful and that Diane would be fine. But I also worried, "Well, what *if*?" That was the cognitive dissonance inside me. It was like, "I don't *want* to hear the results. But I *need* to hear the results because I want it to be good news. But I'm afraid that if I hear the results, and it's *bad* news—." See? My self-talk was telling me to avoid the truth. We all have the tendency to want to avoid whatever makes us uncomfortable. But it's essential to always see the truth, so I finally said, "I'll just sit here and wait. And I'll stop worrying. Whatever comes, I'll be ready for it."

Keep in mind that you never really know if you will be ready to handle a tragedy or disaster. I thought I could handle this, but my anxiety kept triggering doubt. An inner voice was urging me, "*Avoid this call!*" It was interesting, especially during a seminar weekend, to find out that I had a powerful urge to avoid the truth. I had to remind myself: "You can't control events. But you can control your reaction to events."

Finally, the doctor called with a "good news-bad news" report. He said, "We got all the cancer we could see. But we know it's broken loose in her system because we found a tumor on her bladder." He explained that Diane's cancer was in an advanced stage; that she would need chemotherapy and some follow-up radiation treatments; and that, even with treatment, the chances for long-term survival were not good. That hit me right between the eyes. I thought, "Oh God. How do I tell Diane?"

Late Friday, instead of attending the cocktail party we always have at the seminar, I went straight to the hospital to see Diane. I decided to walk the mile or so from the hotel to the hospital because I needed that time to gather myself and prepare what I wanted to say. I wanted to find the right way to tell Diane the truth, and still convey my love, my faith, my hope.

When I left the hotel room, my self-talk was, "Focus your intent," but I was still too nervous to properly prepare what I wanted to say. While waiting for the elevator, I remember imagining what my life would be like without Diane. We've been together since we were sixteen. We've never missed a Christmas together, or a Thanksgiving, or a birthday. For thirty-six years, our goal-setting has been so closely tied that even though we're two separate people, with separate identities, we feel as though we have one mutual destiny.

For an instant, I felt that if the elevator doors somehow opened into an empty shaft, it would be all right if I just fell in. I knew that our kids were provided for, and old enough to take care of themselves, so what difference would it make? I didn't feel desperate or frightened. I had this easy, peaceful, "I quit. I'll go with her" kind of feeling. I'm sure other people have felt this way in similar circumstances, but I had never felt anything like it before—and I never thought I would. See, you can't anticipate feeling that way.

Walking to the hospital, I started to cry because I still didn't know how to tell Diane. I thought, "Do I give up or do I fight?" Normally, my intent would be to fight. For me, that meant all-out-war. I didn't care if I had to give up everything—our business, our home, all we had. But the important decision was Diane's. She had to have the same intent.

At the hospital, I waited for her to come out of the anaesthetic. When she did, I held her hand and said, "Diane, I'm going to tell you the truth. The operation was a success, but the cancer has broken loose in your system. We have a hell of a fight on our hands." She didn't flinch. She looked me straight in the eyes and said, "Okay. Let's get started. What's the first step?"

The next day, people called from all over the world—the U.S., Australia, England, Africa, Japan—to share their concern and prayers for Diane's welfare. We were both overwhelmed by the genuine love that just poured in. I remember Diane saying, "It's very powerful. You can almost feel their energy." I told myself, "I will find ways to multiply this energy, so Diane can feel it every day."

I thought about my friend Gene who, some years earlier, applied many of the principles we teach to help keep his son, Terry, reasonably healthy through a long, tragic ordeal with leukemia. Terry eventually succumbed to the disease, but I remembered the day-to-day positive benefits from Gene's careful regulation of Terry's environment. So I talked to Gene about how we might constructively apply some of those things to Diane's situation.

I wanted to create an emotional climate of normalcy, wellness, and hope around Diane at all times. We started by decorating the room brightly with familiar photos and fresh flowers and many of Diane's familiar personal items. We surrounded her with humorous people; we showed a lot of comedy films in her room, even though, after a chemotherapy treatment, it was tough for her to laugh; we kidded and joked and played lots of games. In other words, we created a light, relaxed, upbeat atmosphere. Diane and I both understood the power of humor and joy to promote physical and mental health, so it was a natural approach for us anyway.

DIANE: When people I knew came to visit me, they brought their prayers and such strong spiritual, positive energy into my room. I could physically feel it inside me. I drew on it during my whole recuperation. But it's important to know that you don't have to take our curriculum to become a positive and constructive person. What made the difference wasn't that the people who came to see me had been through, or understood, our program. It was that they naturally exemplified the concepts we teach. It was just the kind of people they were; they were naturally positive and constructive and they gave me spiritual support.

Actually, there's a lot of constructive information in the negative, too, because you can evaluate and assimilate *all* the information in current reality and make more measured judgments. So it's a mistake to think that this curriculum is Pollyannaish, and everybody is always smiling. It's not that way. It's just that, in stressful situations, a positive atmosphere of lightness and humor and upbeat conversation helps carry the stress from your body so you can strengthen your immune system. With that kind of energy and strength, even in the face of the worst, you're always able to look for the best. And if the worst is all there is, you still know you can learn something from it. Lou and everyone else around me during that period weren't creating a Pollyanna world of "Don't look at the truth, Diane." In fact, they were helping me *find* the truth.

LOU: We also realized that doctors, interns, orderlies, and nurses had their own "Lock On-Lock Out" beliefs and "Who-Saids" of the Greatest Magnitude. I remembered how the hospital personnel had projected their limiting, negative realities into young Terry's mind, and how Gene tried to battle that. Doctors have scotomas. They're sometimes so narrowly focused on their own methods that they don't readily see other options. When they hear information contrary to what they believe, they tend to rationalize it as "an exception to the rule."

They don't mean to be that way. They just believe in their own reality—like I sometimes do in my business, like all of us do—and they aren't aware that they're communicating it. Remember: *Human beings act in accordance with the truth as we believe it.* And we unconsciously project our "truth" through facial expressions, body language, manner, tone of voice. Now, we know that doctors and nurses see patients die every day. That becomes a powerful negative reality: "It doesn't matter what we do. They still die." So we had to be prepared for these people coming into Diane's room, projecting their histories of patients who didn't make it, and regarding Diane as just another statistic.

I regard doctors and nurses as highly skilled, very necessary, even precious—but, ultimately, as just human beings. Quite frankly, many become detached in their statistical reality—like the doctor who broke the news to Diane over the phone. They can easily develop Scotomas of the Greatest Magnitude. But my conviction was this: In life-and-death situations, scotomas and negative "truths" are absolutely unacceptable. So I decided to take extreme measures to counteract the negative realities of all the "Who-Said" experts who would be telling Diane "the truth."

Since we aren't really sure what we control in this world, I decided to take control of darn near everything. First, we needed to overpower the negative affirmations of the experts. We needed to overpower their "doom and gloom" realities. So we began by stressing the idea that, even though others had died from this type of cancer, it wouldn't necessarily happen to Diane. And I made sure that either myself or someone else in our family—particularly our daughters Bonnie, Nancy, and Mary, and my sister Carol—or a close personal friend would take turns being with Diane during all her waking hours. That way, when doctors, nurses, or interns said anything contrary to the goal of success, we would immediately say in front of them, "That isn't necessarily true" or "We don't believe that stuff." Sometimes, the doctors would discuss postoperative treatments with Diane: "You've got to do this" and "This is the way it must be done." And we would say, "We aren't so sure about that." We wanted Diane to become her *own* authority.

It's also very important to always lock on to the end result that you *want* in your life, regardless of the present reality and present circumstances. When you've got all kinds of information that cast doubt, you must be strong enough in your own mind to know that your subconscious draws you to the images you focus on. So, sometimes you may need to deny current reality, deny what your peers and the experts and the people you respect insist is "the truth," and hold the image of what you *want* in the future. That's how high-performance people think. They have the tenacity and resiliency to face the "gloom and doom" and "Ain't it awful" attitudes and not be overwhelmed, or let it destroy their hope.

From the beginning, Diane was extremely positive and focused on the end result of getting well. It wasn't that difficult; Diane is a naturally positive person. In all the time she was ill, she never talked in terms of death or giving up. She always regarded her illness as a temporary setback: "What are my plans for tomorrow?" We know that her positive, future-oriented attitude made a difference. And that's what we worked to support.

DIANE: I never despaired. When I was a child in school, and I got a grade of 92% in spelling, I never thought of it as an 8% failure. I considered it a 92% success. It always irritated me when they wrote on my papers "Minus 8%." I immediately translated it back into the positive. I still do that.

When I was preparing for the surgery, I researched statistics on the cure-rates for my form of cancer, and it was something like 90% failure and 10% success. I always visualized myself in the 10%. If it was only 1%, I would still see myself there. I read somewhere that thousands of people have cancer but don't know it, and they survive to a ripe old age. I also discovered there's no cancer known that someone hasn't overcome. Actually, more people recover from cancer than ever die from it. That's the kind of information I dwelled on. I always saw myself in the "success" category. I thought, "Well, if only one person can beat this, I will certainly be that person." It never entered my mind that it could be any other way.

I was convinced I would get better, but I didn't ignore the possibility of death. I knew I couldn't entirely control what happened inside my body, and that it was possible I could end up in the 90% category. I just never *imagined* myself there. Occasionally, funny little thoughts would seep in—but not in a morbid, defeated sense. Like one time when I wasn't feeling well, I was talking to Lou and I said, completely out of the blue, "Well, that grandfather clock you gave me, I think Glen should have it." It was such a strange remark out of nowhere that we both started laughing.

I never visualized myself dying, so I didn't plan for that eventuality. I knew we had a well-organized will, and that our estate planning was already taken care of. The only contingency I considered came out in a funny conversation I had with Frank Bartenetti—a close friend and advisor, and the director of operations for our company. I said, "You know, Frank, in case anyone in the future might wonder what my opinion would have been on this, here it is. I think our son Glen should have my grandfather clock because he loves clocks and had enjoyed taking my watches apart to see how they worked. And I know there are a lot of women out there who would really love to get involved with Lou." And I showed Frank a list of names and I started pointing to them, one at a time: "Now, this one is definitely out. This one is out, too. But this one would certainly be okay." And we had a great time with it. That was the extent of me talking about "Well, what will happen if I'm not here?"

LOU: Because so many people cared about Diane, we knew she would have a constant flow of visitors after surgery. Here again, each person's negative expectancy could be communicated through body language, manner, tone of voice. And the question most people would ask would be, "How do you feel?" If so, Diane would need to continually affirm how she presently felt. After so much repetition, she might get tired and inadvertantly say one time, "I don't feel so well," or "I'm scared." We wanted to make darn sure that she wasn't set up for negative affirmations like that.

So I placed family members outside Diane's room to greet people before they entered, and to discuss what they should talk about with her. I had meetings at our company about that. I told our people, "We won't leave anything to chance." I told them that I intended to orchestrate and structure Diane's environment so that it was always positive, hopeful, and future-oriented. At home, we had family conferences about how we could help Diane fight her illness. We said we wouldn't ignore the reality of the cancer, but that we considered it temporary. We visualized the way we *wanted* things to be, and the way things would look if Diane didn't have the problem. Pretty soon, everybody painted the same picture of the environment that we wanted to create around Diane.

While Diane had surgery, I posted a sign outside her hospital door that read: "IF YOU'RE HERE TO SEE DIANE, YOU'RE HERE TO *GIVE* HER ENERGY, NOT TAKE IT AWAY. DON'T ASK HER HOW SHE FEELS. ASK HER ABOUT HER GRANDCHILDREN, ABOUT DECORATING OUR NEW LODGE, ABOUT HER UP-COMING TRIP TO AUSTRALIA. *ASK HER ABOUT HER FU-TURE*." This way, we controlled the input of information. I knew that the only people who saw Diane would be talking wellness, hope, and future.

After the surgery, Diane was faced with some very tough decisions about continued treatment: chemotherapy, radiation, how much of this, when to do that. I knew she needed to make those decisions herself. That was very difficult for me. But I understood that she alone should make these decisions because it was her life. Once she made them, she would assume the accountability to make them work. I wanted her to feel, "It isn't up to the doctors. It isn't up to Lou. It isn't up to the treatments. It's up to *me*. *I* am responsible for my own wellness."

I realized that the best way I could help her was to provide her with the best medical information available. So I immediately relieved Betty Tisdale of her regular duties as my personal secretary, and assigned her to direct a "Wellness Command Center" in our offices. Her new full-time objective was to coordinate a world-wide search for the most up-to-date research on successful treatments for Diane's type of cancer. Betty's husband is a physician, and she's a very aggressive, "make things happen" type of person, so I knew she was the right one. I gave her priority access to all our people, who could drop everything they were doing if she needed them.

Betty contacted the most renowned doctors and health care professionals in the world who had success treating this kind of cancer; she called major cancer treatment and research centers for case studies and success ratios—San Diego, Washington, D.C., Idaho, Houston, New York, Montreal, Mexico, Greece, the Bahamas, West Germany, the Philippines, Japan—wherever she had a lead. We pursued every option—people working on projects for a Nobel Prize, faith-healers, immunology projects, metaphysics studies, nutrition and exercise, herbal care approaches, parapsychology, hypnotherapy, the Simonton visualization techniques, best-selling books on cancer therapies.

I convened study groups of speed-readers who devoured relevant literature in magazines, periodicals, journals, pamphlets, and books so we could quickly pass along an abundance of information to Diane. One person would read something, summarize the main points and highlights in a report, and trade with someone else who would read the same stuff and write a second report. That way, we always had a safeguard against being locked on to a particular treatment because of personal bias or a blind spot. Then Betty checked the validity of all this information with the best physicians we knew, so that we didn't make hasty, emotional decisions about what to leave out and what to include. Then we condensed everything into compressed study formats and presented them to Diane. She would study the materials and make her decisions: "Well, let's try this" or "Let's call this doctor and find out more about his method."

We agreed that she wouldn't follow the protocol of any one doctor. So we retained three doctors—which made at least two of them uncomfortable, because "Why are you questioning my judgment? Why are you interfering?" Well, the reason was because we wanted to weigh opinions carefully to try to find the best one. We were searching for the *truth*, so we weren't concerned about bruising someone's ego. Now that takes high self-esteem, because Diane could have easily given up accountability to any one of the doctors: "Doctor, make me well. You know so much more than I do. I will go by your judgment." I think that most people do that. But she knew it was crucial for her to participate in her own recovery. Accountability is a central concept in what we teach: *Take accountability for your own life.* Become your own authority, your own expert, and make your own decisions about your future.

DIANE: I started on a quest to become an expert on what I was about to go through. I read all the research compiled for me, and I gathered materials myself, so I had a multitude of choices. I had an expert surgeon who was one of the best. But I discovered that, in being the best, he was very narrow in his views on how this cancer should be treated. It was like macrophotography where you magnify your subject many times and become focused on small details. I would say he had that view. His total protocol was surgery, then maximum chemotherapy, then maximum radiation.

I started out questioning him, and I never let up. I learned later that one characteristic of typical cancer survivors is that they question things. Many doctors consider those kind of people "difficult" because they're always asking, "Why?" My surgeon said I would need chemotherapy once a month for six months, and I said, "Why six?" And after that, he said I'd need five-and-a-half weeks of radiation treatments. I said, "Why five-and-a-half?"

I finally learned that he was doing a study of ten cancer patients, and they were all on the same protocol. Seven had died already, and I was the eighth. There was another woman who was doing fairly well, and the doctor hadn't found the tenth person yet. I didn't know how long his study had been going on, but I was very irritated that just because he was doing a study, I was "assigned" six sessions of chemotherapy. I didn't want to be a guinea pig. So I said, "Well, I won't say yes to six. I'll say yes to one at a time and see how far I want to go."

I felt an obligation to my family to go ahead with chemotherapy. I had gathered and read enough statistical data on success percentages to know that it was very effective. In fact, I had the first chemotherapy treatment the night of the day I had the surgery. Of course, afterward there was a lot of discomfort and some throwing up. The challenge was to fight off those images and not allow myself to think, "I'm going to be sick again." So I just kept visualizing the chemicals destroying the cancer cells and removing them from my body, and telling myself: "You're getting stronger every day."

This is the period when everybody decorated my room, and people came to visit, and share humor and fun, along with research and upbeat ideas of what to do next. I actually found the process very interesting. I sketched a sort of wellness wheel to depict all the

Figure 16-1.   Diane's Wellness Wheel

positive approaches taken by cancer patients who got well. And as I accumulated more information, I added options to the wheel.

Simply stated, I developed cancer because my immune system was stressed. I used these things Ⓐ to build up and support my immune system to fight the cancer. I worked on these things Ⓑ to recognize and change the basic building blocks in my life which may have contributed to the development of my cancer. I used these things Ⓒ to alleviate the obvious (existing) cancer.

LOU: Diane continued to make her own decisions by choosing to take chemotherapy, which was devastating. Her hair started coming out in clumps. At first, this really bothered her. So we got her the finest wig made. But she wouldn't wear it. She insisted, "No, I'll just look like I look. I want to be myself." Eventually, she lost almost all her hair. But the amazing thing was that she looked absolutely radiant and beautiful anyway. You would look at her and think: "Oh, Diane's trying a fashionable new hair style." And she continued to dress beautifully, just like before. So, to Diane, it was never a negative. She thought of herself, and she *looked*, happy and glowingly healthy. So everybody around her started seeing that, too. It was never, "Oh my God. You poor thing. You've got cancer." It was always, "Boy Diane, you look fantastic!"

DIANE: In the hospital, I had my lipstick and mascara in my little nightstand. I thought, "If I wore lipstick and my mascara yesterday, I'm going to wear it today. I'm in the hosptial, but I'm not going to look sick and pale." I decided I was still me, and that "still me" should be the dominant picture. I remember when Lou and I were just married, and I was in the hospital with kidney problems, I got up the day after surgery and took a stroll because I couldn't think of myself as "hospitalized." I dragged all over the hospital, and I felt much better doing that. The staff was aghast. They found out that I wouldn't allow myself to fall into a passive "patient's" roll: "I'm ill. I can't do anything but lay here and hope for the best." Instead, my attitude was, "I'm getting better and better. What good is in store for me today?"

I always looked to the future. In November, Lou was going to have his fiftieth birthday, but he really wasn't up to doing anything.

So I decided to arrange a big party. To do that, I had to reschedule my next chemotherapy session in advance because, afterwards, I knew I'd be too weak to do anything fun for about four or five days. Well, everybody pitched in to help and we reserved the Garden Court Room and Spanish Ballroom at the Four Seasons Hotel for Lou's party. I was bald at the time, but I got dressed up anyway and had a wonderful time. So it wasn't, "Well, I have cancer. I'm too sick to celebrate my husband's birthday." In fact, planning the party, getting dressed up for it, and enjoying it unfold was very life-affirming for me.

LOU: During this difficult period, Diane was so focused on the future that she designed and helped build the 17,000-square-foot Tice Lodge in the mountains; went to Europe twice and brought back two container loads of antique furniture; decorated and furnished the lodge; threw parties, went shopping, entertained friends, and helped run our company. She changed her diet. She started exercising, even though sometimes she could barely walk. She went to a psychiatrist in case there was some undetected stress involved. In other words, she changed her entire life.

She also sought out unconventional people, like healers, who other doctors referred to as "quacks." They inferred to her, "Why would you go to somebody like that?" Without very high self-esteem, that might have imprinted doubt in her mind. But she decided not to rule out any possibility. She felt that research and decision-making were creative processes. And she knew that the creative process is very stimulating to your total system. So, for Diane, seeking options wasn't just a diversion; it was a stimulation of the total person.

She also had to make some very powerful decisions. Like a decision, at one point, *not* to take radiation, even though the doctor said that radiation was absolutely essential because the cancer had broken loose in her system. It was a tough decision. She had to fight her own mind, she had to think independently, she had to become a risk-taker. A key factor throughout was that Diane took accountability for being sick. She chose not to torture herself with blame or guilt, and not to wallow in self-pity. Instead, she said, "Look, I caused the disease. I can cause the wellness."

DIANE: I began to understand that you don't so much "get" cancer as you develop it. I found out that cancerous cells are present in everyone to greater or lesser degrees. But we have powerful immune systems to keep things stable. If your immune system becomes depressed, it functions at less than optimal levels, and the cancer—or abnormal cells—can proliferate.

Around this time, I also found a wonderful doctor who was not only an oncologist—a cancer doctor—but also an immunologist. He believed in building up the immune system to fight the cancer. He helped me understand how my immune system might have become depressed over many years. What drew me to him was that his approach was more "total," and he addressed the body's own fighting mechanisms. Back in medieval times, they talked about treatments for catastrophic diseases only in terms of "cut, burn, and poison." Well, today, what is the most modern treatment for cancer? Cut, poison and burn. He saw much further than that.

His approach dovetailed perfectly with the concepts that we teach. My reflective thinking was that the immune system was part of me, so building it up would give me a personal feeling of accountability in the fight. I felt that if I built up my immune system, I could control the cancer. But I didn't give up the surgery and other traditional approaches. I just added a whole bunch of other options. Which is significant. I think too many people deny unorthodox or nontraditional options. I'm not suggesting that you should give up surgery or chemotherapy. But neither should you rely only on traditional methods without also exploring as many alternatives as possible.

So, even while I was undergoing chemotherapy treatments with one doctor, I continued seeing an extraordinary healer who was able to describe very accurately the cancer cell activity in my body. At the same time, I kept following the regimen of my immunologist who provided megadose vitamins, an exercise program, and a diet that helped build my immune system and depress the cancer. I also intensified my own research to find out about carcinogenic foods that you shouldn't eat, and immune-building foods that you should eat. I remember discovering little tips here and there, like the idea that cancer cells are weak cells that thrive in a saline environment in your body, but wither in a potassium environment. That's how I discovered it was best to cut out extra salt in my diet and add more potassium.

I ate mainly fresh vegetables, fresh fruits, whole grains, and limited amounts of lean meat, such as turkey and some wild game and chicken—but not Arkansas chicken, which is full of hormones. I had immune-building shots, I took special vitamins every day— Vitamin A, Vitamin C, Vitamin E—and I took Vitamin B-12 shots once a month. The vitamins had a very ironic effect; they helped my fingernails grow long! That was the accidental realization of a life-long dream.

There are reasons your immune system gets stressed. I learned a lot about that by researching the work of Dr. Carl Simonton, who does work that's closely related to what we teach. In his book, *Getting Well Again*, he explains the cancer healing process in terms of positive thinking, visualization, and affirmations. He even has a course that teaches children how to deal with their cancer through visualizations, like picturing little cowboys riding through their bodies shooting the cancer cells and carrying them out of the body. Those tools are very effective, even if people do nothing else.

Simonton also developed a psychological profile of the typical cancer patient who beats the odds by stabilizing or going into complete remission. He called those patients "Superstars." So I sent for the study and learned from it. According to Simonton, "Superstar" patients are assertive, obstinate, and highly creative. They have strong ego needs; they never give up; they are open-minded, inquisitive, and confrontive; they have a strong sense of reality, self-confidence, and a lack of ethnic prejudice; and they believe they control their own lives.

From Simonton's list, I made a list of my own affirmations to guide me closer to the profile. They were a mainstay in my recovery.

My "Superstar" Affirmations

The following list of affirmations are based on *Psychology of the Exceptional Cancer Patient; A Description of Patients Who Outlive Predicted Life Expectancies*, by Jeanne Achterberg, Ph.D., Stephanie Matthews-Simonton and O. Carl Simonton, M.D.

I am a non-conformist.
I am a fighter.
I am psychologically aggressive.
I have ego strength.
I have a strong sense of reality.
I have feelings of personal adequacy and vitality.
I have a non-judgmental morality—everyone doesn't have to have my lifestyle and they're still O.K.
I treat all people with dignity and respect.
My locus of control is self.
I laugh at myself and I don't take life too seriously.
I am free each moment to choose my direction.
I balance recognizing my malignancy with the belief that my body has a built-in mechanism to fight disease and return to a homeostatic condition of health.
I seek new worlds to conquer.
I exercise forced physical activity daily, as it retards tumor growth.
I seek my priorities and strengths daily.
I am learning to receive.
I have freedom from conventionality.
I demand and seek information about my disease.
I seek the finest traditional medical treatment as well as other diverse well-substantiated cures.
I am physically active at work and play.
I grow intellectually and emotionally.
I find routes to combat events in my life that cause life to lose meaning, so I do well psychologically.
I have psychological insight.
I enjoy great flexibility in my life.

I found out that positive thinking is an excellent immune system booster, because the mind and the immune system are strongly linked. Studies show that what happens in the mind invariably affects the body. It's exactly like our concept of "The Placebo Effect": If you can get sick on a negative placebo, you can get well on a positive placebo.

I worked on my weak areas. I remember a funny incident: I was always an easy-going person, so I especially needed to affirm my assertiveness. Well, finally, I became more assertive than necessary. At a party, during the period when I was still having chemotherapy, Lou took me aside gently and said, "Diane, your affirmations on assertiveness are working beautifully. But could you add a little something about *tact* in there, too."

Getting well is really so much a matter of self-esteem, self-worth, and self-assertiveness. If you feel good enough about yourself, you'll take care of yourself. If you don't feel good about yourself, you'll only do so much and that's enough. It's important to feel good enough about yourself that you'll go to extremes to get better—like learning about the crucifer winter vegetables that help increase the body's output of tumor-inhibiting enzymes, why you don't eat spinach and beets, and which foods provide immuno-stimulating nutrients.

I went all-out to build myself up psychologically and physically. I found out that oxygenation of the body is crucial to building strong cells. So I started doing vigorous exercise every day. When I was doing chemotherapy, it consisted of just walking downhill to the beach behind our house, because I was too weak to do more. But I knew that if I walked to the beach area, it would force me to walk back uphill to get back in the house—and that was enough exercise during those periods. Later, I started swimming at an athletic club. While I swam, I planned, in my mind, all the fun things I would do the rest of the day or the rest of that week, and I'd review my affirmations. At the time, we were building our ranch lodge in the mountains, so I would visualize the rooms and the furniture I wanted in each one, and where I would travel to find that furniture.

That was especially beneficial because it was a creative project, which was energizing. But you don't need a project as expansive as that; you can just visualize simple things, like planting bulbs that will come up in the spring, and seeing the bulbs in bloom. I had a flower garden, which was in poor shape, so I ordered a lot of lilly bulbs that wouldn't come up until the next year, and I would imagine what they'd look like when they came up.

I also visualized and planned for future family events: "Who's coming for Thanksgiving? What will we be doing at Christmas?" Even if something was eight months away, I visualized being part of it. I envisioned the decorations, the activities, the people we'd invite. I also made sure I called my sister regularly, so we could continue going out to lunch together. And I didn't give up on buying clothes; I went shopping a lot. If you have the idea that you won't be around very long, you aren't going to buy that winter suit you'll need for the next six months. So I deliberately included long-range goals like that in my daily planning, instead of subconsciously eliminating them by thinking: "Well, I don't need that anymore. I won't be here to use it." Instead, I'd think, "That's a beautiful winter coat. I'll wear that up at the ranch this year."

I also realized it might be important to have a psychological evaluation of my life to see what things I'd need to change. Early life traumas can subtly suppress your immune system over a long period of time, and gradually lead you downhill until you reach a point of low resistance. There's a song that says, "I made it through the rain." Well, you can make it through the rain if you make constructive psychological changes along the way. If you don't, it might just keep raining on you. If you don't get cancer again, it will be something else.

My immunology doctor did lab tests every month to check the cancer cell activity and the strength of my immune system. Each month, I saw that the cancer cell activity was diminishing while my immune system grew stronger. I continued going to my healer, who reassured me about my blood chemistry, and told me where I still had cancer, what stage it was in, and whether it was growing or not. He was an amazingly gifted person; everything he told me matched the lab reports—which he never saw. Eventually, I got him and my immunology doctor talking together, and I was able to balance what one told me against what I learned from the other. When I was through with chemotherapy, I *knew* I was getting well.

I also used visualization every day. I would first still my entire body, start deep breathing to relax, and then remind myself of the reality of the present moment—that there was still the possibility I had cancer in my body. I visualized the little spots of cancer that might still be present. Then I visualized an army of immune cells exploding like popcorn and multiplying, then attacking and devouring the cancer cells. I also visualized a little river that these cells flowed into, which ran the cancer spots out of my body.

Each time this happened, I would visualize myself walking up a hill and standing at the top. Then, as if I were outside myself, I would see myself looking through my body, which was lit up and transparent and totally clean. That was my symbol of total wellness; the transparency represented a cleaning out of the cancer. Every other visualization revolved around that image; they were different avenues that led directly to that one place.

I had to discipline myself to do these visualizations at least twice a day. So I pretended it was a business appointment with myself. That made it a priority because I wouldn't lightly cancel a business appointment. You need to be undistracted when you do your visualizations, so I'd often drive to the park and do them in the car. I would visualize different states of wellness, energy, and strength. I would try to visualize the various "Superstar" characteristics. For example, I'm a nonconformist, so I would visualize myself not conforming to certain expectations. Or for assertiveness, I'd sometimes imagine someone doing something unwise, and me making a point to say something about it.

Self-talk was also very important because I was alone a lot, especially during my chemotherapy period. Though a lot of people spent time with me, I was the only one who stayed in the hospital while everyone went home at night. Driving home, I was the only one looking for places off the side of the road where I could throw up. When I was recovering at home, I was the only one laying in bed, feeling sick, while everyone left because they didn't want to bother me. For five days after chemotherapy, I would experience the sickness and all the throwing up. I kept telling myself, "There are people who don't have any of these symptoms. You can control them if you try." I needed to continually reinforce my optimism, or else I might've created a negative self-talk cycle of "Oh, I'm sick. I'm throwing up. I'm going to throw up again and again and again."

Through positive self-talk, I controlled postchemotherapy sickness a lot, but I didn't totally eliminate it. My hair kept falling out. That didn't bother me so much, so I didn't bother to intensely visualize taking the treatment without my hair falling out. Maybe if I had done that, I could have controlled it a little more. But I didn't spend as much time and energy on those kinds of things as I did on just getting well.

Right after the last chemotherapy session, my surgeon told me that I should start periodical radiation treatments within three days, which meant I couldn't take my overseas trips. He was very explicit about all of the possible negative side effects. He mentioned everything from permanent intestinal damage to effects on my sex life. I thought, "Boy, I'm not gonna let those things happen to me." So I didn't take the radiation. Three months later, he sent me a letter: "It has come to my attention that you did not follow my protocol. Don't you realize how serious this is?" He went on for two pages and said at the end, "Would you at least come in every six months so I can see how you're doing?"

My immunologist thought I needed radiation treatments, too. But I said, "The last tests showed that cancer cell activity is almost nil, and my immune system is growing steadily stronger. I don't think I need this treatment. I'll take my lab test every month and, if anything changes for the worse, I'll come in for radiation treatments." Also, my healer had been giving me feedback that indicated my immune system was killing off the cancer cells, so I figured my immune system was taking care of it. We left it at that.

My decision was right. For the last four years, they haven't found any cancer cell activity of any kind, and my immune system is very strong. Recently, I took a Cat Scan test to prove I was totally clean—and I am. I haven't even caught a cold.

LOU: When I think of this whole ordeal, I always think of the special moment between Diane and I when we were driving to the Swedish Hospital for her last chemotherapy treatment. Since we were married at sixteen, we had gone through all kinds of setbacks, and we always told each other that whenever we stood up to those challenges, great things occurred on the other side. So, just as we approached the freeway, I said to her, "I can hardly wait for you and me to get through this. Because every time we've come through something, great things have happened on the other side. We have never faced something this devastating before, so it *has* to be really good on the other side. I can hardly wait to get there."

As we pulled up to the hospital, I smiled at Diane and she said, "Remember what I always say about adversity: '*When you come through a tough crisis, it just gives you longer legs for bigger strides.*' "

If you are planning for
a year
                    sow rice,
If you are planning for
a decade
                    plant trees,
If you are planning for
a lifetime
          educate people.

Chinese proverb